D0943397

IN THE FOOTSTEPS OF LE CORBUSIER

IN THE FOOTSTEPS OF
LE CORBUSIER

Edited by Carlo Palazzolo and Riccardo Vio

RIZZOLI
NEW YORK

ACKNOWLEDGMENTS

The editors wish to thank all who have favored the progress of this book. While it is of course impossible to mention everyone, we acknowledge the staff of the Fondation Le Corbusier, and particularly Evelyne Trehin, Caterina Perre of the library of the DPA of the Istituto Universitario di Architettura di Venezia, M. Morizet of CCI in Paris, and Umberto Tasca of Zanichelli Editore of Bologna.
We were greatly assisted by Annalisa Avon, Gianluca Bazzan, Paolo Berdini, Flavio Cesaro, Massimo De Luca, Francesco Donato, Enrico Fedrigoli, Sebastiano Gerardi, Giorgio Marastoni, Francesco Messori, and Renato Rizzi.
Special thanks are due to Giovanni Leone and Luigi Marastoni.
Finally, the advice of the authors has been invaluable, particularly that of Giuliano Gresleri, Bruno Reichlin, and Francesco Venezia.

First published in the United States of America in 1991 by
RIZZOLI INTERNATIONAL PUBLICATIONS, INC.
300 Park Avenue South, New York, NY 10010

Library of Congress Cataloging-in-Publication Data

Sulle tracce di Le Corbusier. English.
In the footsteps of Le Corbusier / edited by Carlo Palazzolo and Riccardo Vio.
p. cm.
Translation of: Sulle tracce di Le Corbusier.
Includes bibliographical references.
ISBN 0-8478-1219-7 (pbk.)
1. Le Corbusier, 1887-1965—Criticism and interpretation.
2. Le Corbusier, 1887-1965—Influence.
3. Architecture, Modern—20th century—France.
I. Palazzolo, Carlo. II. Vio, Riccardo. III. Title.
NA1053.J4S913 1991   90-52935
720'.92—dc20   CIP

The essays beginning on pages 37, 59, 73, 93, 133, 149, 177, 189, 197, 209, were translated by Hanna Hannah.
The Foreword and the essay beginning on page 263 were translated by Doron D. Sherwin.

Printed and bound in Italy

CONTENTS

FOREWORD

An architect . . . cannot and need not be a Grammarian, as was Aristarchus, though he ought not to be illiterate; nor need he be a Musician, as was Aristoxenus, though he should not lack some acquaintance with music; he need not be a Painter, as was Apelles, though he should not be ignorant of drawing, nor a Sculptor, as were Myron or Polycleitus, though he must not be without some understanding of sculpture . . .

Vitruvius

The architectural work of Le Corbusier defies any attempt at synthesis; to recall the innumerable disciplines to which he applied himself in order to explain its complexity would be equally insufficient.

Given the lack of an univocal legacy, we have decided against a reconstruction of his personality, preferring instead to propose an "exploded reality" in which each single fragment has become a new world. In selecting the various essays, or in commissioning new ones, we have sought to bring out as much as possible the affinities between some particular aspect of Le Corbusier's work and those of the architects-authors of these essays. It is no coincidence that for some of them the published essays actually represent, or have represented at one time, an architectural declaration of principle.

To whomever wished to follow the path *Vers une Architecture*, Le Corbusier recommended not only to free the spirit from any formula—"to open one's eyes"—but also knowledge, experience and direct contact with the great architectures of the past. Only an immersion in "the world of forms" renders possible the acquisition of the architect's sensibility—so difficult to learn, to define, to communicate. It is precisely this sensibility that is the common denominator of the essays collected here.

The reader should not expect any critical-scientific or philological-historical analyses from this book. This would be far from the scope of its intentions. Let him rather be satisfied to be guided along through the "Le Corbusier universe" by subjective readings, even though these may, at times, inspire his mind to wander—to *dream* new architectures.

IN THE FOOTSTEPS OF LE CORBUSIER

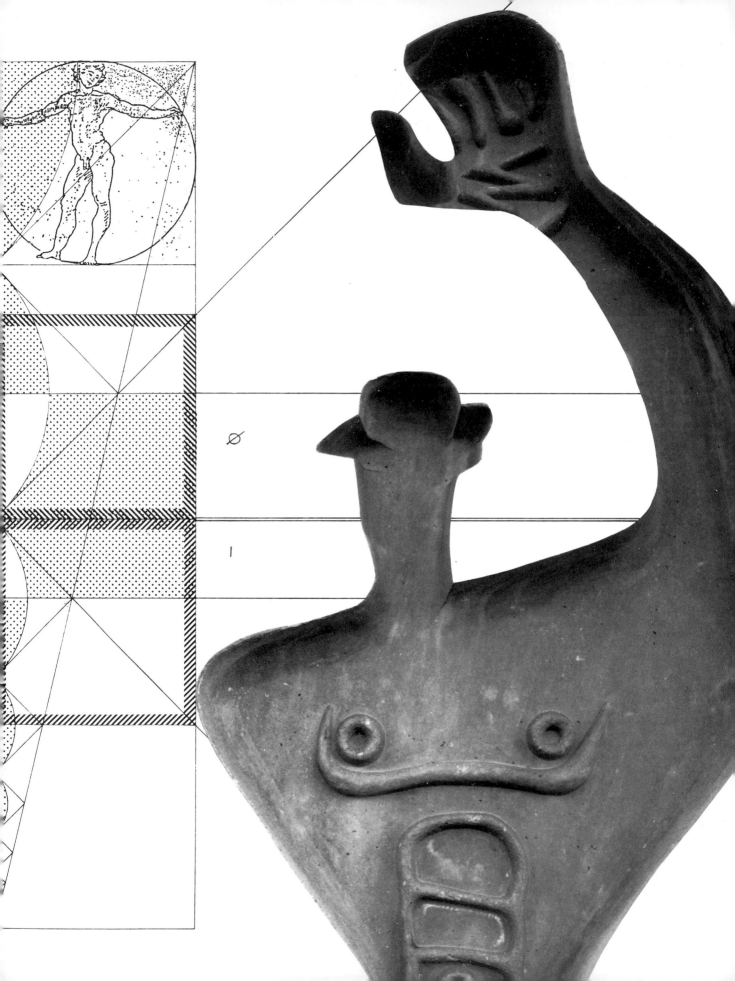

LE CORBUSIER'S MODULOR

Rudolf Wittkower

At a recent meeting at the Royal Institute of British Architects in London to which I was a party (June 18, 1957), the motion was before the house "that Systems of Proportion make good design easier and bad design more difficult." The motion was defeated. But in the debate Le Corbusier's Modulor was constantly referred to, and the distinguished architect, Misha Black, even said apologetically that "it must inevitably be in our minds as we discuss the motion." Indeed, after the Modulor we must be for it or against it; it would mean deluding ourselves if we tried to be escapist or neutral.

In 1948 Le Corbusier surprised the architectural world with his *Modulor*. The book was quickly sold out. Le Corbusier himself, whom I may (perhaps not too charitably) describe as a cross between a prophet and a salesman of rare ability, brought the story up to date in 1954, with the publication of his *Modulor 2*.

What was the reason for the world-wide response to the Modulor? Was it due to Le Corbusier's prophesy or his salesmanship? Each may have played a part, but many a prophet has cried in the wilderness, unheard. In all fairness, we must admit that the time was ripe for the Modulor.

The Beaux Arts tradition, according to which proportion is something vague, indefinable, irrational—a "something" that must be left to the individual architect's sensibility—that tradition is as dead as a doornail. If it is not, it should be.

Be that as it may, I find it difficult or even impossible to give paternal advice to practitioners regarding the suitability of the Modulor for the design of, say, skyscrapers. As an historian I am concerned with the past rather than with the future, and I can only discuss the Modulor in its historical context. Such an investigation may at least help to assess the validity of Le Corbusier's basic assumptions.

So far as I can see, the belief in an order, divine and

11

1. F. Gafurio. Pythagoras and the Greek musical scale.
2. Francesco di Giorgio Martini. Figure of a man superimposed over the plan of a cathedral.

human, derived from numbers and relations of numbers was always tied to higher civilizations. All systems of proportion are implicitly intellectual, for they are based on mathematical logic. Without a grasp of geometry and the theory of numbers, no system of proportion is imaginable.

It must be regarded as one of the most extraordinary events in the early history of mankind when a bridge was created between abstract mathematical thought and the phenomenal world that surrounds us; when geometry and numbers were found to govern the skies as well as all creation on earth. The Bible reflects this remarkable alliance between life and mathematics, between endless variety and numerical limitation. In the *Wisdom of Solomon* (XI, 20), we read, "By measure and number and weight thou didst order all things."

The intellectualism of this daring hypothesis must not lead us astray, for in reality we are here faced with a biologically conditioned sublimation. The quest for symmetry, balance, and proportional relationships is deeply embedded in human nature. Modern antagonists always claim that systems of proportion interfere with, and even impede, the release of creative energies. In actual fact, however, such systems are no more, and no less, than intellectual directives given to an instinctive urge which regulates not only human behaviour but even the behaviour of higher species of animals.

Man's predisposition for ordering complex sensory stimuli can easily be tested. For instance, we interpret automatically irregular configurations as regular figures (see Arnheim, *Art and Visual Perception*, fig. 44). Such incontestable observations permit us to conclude that we seek ordered patterns; systems of proportion are the principal vehicles to satisfy this urge.

All systems of proportion in Western art and architecture, the only civilization we are concerned with, are ultimately derived from Greek thought. Pythagoras, living in the sixth century B.C., is credited with the discovery that the Greek musical scale depends on the division of a string of the lyre in the ratios 1:2 (octave), 2:3 (fifth), 3:4 (fourth), and 1:4 (double octave). In other words, the ratios of the first four integers 1:2:3:4 express all the consonances of the Greek musical scale. This discovery of the close interrelationship of sound, space, and numbers had immense consequences, for it seemed to hold the key to the unexplored regions of universal harmony. Moreover, if the invariable of all octaves is the ratio 1:2, it must be this ratio, the Greeks argued, that is the cause of the musical consonance.

Perfection and beauty were therefore ascribed to the ratio itself.

Plato, in his *Timaeus*, expounded a geometrical theory which was no less influential. He postulated that certain simple figures of plane geometry were the basic stuff of which the universe was composed. I have no doubt that it was mainly owing to Plato's never-forgotten cosmological theory that such figures as the equilateral triangle, the right-angled isosceles triangle, and the square were charged with a deep significance and played such an important part in the Western approach to proportion.

We have overwhelming evidence that many medieval churches were built *ad quadratum* or *ad triangulum*, reflecting a platonic pedigree. Milan Cathedral is a well-known example: discussions on whether the church should be erected according to triangulation or quadrature dragged on for years.

From the fifteenth century on, attention was focused on musical proportion. Although never entirely excluded from consideration, the Renaissance and post-Renaissance periods preferred an arithmetical theory of proportion derived from the harmonic intervals of the Greek musical scale, in contrast to the Middle Ages, which favoured platonic geometry. The Renaissance, in addition, fully embraced ancient anthropometry. Following Vitruvius (whose treatise reflects Greek ideas), Renaissance theory and practice pronounced axiomatically that the proportions of architecture must echo those of the human body. This ancient theory lent itself to being incorporated into a Christian conception of the world. The Bible tells us that Man was created in the image of God. It logically follows that Man's proportions are perfect. The next axiom appears unavoidable: man-made objects, such as architectural structures, can only be attuned to universal harmony if they follow man's proportions. You may approve or disapprove of these deductions; you may find Renaissance architects' demonstrations of the connection between man and architecture naive and even funny, but some of you may detect that we are moving close to the Modulor. Moreover, because of—or in spite of—such convictions, the world was enriched by most beautiful buildings.

To postulate such a relationship between human and architectural proportions is, perhaps, not so far-fetched. The human body lends itself to an investigation of metrical relationships between parts and between the parts and the whole. You can express the parts in terms of submultiples of the whole; or you can operate with a small unit of measurement such as the

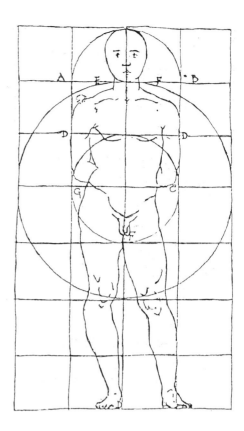

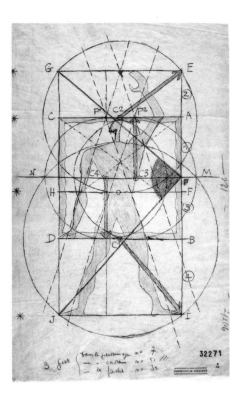

3. Standing man, his arm raised; drawing for the illustration for *Le Modulor*, 1948 (FLC 32271).
4. Matila Ghyka. Studies of the Golden Section.
5. The two constructions of the Golden Section, the one added to the square (the red series), the other removed from the double square (the blue series).

face or the hand as a module, the multiples and submultiples of which guarantee metrical coordination.

Precisely the same principles may be applied to architectural structures: all the parts may be metrically interrelated by making them submultiples of a grand unit or multiples of a small unit. For the Renaissance, the *tertium comparationis* between man and buildings consisted in this: just as the beauty of the human body appears to be regulated by and derived from the correct metrical relation between all its members, so the beauty of a building depends on the correct metrical interrelation of all its parts.

In the eighteenth century the old approach to proportion broke down. Enlightenment and empiricism militated against the notion that mathematical ratios as such can be beautiful. Romantic artists had no use for intellectual number theories which would seem to endanger their individuality and freedom. In the nineteenth century it was mainly scholars who kept the interest in problems of proportion alive.

The mid-nineteenth century, however, saw two events which had a direct bearing on the modern approach to proportion—and on Le Corbusier's Modulor. First, Joseph Paxton built the Crystal Palace in London, the first structure of colossal size erected of standardized units over a grid. The logic inherent in the industrial revolution enforced a dimensional order. Secondly, the German, Adolf Zeising, published a book, *Neue Lehre von dem Proportionem des menschlichen Körpers*, 1854, in which he persuasively argued that the Golden Section was the proportion pervading macrocosm and microcosm alike.

The wonderful properties of the Golden Section, of course, had been known to the Greeks. The Golden Section is the only true proportion consisting of two magnitudes (instead of 3 or 4), and in it as you know, the ratio of the whole to the larger part always equals that of the larger to the smaller part:

$$\frac{a}{b} = \frac{b}{a+b} = \frac{.618}{1} = \frac{1}{1.618}$$

In the early thirteenth century Leonardo da Pisa, called Fibonacci, discovered that on a ladder of numbers with each number on the right being the sum of the pair on the preceding rung, the arithmetical ratio between the two numbers on the same rung rapidly approaches the Golden Section. Thus, for practical purposes, the Golden Section may be approximated to such ratios as 5:8, 8:13, 13:21. (Expressed algebraically, the Fibonacci series runs: a, b, a+b, a+2b, 2a+3b, 5a+8b. . . .)

Although the Golden Section remained a treasured heirloom of Western thought, it played no significant part in art and architecture. But after Zeising, the Golden Section found enthusiastic partisans, and a straight line leads from him to Hambidge's *Dynamic Symmetry* (1917) and to Matila Ghyka's books in the nineteen-twenties and thirties—from Ghyka to Le Corbusier.

Here briefly are the constituent elements of the Modulor one after another:

First, the Modulor is a measuring tool based on the human body. Anthropometry is its essence. Le Corbusier is thus in line of descent from Vitruvius and the Renaissance. When you look at his design of the "Stele of the Measure," built at the Unité d'Habitation at Marseille, you are right back at the anthropometric Renaissance exercises which seemed so strange before.

Secondly, basic geometrical units, the square and the double square, form Le Corbusier's point of departure. Quadrature, we saw, played an overwhelming part in the Middle Ages, and the square and the double square with their ratio of 1:2 has Pythagorean connotations. Le Corbusier saw these units in their relation to man: the solar plexus lies at the centre of a man with arm raised. Needless to say, this was well known to Renaissance artists.

Thirdly, two Golden Section means are introduced, one added to the square, the other subtracted from the double square. The Golden Section added to the square determines the relationship between the two parts of the body, up to the solar plexus and from there to the head. The Golden Section subtracted from the double square determines the relationship from the foot to the fork and from the fork to the tips of the fingers of the upraised arm.

The proportions of the human body defined in terms of the Golden Section were derived by Le Corbusier from his erroneous belief that "it has been proved, particularly during the Renaissance, that the human body follows the Golden Rule." In actual fact, Renaissance artists found in the human body only commensurate musical proportions. Le Corbusier's implicit acceptance of the Golden Section stems from the mystique of Matila Ghyka.

Fourthly, the Modulor is no module in the ordinary sense. It consists of a scale of dimensions derived from

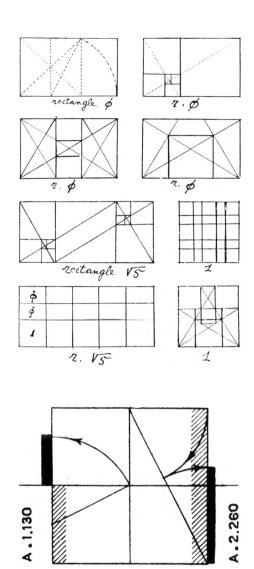

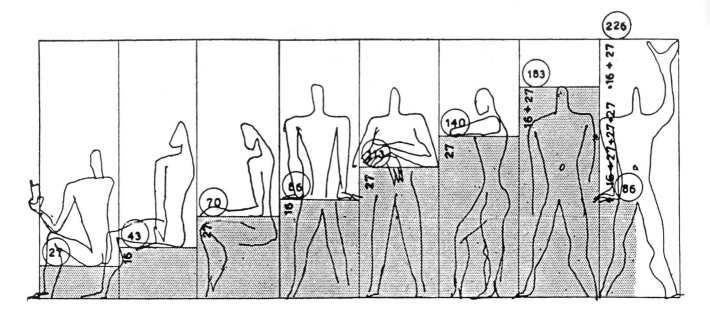

6. Dimensioning of the positions typical of the human body in space according to the Modulor.

the six-foot man. As we have seen, the irrational divisions of the Golden Section can be approximated by numbers of the Fibonacci series (Le Corbusier used centimeters, but he may as well have used inches). In his Modulor, the figures 43, 70, 113 belong to a Fibonacci series which originated from the square (the red series, in Le Corbusier's terminology), and 86, 140, 226 belong to another Fibonacci series, which originated from the double square (the blue series). In other words, the ratio of 1:2 is always present.

By combining the two series, one arrives at a series the terms of which have a special bearing on man in space, as Le Corbusier attempts to demonstrate. These Fibonacci series, single or in combination, may be prolonged in both directions. An illustration published by Le Corbusier shows that each series can be drawn as a grid which engenders a great variety of spatial shapes.

Another figure gives the points of intersection of the superimposed red and blue series, and here the interweaving of the original unit, the double unit and the Golden Section may be noticed.

For the Modulor, Le Corbusier makes some special claims: First, the spatial combinations obtained by the Modulor are infinite. Secondly, the Modulor is a perfect means of unification in the mass production of manufactured articles. In contrast to an arbitrary module, it offers the possibility of harmonious integration of standardized products. Such considerations show Le Corbusier in line of descent from Paxton and competing with the propagators of standardization through modular coordination. Thirdly, in contrast to the technologists among architects, who consider a module esthetically neutral, for Le Corbusier

16 Rudolf Wittkower

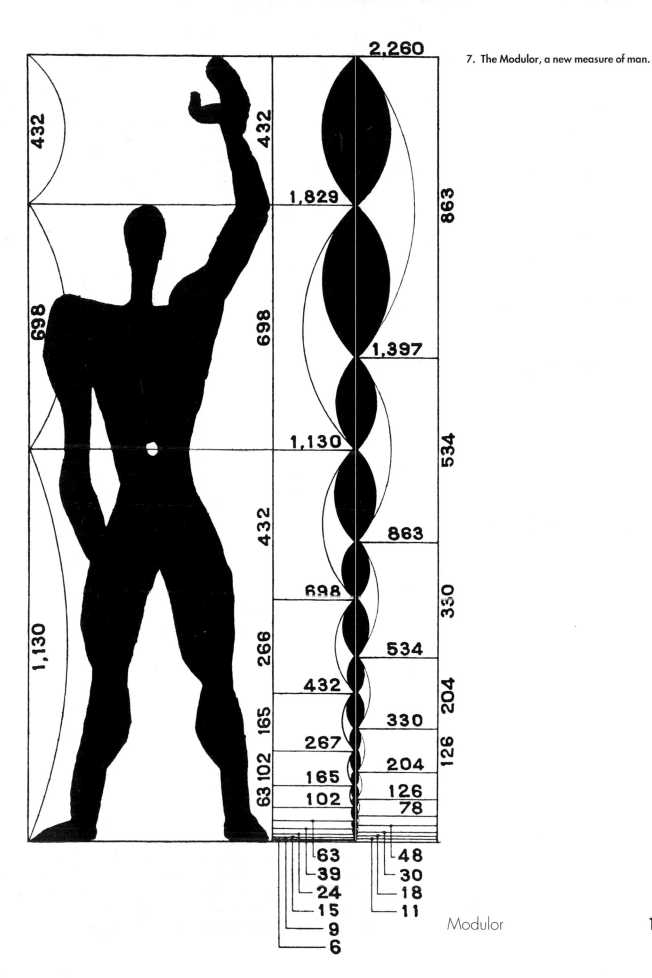

7. The Modulor, a new measure of man.

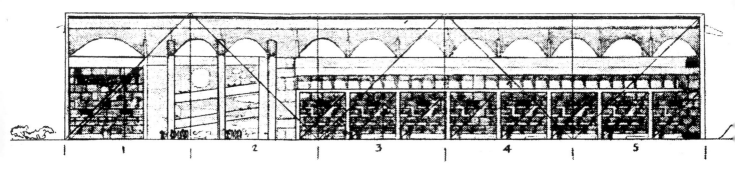

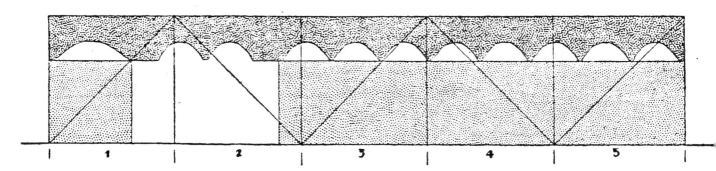

8. Chandigarh, High Courts, section and proportional scheme.
9. The "Stele of the Measure" at the *Unité d'habitation* in Marseille.

esthetic satisfaction overrides all other considerations. Harmony, regulating everything around us, is his ultimate quest. His aesthetic judgment is buttressed, thus, by a metaphysical belief in a divine order of things. Fourthly, the Modulor is a precision instrument, comparable to the keyboard of a piano; like the keyboard, the Modulor does not interfere with the individual freedom of the performer. Nor does it help to make bad designs good.

Meanwhile, modular coordination is on the march. An almost unbelievable amount of research has been devoted to it in recent years. The main purpose of these enterprises is to economize on all levels: in the architect's and the contractor's office as well as in the factory. Designs consist of multiples of the basic module, and since F. Bemis's *Evolving House*, published in 1936, the four-inch grid has been given preference in this country. The difference between the static—sterile, one is tempted to say—quality of the normal modular grid and the dynamic quality of Le Corbusier's grid is most striking.

What is the balance sheet? As I see it, Le Corbusier's Modulor, the creation of one man, has to assert itself against the combined efforts of hundreds or even thousands working on modular coordination. The odds favour the advocates of modular coordination: their work is scientific, sober, and objective. It is to the point, easily intelligible, and eminently practical.

Rudolf Wittkower

Le Corbusier's is the opposite in every respect: it is amateurish, dynamic, personal, paradoxical, and often obscure. When you think you have it all sorted out, you wonder how practical the Modulor really is. Le Corbusier's own buildings at Marseille, St. Dié, Algiers, Chandigarh, supply the answer.

Nevertheless, all his claims have been challenged. Against his faith in the immense variability of design offered by the Modulor, it is said that its range enforces an unsatisfactory limitation. Against his canon derived from the six-foot man, it is claimed that in order to be universal, other human heights should be taken into account. His assertion of freedom of design guaranteed by the Modulor is dismissed as "just another rigid academic system." His play with the Golden Section and the Fibonacci series is criticized as schoolboy mathematics wrapped in a cloak of mystification.

I do not want to continue this list of censure, for when all is said and done, it is only Le Corbusier whose instinct guided him to the sources of our cultural heritage; who transformed it imaginatively to suit modern requirements; who attempted a new synthesis, and once again, intellectualized man's intuitive urge with which I began. It is only Le Corbusier who brings to bear on the old problem of proportion a prophetic, unceasingly searching, and, above all, poetic mind . . . the poetic and illogical mind of a great artist.

Since the breakdown of the old systems of proportions, no architect has been so deeply engaged and none has believed so fervently that "architecture is proportion."*

* This paper was first presented at a conference at Columbia University in New York in the spring of 1961. It was published in *Four Great Makers of Modern Architecture: Gropius, Le Corbusier, Mies van der Rohe, Wright,* New York, Trustees of Columbia University, 1963, pp. 196–204.

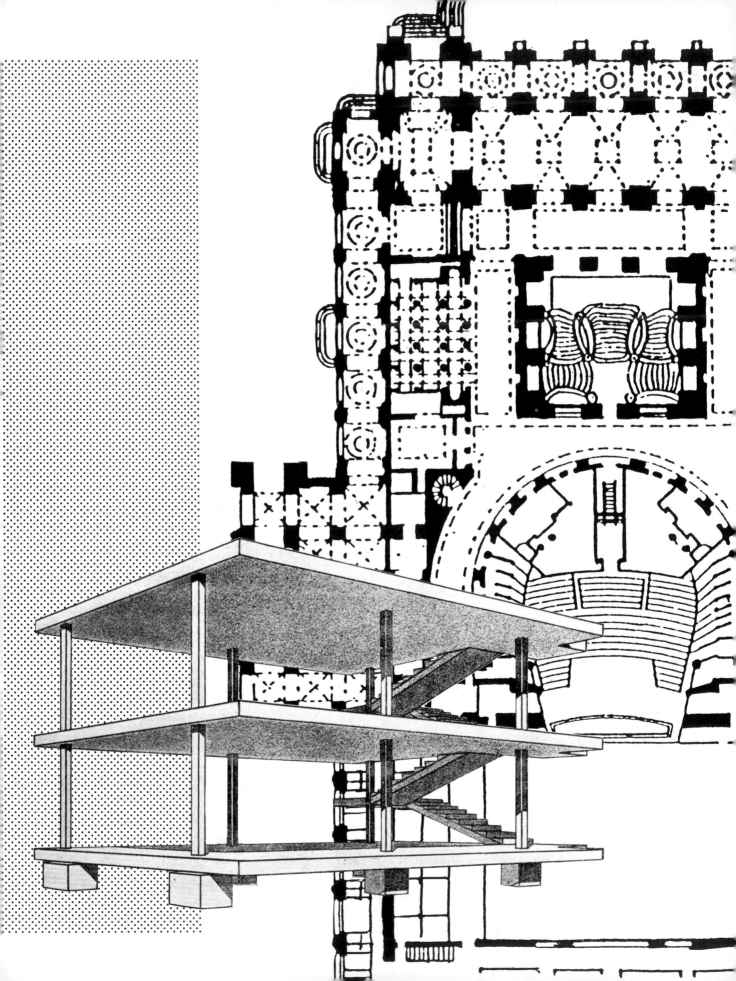

LA MAISON DOM-INO

Peter Eisenman

AND THE SELF-REFERENTIAL SIGN

The modes and identities of representation, so weighted down with their own material history, have ceased to express the order of being completely and openly.

Michel Foucault

It can be argued that all changes in architecture can in some manner be traced to changes in culture. Certainly, the most tangible changes in architecture have been brought about by advancements in technology, the development of new conditions of use, and the change in significance of certain rituals and their domain of performance. Thus, it would seem that the nature and significance of the architectural object should reflect the gradual shift in man's consciousness that occurred between the mid-fifteenth century and the twentieth century, from a theocentric to an anthropocentric conception of the world.

Such changes in architecture are most abstractly recorded in spatial manipulations of plan and section, which become the physical manifestations of developing formal strategies made possible by new conceptions of notation and representation. While more superficial stylistic changes are easily grafted onto the facade like applied icons, such changes in elevation are never so fundamental as changes in plan and section; plan and section have been, since the development of orthogonal projection, the repositories of the animating principles that define architecture in the classical Western sense. They are the primary notational devices that reflect both changing concepts of use and meaning and the technical capacity to produce such changes. One has only to compare a plan of Palladio (fig. 11) to one of Bramante (fig. 10), or one of Scamozzi (fig. 12) to one of Palladio, to see in the movement from the external expression of the cruciform to its envelopment in a

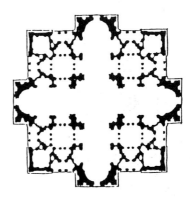

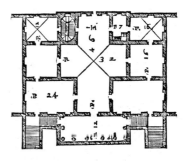

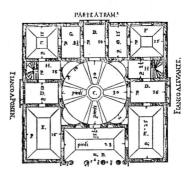

10. Early plan for St. Peter's, Rome. Bramante, c. 1506.
11. Villa Foscari (La Malcontenta), Malcontenta de Mira. Andrea Palladio, 1560.
12. Plan of Villa Pisani alla Rocca. Scamozzi, 1576.

21

platonic square or rectangle and finally the cruciform's complete dissolution, evolving spatial conceptions of an anthropocentric society.

The record of the later history of Western architecture, from the early nineteenth century to the present, also documents the changes which have occurred in man's conception of his object-world as they come to be reflected in his architecture. For example, if one examines the difference in conception between two buildings like Charles Garnier's Paris Opera House and Le Corbusier's Maison Dom ino admittedly of widely different use and significance but nevertheless typical—one witnesses an alteration of space so fundamental as to announce historical rupture. The abandonment of the plaid grid of the opera house for the free plan of Dom-ino, possibly one of the most critical changes ever in the continuous cycle of changes, appears to herald a decisive cultural phenomenon: the birth of a Modernist sensibility that is to parallel and even supersede classical Western thought.

Modernism is a state of mind. It describes the change that took place sometime in the nineteenth century in man's attitude toward his physical world and its artifacts—aesthetic, cultural, social, economic, philosophical, and scientific. It can be interpreted as a critique of the formerly humanist, anthropocentric attitude, which viewed man as an all-powerful, all-rational being at the center of his physical world.

In the arts other than architecture, where Modernism has signaled a profound change, it is fairly easy to distinguish a condition of objecthood and sign which can be labeled "Modernist." In each case, this condition is characterized above all by the object's tendency to be self-referential. Thus the change from narrative to non-narrative prose or from tonal to dodecaphonic music reflects in its historical evolution a change in the *conception* of the relation of man and his object world, a relation where the writer or composer is no longer necessarily interposed between the object and the reader or listener. Man is seen to be in both a more direct and also more relativistic condition vis-à-vis his object world—the "peer" of rather than the determiner of his works. Modernist prose and music incorporated not only this new relation of the object/maker, but also of the object's signification, that is, how the object reveals its condition of being and its manner of coming into being, how these are recorded and the inherent condition of such notations. Since the object of prose, music, painting, and

Peter Eisenman

sculpture is no longer merely a narrative record and mimetic representation of man's condition, it becomes more fundamentally concerned with its own objecthood, with an existence outside of (if parallel to) its inescapable origination by, and traditional representation of, man. This new conception of the object world naturally opens a potential for uncovering entirely new modes of existence within the object world itself.

But what is curious about most interpretations of modern architecture, and in particular those of Le Corbusier—supposedly the most modern (i.e., abstract, painterly) of all the modern architects—is that they do not view their subject in very modern terms. In fact, far from establishing the tenets of a Modernism in architecture, they seem intent on seeing modern architecture as a continuation of the Renaissance tradition. For example, up to now the most significant critical and theoretical writings on Le Corbusier have been by Colin Rowe. However, one has only to look at the titles of some of his texts to see that their thrust is decidedly anti-Modernist. In fact, of his five major texts dealing with Le Corbusier three of them contain key words in their titles which link Le Corbusier with Renaissance thought— "Mathematics of the Ideal Villa," "Mannerism and Modern Architecture," "The Architecture of Utopia"—and all of them develop an attitude toward space which has its origins in the sixteenth century. From a reading of these texts, there is little question that while Rowe exhibits a consistent respect for Le Corbusier he simultaneously sustains only a fragile tolerance for modern architecture and for that matter much of what can be called Modernist thought. And since Colin Rowe has provided one of the few critical matrices for analyzing modern architecture, it may be well to ask how much of his thinking has conditioned our received view of Le Corbusier, and thus even much of second generation modern architecture; and conversely, how much of his thinking is in fact a product of modern architecture itself, which it can be argued is not necessarily modern or Modernist, but rather a phenomenon of late humanism; and finally, how much the free plan, supposedly the 'canonical' spatial diagram of modern architecture, is merely a manifestation of a late Enlightenment view of man, and how much the free facade is merely an icon of Le Corbusier's technological genius.

Once these questions are admitted, then it can be argued that Rowe's ideas have in fact obscured the one aspect of Le Corbusier's work that makes it truly Modernist: that is, its aspect as a self-referential sign, its existence as *an architecture about architecture*. In the interpretation of modern architecture put forward by Rowe and others, while the style preference changed and new descriptive metaphors were used, the conception of what architecture was and what it could be remained relatively constant. Architecture remained conceived by man, representing man and his condition. It assumed physical structure and shelter to be absolute conditions of architecture, and when it considered signification it was in terms of a meaning which was *extrinsic* to architecture itself; that is, to ideas which related architecture to man, rather than to intrinsic ideas which explained architecture itself. It continued to rely on the traditional drawing modes of plan, section, and elevation to conceptualize its values. But if, as Saussure has suggested of language, words tend to divide a conceptual spectrum in arbitrary and specific ways, similarly the continuing representation and conceptualization of architecture in plan, section, and elevation can be said to have determined and probably also obscured many aspects of architecture.

As a plan and a section diagram, Dom-ino seems a rather simple and straightforward statement. Perhaps for this very reason—its apparently extreme clarity—it is often taken as an icon and a structural paradigm, an example of the potential of the then new technology, a prototypical unit expressing ideas of mass production, repetition, and so on. The famous perspective drawing is cited by Rowe as the initial didactic statement of the spatial concepts of the Modern Movement (p. 20). He argues that here in the concentrated energy of a few simple gestures are contained implications which for the next twenty-five years are to condition the development of modern architecture. But it is only within the context of a Renaissance conception of space, rather than a Modernist one, that the Maison Dom-ino can be considered a canonical spatial diagram. For in a Modernist context the Paris Opera House and the Maison Dom-ino appear merely as successive variations of the same phenomenon: historical change mirrored in unchanging modes of representation. 'Modern' in Rowe's context seems merely to indicate the new style of supposed abstraction and the symbology of the machine rather than to signal changes apparent in the notations of plan and section which might suggest a fundamental change between man and object. Thus, if we see Maison Dom-ino through the eyes of

Peter Eisenman

Rowe as the canonical free plan diagram, a certain category of conceptions about architecture is made available to us, but within this category only a limited concept of change can be discerned.

Moreover, while the canonical spatial diagram of Dom-ino is often alluded to as if its invocation was sufficient to support its supposed lucidity, it has never been formally analyzed in any systematic way. The general acceptance of Rowe's thesis suggests that the recognition of an obvious and compelling truth, which in turn suggests that in the diagram itself there must exist, in the few elements and their precise size, shape, number, and location, a level of communication that goes beyond the mere fact of their existence. While this communication has been described in one way by Rowe, it is also possible to read the particular configuration of the diagram in terms of an *other* condition of representation, an *other* significance, an *other* realm, which exists simultaneously with the accepted interpretations. It is precisely the simplicity and clarity of the diagram taken together with the fact of its impact in the history of modern architecture that leads us to look for this 'otherness', which might be defined as a Modernist context for Dom-ino.

Thus, looking now at Maison Dom-ino with a different lens, proposing a different conceptual spectrum, it is possible to see in the precise selection, size, number, and location of the elements in the Dom-ino diagram the incipient presence of the self-referential sign. Such a sign notion as initiated in the Maison Dom-ino may begin to define not only a Modernist condition of architecture, but beyond that, insofar as this notion of sign is different from that which is classically thought to be architectural, to define certain minimal conditions for any architecture. Our analysis must begin with the basic elements—the three horizontal slabs, six box-like footings, six linear columns, and one staircase in a primitive geometric configuration. First, it can be assumed that in any such diagram of architectural elements, the columns and slabs and their positioning have something to do with holding things up—probably also with some primitive intention to shelter, enclose, and divide, but fundamentally with obeying the laws of statics and physics. This much can be taken for granted. Thus, the configuration is initially seen as the result of necessity rather than any other intention; the columns and slabs are not read as signs, but merely as "integers" of construction.

Yet a floor slab or a door, a window or a wall may be

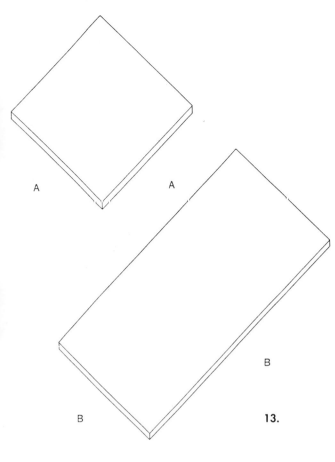

13.

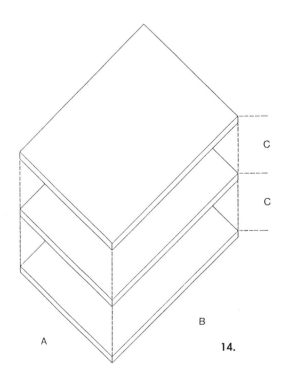

14.

necessary conditions for building or function but they are not sufficient in themselves to define 'architecture'. Because while all buildings have doors, windows, walls and floors all buildings are not necessarily architecture. Equally all of these elements, as physical entities, necessarily have three spatial dimensions, but these, no matter how pleasing their proportions, which may be recorded and understood geometrically, are not necessarily architecture.

If architecture is not geometry, it must in some way be differentiated from it. In order to distinguish any one class of objects from any other, it must be possible not only to signal the difference of that class from all others (a negative signal) but to signal or identify the presence of the particular class itself (a positive signal). While all Ford Motor cars, as a class, may say something about movement, vehicles, etc., any single motor car is not necessarily the sign of another nor of the general category of motor cars. Similarly, any column, wall, or beam, while it may be saying something about structure and statics, is not *per se* a sign either of itself or of any general category which could be considered architecture. It is merely a column, wall, or beam.

The dimensions of any rectilinear plane, whether floor, wall, or column, can be designated simply by two notations: A A or A B; that is, either the two perpendicular sides are equal or they are unequal (fig. 13). However, if the dimensions of a plane are A B, and this dimension is *marked*, that is, *designated in some way as different*, then this marking can be considered to be a sign of that condition. The presence of an intentional sign may be the most important quality which distinguishes architecture from geometry, distinguishes an intention to be something more than a notation of a physical presence from the facts of literal existence. The three horizontal slabs of the Maison Dom-ino have an A B relationship of end to side. Initially, we do not know if this A B relationship is intentional, since such a relationship in any non-square plane is always literally there, so we begin to look for its marking as a sign. We also notice that the particular relationship of the three slabs suggests a geometric condition which can be defined by a set of proportional relationships. Of course, any number of arbitrary proportional relationships which still respect the laws of gravity can be made from these particular elements. For example (fig. 14), the three horizontal elements can be placed one over another with their corners in line so that they are equidistant

Peter Eisenman

from one another. They can also be placed so that while they remain equidistant from one another vertically and the two sides remain in alignment the planes step away from one edge at equal intervals (fig. 15). Alternatively, still leaving edges aligned, the interval between horizontals can be changed so that they are no longer equidistant but rather in a proportional ratio (fig. 16). These examples are merely three of many simple variants of a regular ordered geometry, but of course an almost infinite number of such alternatives could be posed. Each can be described by a different set of proportional systems and placement rules. These in turn can be explained by a simple rationale or strategy, and plans and sections can be drawn for them.

But are any or all of these variations anything more than geometry? And even in terms of their use as floor levels and the necessity to enclose them so as to provide shelter, are they anything more than a set of geometric relationships plus this use, which together in some way approximate what we have always thought architecture to be? And if we answer in the affirmative that they do constitute architecture, then do all such variations of these elements when combined with their uses constitute architecture? And if it immediately appears clear that not all of the examples qualify, then how do we begin to distinguish between those that do and those that do not? Or if none of the variations are considered architecture, how do we begin to identify at what point these primitive configurations become architecture and when in this process they become a canonical spatial diagram of modern architecture? Beyond this, what, if anything, might make them a Modernist as opposed to a classical architecture?

Clearly each diagram is potentially a framework for architecture, but no more or no less than any other three dimensional configuration. In fact, a highly simple geometric scheme is perhaps less likely to transcend its existence as mere geometry than a more complex one since it is more difficult to change it — to add or to subtract any element—without changing its decription and its rationale (that is, without transforming it into some other geometric structure); the elements tend to be the manifestations of a closed system which allows for no alternation or interpretation except for more or less minor changes in their size and shape. Thus, in cases where a simple geometry exists as a basic diagram, the 'architecture' seems to be reduced to the decorative grafting of some aesthetic skin or the insertion of a particular use into

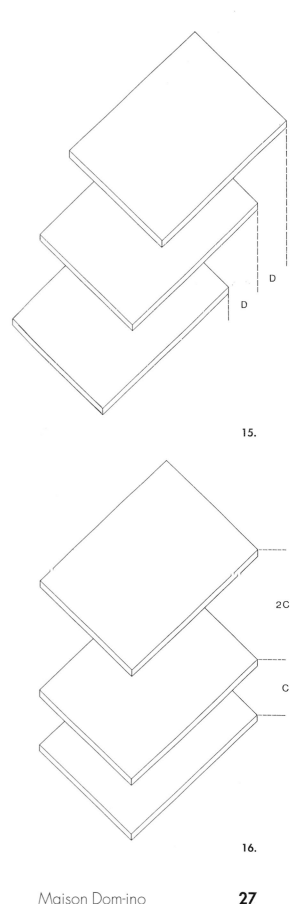

15.

16.

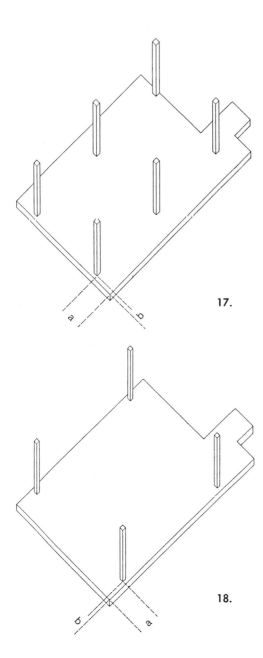

17.

18.

the given geometry. Likewise, if we reverse the proposition and begin with some program of use or a site context which logically suggests a simple order, the question of whether the diagram is any more or any less architecture would remain exactly the same.

But let us return now to the original Dom-ino elements and their precise configuration in the Dom-ino diagram. If we analyze this configuration we begin to see that the elements together with their precise size and location exhibit an articulate level of intentionality. This cannot be seen in the configuration of the slab alone, but only in the relationship of slab to columns. Once more, one has to imagine a range of possible or reasonable column locations and a set of alternative shapes—round, square, or recti-linear. The fact that the three pairs of columns are set back at an equal distance from the long sides while on the ends they coincide with the edge of the slab provides the clue to the fact that they are more than simple geometrical notations (fig. 17). First, because the columns are also in an A B relationship to the edge of the slab they can be seen to reinforce the difference between side A and side B of the slab itself. Second, while in themselves A and B are only a notation, a proportional difference—the literal fact that the slab is not a square—it can also be seen that the envi-sioned function—house—is not the determiner of the proportional relationship since most functions can be accommodated in any simple shape. For example, a house can just as easily be accommodated in a square as in a rectangle. Third, an equivalent A B distinc-tion, if that had been the only proportion, could have been made by setting the two pairs of end columns back from the side and the side columns flush with the front and back of the slab (fig. 18). Again, the col-umns could have been set back equally, the same distance on the ends as on the side (fig. 19). In this case, it would have been only the unequal sides which would have marked the A B distinction; all the col-umns would have been seen in an equal A A relation-ship to the edge. Finally, the length could have been marked as a function of the width A by inserting another pair of columns (fig. 20), providing two equal increments of width A. All—and of course any number of others—would have worked equally well from the point of view of structure, function, and geometry.

But again, since only one of these possibilities is in fact the case, we must assume an intentionality in the particular configuration with respect to all other permutations, and insist that the precise location of the columns with respect to the slab reveals the presence of an intention to treat the column-slab relationship as a sign and the precise location of the columns as a mark of that intention. The idea of marking and the presence of the column as a mark as opposed to a mere division or structural element are understood through the general linguistic concept of *redundancy*. Thus, when the column locations act *to reinforce the original geometric A B relationship which in itself is so clear as not to need reinforcement*, one interprets this as an intention to underscore a condition of being, that is as a significant redundancy. While A and B are literally present, there is also an intention to have A and B become something other than their actual presence. The redundancy of the mark thereby signals that there is something present other than either the geometry or the function of the column and slab.

There is then an unintentional, or literal, reading of column and slab which posits A and B as unequal sides of the slab, and then an intentional reinforcement through the location of the columns, which makes A and B take on an additional presence. Thus, the fact itself—the slab—plus the spatial marking—the location of the columns—suggest an idea about sides A and B which is an idea only about itself, a self-referential statement. This then may be a primitive though truly Modernist phenomenon, one that speaks about its mere existence and its own condition of being.

A second aspect of the Dom-ino diagram which can be called self referential is the horizontal datum. The notion of a datum in the traditional architectural sense is not Modernist but an attitude to the vertical plane which seems to have originated in the sixteenth century. A datum was something which existed by virtue of its dominant configuration or location, and acted to inform and direct the observer's experience of the object. This can be understood if we look at Le Corbusier's villa at Garches, where the strong condition of frontality derives from the sixteenth century. It is true that its peripheral as opposed to centric composition—its conceptual "density" at the edges—seems to define it as "modern," but peripheral composition also existed in the sixteenth century, although the idea was lost in the centralizing tendencies of the Beaux-Arts. But again, the modernity, if it may be called that, exists only in the sense of the structure or composition of the image and not in a changed condition of object-viewer in relation to both the sign and the object. Garches can be said to be

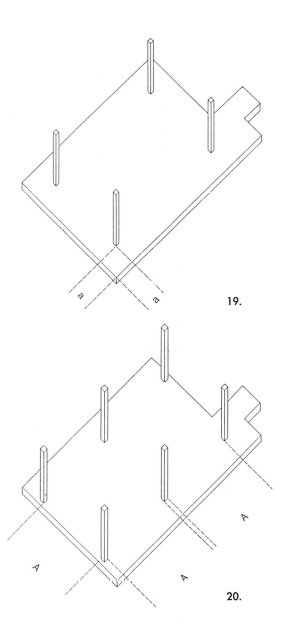

19.

20.

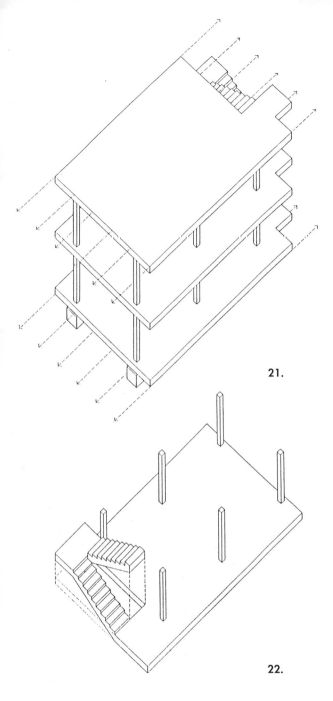

21.

22.

Modernist only when the front facade is considered as a frontal datum, as the collapsed energy of the other three sides being projected on the single plane. For in these terms it is a self-referential datum. It fixes a new object-man relationship, that is, man is no longer required to walk around the building to understand the object. Rather conception is from a single static position. It differs from the classical conception of frontality and datum in the sense that while the Renaissance datum fixes a preferred viewpoint of man to object, it does not imply the collapse of the other three viewpoints into a single position.

Dom-ino places primary emphasis on the horizontal as opposed to the vertical datum. Setting the column grid back from the edge of the horizontal plane provides a dominantly sandwich-like character to the space. And, it is the location of the columns on the front, back, and sides which reveals the self-referential nature of the datum. In the equality of the setback there is the suggestion of symmetry and stasis, i.e., that the long sides are complete and will not grow (fig. 21). At the same time, the location of the columns flush on the ends marks an opposition to the setback columns on the sides, and further suggests that the ends of the slab have been cut off, implying the possibility, or former condition, of horizontal extension of the slab on the long axis. Horizontal extension is an idea about horizontality, in fact about "horizon." And since extension is implied in only one direction of the horizontal axis, the differentiation of extension and stasis themselves is what is being marked. Thus, the horizontal plane becomes a datum carrying the idea of both an infinite *extension* of space in longitudinal vectors and the denial of the same proposition in lateral vectors. Moreover, since its reference is only to horizontality, to spatial extension or compression which are intrinsically architectural ideas, it differs from both the concept of datum of Garches and the traditional datum of classical Western space. For in both of these, datum is primarily concerned with relating and structuring the perception of a viewer to an object. Datum provided the viewer with a physical reference to understand both the narrative of his movement to, around, and in an object as well as his static position at certain points along that movement. In both cases datum structured the experience of man. In this sense it speaks outside of itself and can be seen as extra-referential. The horizontal datum of Dom-ino speaks only of its own physical condition. It is a sign of that condition and nothing more. In this sense it is self-referential. It exists as a mark of its own condition and is only known through its own marking. This conception of datum at Dom-ino also begins to alter the conception and definition of architecture.

This brings us to the next element of the Dom-ino diagram, the staircase. Since Le Corbusier himself shows it in subsequent drawings as the element by which the units clip together, it is always assumed that its particular location derives from this intention. However, again attempting a different kind of interpretation, it is possible to find in the particular location of the staircase with respect to the slab a third self-referential notation. There are three interpretations of this relationship. First, the slab can be read as extending to the outer edge of the staircase (fig. 22); in this case, the void in the corner is read as a cut-out in the slab. Second, the slab can be read as terminating at the inner edge of the staircase; in this case, a small square piece can be read as added to the slab (fig. 23). Third, the slab can be read as extending to the mid-point of the stair; the stair being seen as half inside and half outside the slab (fig. 24). In this case both cut-outs—subtraction, and addition—can be read simultaneously. While the actual location of the staircase in relation to the slab establishes a series of vertical layers perpendicular to the long axis, it also establishes a sign notation which calls attention to the actual addition and subtraction. These, like extension and stasis, involve both the actual object and the ideas about architecture itself. There is also the counter proposition inherent in the placement of the staircase; one which expresses the integrity or wholeness of the horizontal plane. For one must leave one plane in order to go up, re-entering the next plane from outside rather than puncturing its surface from within. Thus, the location of the staircase produces two propositions which are in opposition but together refer only to the nature of the horizontal surface itself (fig. 25).

Finally, one must consider the six square base elements in relation to the first horizontal slab. Certainly their size, shape, and location suggest something more than support because, as one can easily see, other configurations could have provided equivalent support. For example, the slab could have been set on the ground (fig. 26), so the mere gesture to raise it and place it on a base makes a first, although conventional, distinction between ground and slab; but second, the particular way that the slab is raised on what seem to be traditional construction footings, which eqully could have been buried, suggests an-

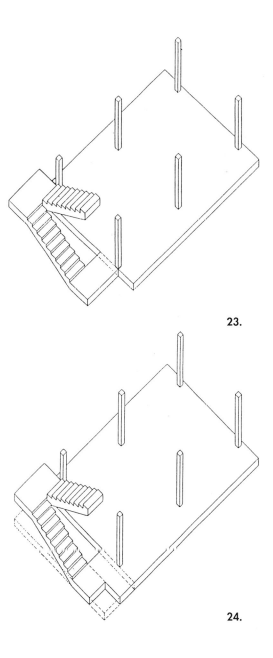

23.

24.

Maison Dom-ino　　**31**

other intention for them. The most obvious gesture would have been to continue the columns through the lower slab as *pilotis* (fig. 27). But in this case there would have been no distinction between the way the vertical element meets the top and bottom of the slab. It is precisely because the columns do not continue through the slab and instead become block-like elements that the notation is self-referential. It marks not only the literal difference—that which exists between the top and bottom surfaces of the slab in structural terms—but it also marks the bottom slab as something other than the two upper slabs. This marking indicates that the shape, size, and location of the footings are something more than structural. They function, but at the same time they *overcome* their function, an idea which begins to suggest another primitive condition for an architecture.

For if architecture can be distinguished from geometry on the terms we have suggested, what distinguishes it from being sculpture? We know that sculpture too is more than simply geometry in three dimensions, it is more than a physical representation of some mathematical concept. It may, like architecture, contain geometrical orders and be explained in certain cases by them (although unlike architecture, since sculpture is not necessarily intended to be walked on and in, it does not demand surfaces which in their flatness and horizontality are determined by the laws of gravity, and hence by some form of rectilinear geometry). Sculpture then seems to contain all of what has so far been said to be the sufficient conditions of architecture without any of its necessary conditions: like architecture, it is concerned with objecthood—with physicality and spatiality, and it is also concerned with the characteristics of sign which distinguish it from geometry. But while the two have a similar relationship to geometry what distinguishes them from each other is their relationship to use. Sculpture does not have walls, except in a metaphorical sense. It is this difference which defines a necessary condition for architecture distinct from sculpture.

'Planeness' is a quality of all planes and thus all walls. It involves dimension, physicality, and extension; it signals division and contiguity. But 'planeness', as opposed to 'wallness', is not a sufficient or distinguishing condition of architecture because sculpture has 'planeness' too; moreover, it does not intrinsically imply shelter, support, and enclosure, aspects of function which we have said constitute the minimum traditional necessary conditions of archi-

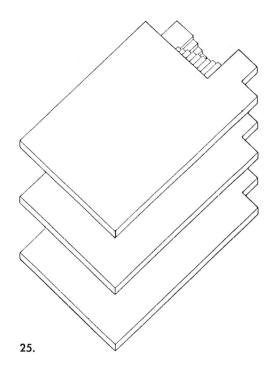

25.

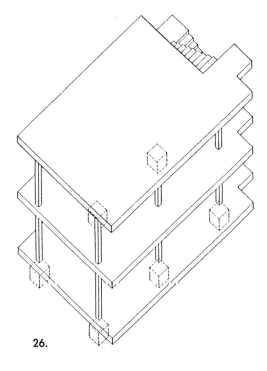

26.

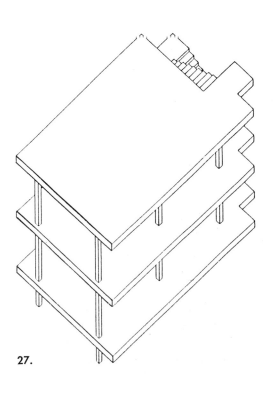

27.

tecture. 'Planeness', then, is not a necessary or sufficient condition of architecture. 'Wallness', on the other hand, contains those qualities which supply the necessary distinction between architecture and sculpture; but, by definition once again, these are merely necessary but not sufficient conditions of architecture since while they distinguish architecture from sculpture, they fail to distinguish it from mere building. As has been seen, to distinguish architecture from building requires an intentional act—a sign which suggests that a wall is doing something more than literally sheltering, supporting, enclosing; it must embody a significance which projects and sustains the idea of 'wallness' beyond mere use, function, or extrinsic allusion. Thus its paradoxical nature: the sign must overcome use and extrinsic significance to be admitted as architecture; but on the other hand, without use, function, and the existence of extrinsic meaning there would be no conditions which would require such an intentional act of overcoming.

In sum, a collection of planes and lines as projected in geometry or as materialized in sculpture can never be architecture precisely because they do not have inherent conditions of use and significance which must be overcome and subsumed. That same collection of planes and lines once they are also invested with 'wallness' and 'beamness' may become architecture when there is the presence of an additional intention to mark the 'wallness' and 'beamness' as architecture. The marking itself, the intentional recording of a condition beyound use, geometry, and extrinsic meaning, reveals that the 'sufficient' component of architecture is not merely the adding together of everything else, but rather exists as a separate, parallel, and potentially intrinsic condition of any space.

Thus, architecture is both substance and act. The sign is a record of an intervention—an event and an act which goes beyond the presence of elements which are merely necessary conditions. Architecture can be proposed as an ordering of conditions drawn from the universe of form together with the act of designating conditions of geometry, use, and significance as a new class of objects.

In this sense the Maison Dom-ino is a sign system which refers to this most primitive condition of architecture, which distinguishes it from geometry, or from geometry plus use and meaning. But more importantly in this context, the Maison Dom-ino can be seen to reflect a Modernist or self-referential condi-

Peter Eisenman

tion of sign, and thus a true and seminal break from the four hundred year old tradition of Western humanist architecture.*

* This essay first appeared in *Oppositions*, no. 15/16 (Winter/Spring 1979), pp. 118–28.

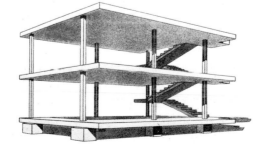

Maison Dom-ino

THE SINGLE-FAMILY DWELLING OF LE CORBUSIER AND PIERRE JEANNERET AT THE WEISSENHOF

Bruno Reichlin

On October 5, 1926, Mies van der Rohe sent Le Corbusier the official invitation to participate in the construction of the experimental Siedlung Am Weissenhof. In the invitation the request was still circumspect and vague: he mentions "The plan for a group of single-family houses." But the "building program" consigned to Le Corbusier and Pierre Jeanneret already foresaw two constructions on the definitive site.[1] There are no doubts about the strategic importance of the site: if Mies's large block of lined-up houses marks the northwest boundary and constitutes the "visual limit" for the building, it thus assumes the function of "Stadtkrone" (city crown);[2] the powerful "terrace house" by Peter Behrens and the two high constructions by Le Corbusier complete the composition of the experimental neighborhood in relation to the northern and southern ends. And if the main access to the experimental neighborhood of the city proceeds along the avenue Am Weissenhof, pointing directly at Mies's block, the two houses by Le Corbusier and Jeanneret characteristically signal the image of the Siedlung from which the important Friedrich-Eber Street descends as it turns toward the panoramic Rathenau Street. Edgar Wedepohl comments with admiration and irritation at the same time: "the position of Le Corbusier's houses on the extreme edge of the Weissenhof Siedlung produces a completely symbolic effect. These buildings, also in confrontation with all the others, are truly an innovation."[3]

The "concept of the show" sent to the participants—even marked "Confidential! Not intended for the public"—states the optimistic and ambitious expectations of the promoters quite well: "The show . . . is a systematic attempt at a solution for the new dwelling and all the structural, technical, and hygienic problems of the organization of space that come together in it";[4] moreover, it is specified that this neighborhood is "an experimental colony for establishing the basis for mod-

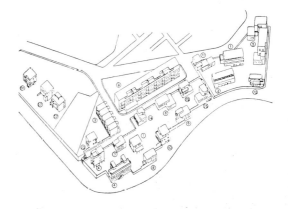

29. Stuttgart, Experimental Siedlung Am Weissenhof, 1927 (the houses by Le Corbusier and Pierre Jeanneret are marked no. 4).

[1] It almost certainly refers to the "Lageplan" in 1:200 scale, Fondation Le Corbusier (hereafter FLC) 7678.
[2] Jürgen Joedicke and Christian Platz, *Die Weissenhofsiedlung*, Stuttgart, 1968, p. 10.
[3] Edgar Wedepohl, "Die Weissenhof-Siedlung der Werkbundausstellung 'Die Wohnung', Stuttgart, 1927," in *Wasmuths Monatshefte für Baukunsl*, 1927, p. 397.
[4] FLC, Dossier "Wiessenhof," document: "Werkbund Ausstellung 'Die Wohnung', Stuttgart, 1927," p. 5.

37

[5] FLC, quoted document.
[6] *Le Corbusier et Pierre Jeanneret—Oeuvre complète 1910–29*, edited by W. Boesiger and O. Stonorov, Zürich, Girsberger, 1929, p. 23.
[7] Le Corbusier, *Précisions sur un état présent de l'architecture et de l'urbanisme*, Paris, Crès (coll. Esprit Nouveau), 1930; Paris, Vincent Fréal, 1960, p. 56.
[8] This refers to the following publication: Alfred Roth, ed., *Zwei Wohnhäuser von Le Corbusier und Pierre Jeanneret*, Stuttgart, 1927, and *Bau und Wohnung—die Bauten der Weissenhofsiedlung in Stuttgart errichet 1927 nach Vorschlagen des Deutschen Werkbundes im Auftrag der Stadt Stuttgart und in Rahmen der Werkbundausstellung "Die Wohnung,"* Deutschen Werkbund, Stuttgart, 1927.
[9] Alfred Roth, ed., *Zwei Wohnhäuser ... op. cit.*

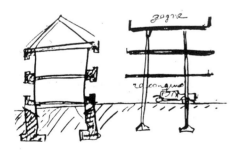

30. Notes by Le Corbusier on the back of the "program of the exposition" (FLC).
31. "La 'coupe symbole' de la révolution architecturale contemporaine" (*Précisions*).
32. Maison Citrohan, sections and plans (from *O.C. 1910–29*).

ern serial construction" and that "the fundamental principle is ascertained by new domestic functions due to the use of new materials."

On the other hand, its promoters have to refute the current opinion "that an industrialization of the building means the violation of the individual. This is why the industrial manufacturing of the apartment buildings or houses *in toto* is not aspired to, but only the mass-production of building units and standardized details . . . transmitting elements that are clearly definitive and determining; thus different types of houses can be defined according to the inhabitants' needs, unlimited variations can be obtained." Here, as in inumerable circulars that followed, and in the publicity build-up mounted by Werner Gräf, the accent is placed on the fact that the exposition was intended for the purpose of experiment and demonstration.

Paradigms of a search: "Citrohan" and "Dom-ino"

For Le Corbusier this invitation was the opportunity for much-coveted time; to judge from his hasty annotations on the back of the program folio, his reaction must have been immediate.[5]

The note says: 1 citrohan
           1 domino

Some only partially legible writing follows, concerning a "brévet allemand pour [?] des pavés vitrés sans fenêtres [?]" (German patent for glass blocks without windows), the demonstrational stand underscored again in the phrase: "on demande *maison montée à sec*" (they are asking for a dry-mounted house); then underneath there follow instructions for his cousin Jeanneret: "Pierre réaliser [?] les diverses sortes de sièges" (Pierre to realise [?] different kinds of chairs), with some sketch-idiograms that show chairs, beds, and something else. Finally: "Fenêtre sans brévet / avec double vitrage écartement théorique 9mm / Demander St Gobain verre / dalle perforé [?]" (Window without patent / with double glass / theoretical space 9 mm / Ask for St Gobain glass / perforated flagstones) and another hard to read sketch.

Now, "Citrohan" and "Dom-ino," together, assume the main part of a search for the element types of the new architecture that Le Corbusier had brought forward since 1914.

"System and structure—framework—completely independent from the function of the house's construction plan,"[6] the "Dom-ino" is the presupposition from which Le Corbusier would define the revolution of modern architecture triggered by the use of new construction methods: "ossature indépendante, plan libre, façade libre" (independent framework, free plan, free façade), summarized as "la coupe symbole de la révolution architecturale contemporaine" (the cutting symbol of the contemporary architectural revolution).[7] By extension of the terms, various successive housing projects in 1914 characterized by the use of an oriented structural grid, would be designated as "Maison Dom-ino."

From the beginning "Citrohan" designated a type of house with its own structural, distribution, and spatial characteristics, even if soon after the spatial organization was determined to be a "strong" element; the "Maison Citrohan" is a parallelepiped box with its walls supporting its larger sides, vertically subdivided inside by an intermediate floor against the supporting walls, articulating space in different areas at a single or double height, according to use.

Making brief note of "Citrohan" and "Dom-ino," Le Corbusier seizes the opportunity presented by an extremely didactic and demonstrational exposition to confer a paradigmatic formulation on the terms bearing on his research. Not by chance that the two houses in Stuttgart would be the object of an independent publication that gives account, down to the most minute details, of the concept that informed them; in this, as in the official publication of the exposition, the famous "5 points d'une architecture nouvelle"[8] are articulated for the first time. In magazine articles, in radio interviews, or conferences,[9] Le Corbusier would turn many times to the significance of these two houses. For a long time they were his most talked about works, despised and celebrated by the press and by the public at large. But the tenor of these testimonials leads us to doubt what message Le Corbusier truly had intended.

The "architectural message" according to Le Corbusier

In this section I intend to investigate that "message" in all its multiple implications.

The pamphlet published by Alfred Roth in Stuttgart in 1927, *Zwei Wohnhäuser von Le Corbusier und Pierre Jeanneret* (Two houses by Le Corbusier and Pierre Jeanneret), renders a careful and exhaustive account of the "contents" of the two buildings, but it only concerns itself with an inventory of "objects": materials, techniques, spatial and formal distribution, and the procedures and intentions that have come together in the installation of the building. He investigates, on a small scale, the modalities—the how—of this "installation," considered from the point of view of

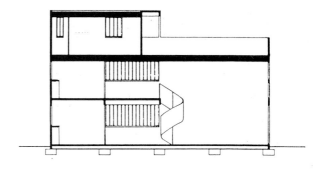

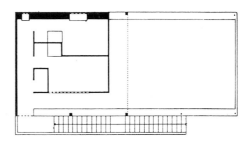

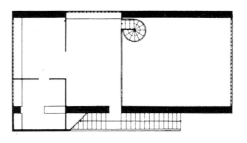

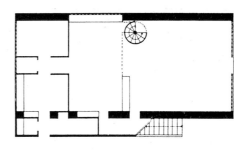

[10] Le Corbusier, *Urbanisme*, Paris, Crès (coll. Esprit Nouveau), 1925, p. 59.

[11] See Umberto Eco, *Lector in fabula—la cooperazione interpretativa nei testi narrativi*, Milan, 1979.

[12] See the famous tripartite division proposed by Erwin Panofsky in his *Studies in Iconology: Humanistic Themes in the Art of the Renaissance*, New York, 1939, pp. 3–31; also the various critical texts that referred to it insisting particularly on the problematic status of the so-called preiconographic sign; see Hubert Damisch, "Sémiologie et iconographie," in *Francastel et après*, Paris, 1976; Giuseppina Bonerba, "Presupposti semiotici nell'iconologia di Panofsky," in *Versus—Quaderni di studi semiotici*, no. 33, 1982, pp.131–44; Adolf Max Vogt, "Suspension eines Körpers im Leeren—Zur präikonographischen Schicht in der Architektur," in *Das Architektonische Urteil*, forthcoming publication from GTA-Institut of the EHT in Zürich.

[13] For the term "encyclopedia" see Umberto Eco, *Lector in fabula*, pp. 37–40; also from the same author: *Trattato di semiotica generale*, Milan, 1975; and "Dizionario versus enciclopedia," in *Semiotica e filosofia del linguaggio*, Turin, 1984.

[14] Alfred Roth, ed., *Zwei Wohnhäuser*, op. cit.

[15] Le Corbusier, *Almanach d'architecture moderne*, Paris, 1926, pp. 102–3.

[16] See the essays collected by Christopher Jones and D.G. Thornley in *Conference on Design Methods*, 1963; by G. Susani in *Scienza e progetto*, Padua, 1967; by Alberto Rosselli in *I metodi del design*, Milan, 1973. The distinction used by Abraham Moles between functional and structural classification of the machine, seems particularly pertinent to me in characterizing Le Corbusier's analytical approach toward the architectural object; see the lecture held on June 10, 1964 at the Hochschule für Gestaltung of Ulm, partially taken up again by Rosselli. This distinction must already have had a certain success in the last century, if Georg Hirth, in his *Das deutsche Zimmer*, Munich, Leipzig, 1886 (third expanded edition), recommends it to his readers in the introductory pages "Die Hauptstücke der Dekoration." Hirth writes: "Like us, criticizing our making and license to make, we oppose our egotistic interest in those like us. In an analogous way we can also distinguish subjective functions, even those in the material and technical nature of the object and necessary to its conservation; and objective functions, through which the object satisfies our needs: the practical necessities, our sense of humor or beauty, our desire for illusion and symbols, and finally, our aesthetic canons. Whoever takes the pain to clearly grasp the reciprocal rapports that run through these two types of functions in each decorative element, finds himself on the right path toward sounding the secret of all the arts. But one must guard against giving one or the other function priority over the others: the two series form a linked rule in each way, without which we cannot extract any factors without destroying the example."

its performance, arousing in its qualified consignee (in the semiotic sense) that kind of enjoyment that Le Corbusier had so admirably defined in one of the pages of *Urbanisme*:

"Behind the eyes there is this agile and generous, fecund, imaginative, logical, and noble thing, the spirit . . . Prestigious machine that unleashes knowledge and creation. Symphonies. To be caressed by forms, then to know how they have been generated, in which relation they have been joined, how they respond to an intention that reveals itself, how they are classified in the collection that is constituted of chosen images. To measure, to confront one's own spirit, to look: to participate oneself in the author's delight and in his torments . . ."[10]

Seemingly nothing, these few rules propose a true and actual "map" of the "interpretive cooperation"[11] in the confrontation of an architectural object—of its mind—considered a semiotic *sub specie*: the sensual, "naive"—preiconographic[12]—approach: "to be caressed by forms"; the conscious and true decodification; to recognize the parts of an object, to infer its organization, the relation between cause and effect: "then to learn how [the forms] have been generated, in which relation they have been reunited." This knowledge sets in motion the "encyclopedia"[13] of those who enjoy it: "to know how [the forms] have been classified in a collection that is made up of chosen images. To measure, to confront one's own spirit," to that, finally, which could possibly be defined as the metatextual comprehension of the work: to recognize the cultural, ideological, artistic, social, psychological construct of the external world in its physical concreteness, in the unity of the object, such as the author sees it, experiences it, and transposes it in his work: "to know how [the forms] respond to an intent that is made manifest" and "to participate oneself in the delights of the author and his torments."

I will now limit myself to the study of the single-family dwelling at Bruckmannweg 2, which in Le Corbusier's work represents a further development of the "Maison Citrohan."

"La fenêtre est l'élément mécanique-type de la maison"

"The structural skeleton consists exclusively of a framework of reinforced concrete," states Alfred Roth and goes on to specify: "The distances between the pilasters are given from the beginning. They are determined by the use of the sliding-window element."[14]

APPEL AUX INDUSTRIELS

Voici les vides que nous donne naturellement le ciment armé.

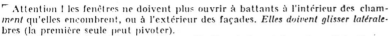

⌐ Attention ! les fenêtres ne doivent plus ouvrir à battants à l'intérieur des cham-
bres qu'elles encombrent, ou à l'extérieur des façades. *Elles doivent glisser latérale-
ment* (la première seule peut pivoter).
Si j'ai 10 de surface éclairante, il me suffit d'avoir 3 ou 4 de surface d'aération.

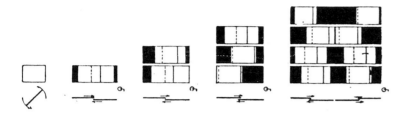

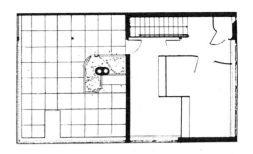

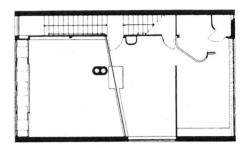

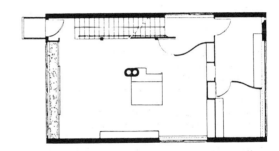

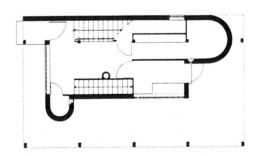

A close but directed relation between structural openings and framework is then established and the given subordinate is the framework: "the sliding-window element is standardized at 2.5 meters in length and 1.1 meters in height. The length is determinant: the pilasters are thus arranged on two rows, at 2.5 meters from each other. The distance between the two rows adds up to the two window units, that is, 5 meters." This subordinate relationship at least breaks the habit of thinking that leads to the retention of the structural given as primary, because in fact it is first to be built and is the material premise of the building.

But in Le Corbusier's eyes, the window elements boast of nobility. With his "Appel aux industriels" (A call to industrialists)[15] launched from the pages of the *Almanach*, Le Corbusier had indicated the window as the "élément mécanique-type de la maison" from which to begin. The privilege given the window element can be explained. In defining the requisites that have to be satisfied to formulate the solution, Le Corbusier had furnished an actual demonstration of a method that anticipated the fundamental criteria of functional and structural analyses of the design methodologies that became established in the 1950s and '60s, especially in the field of industrial design. Here the functional points to the modalities of factual and symbolic use of the object, while the structural analyses define its material and technical requisites: solidity, compatibility with other elements (of the building, of the machine), production, etc. [16] And it is in this way that Le Corbusier

33. The scheme exemplifies the possible combinations of the window element industrially produced and conceived as the "élément mécanique-type de la maison" (from "Appel aux industriels," 1926).
34. Single-family house at the Weissenhof, final design, plans (from FLC 7645, 7646, 7647, 7649, and from *O.C. 1910–29*).

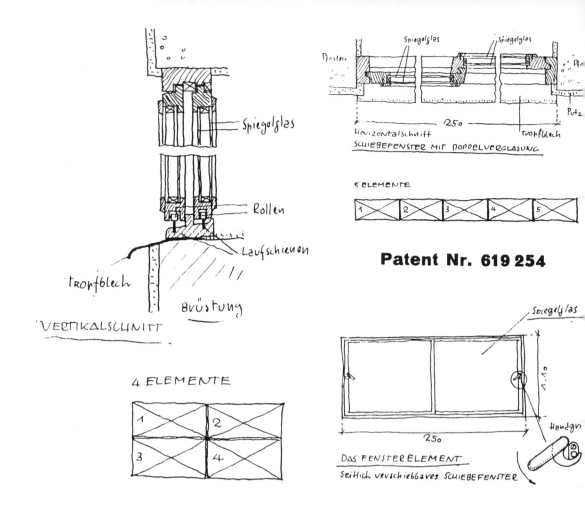

Spiegelglas

Rollen

Laufschienen

Tropfblech

Brüstung

VERTIKALSCHNITT

Spiegelglas   Spiegelglas

Posten

Pfo

Putz

2.50

Horizontalschnitt   Tropfblech

SCHIEBEFENSTER MIT DOPPELVERGLASUNG

5 ELEMENTE

| 1 | 2 | 3 | 4 | 5 |

Patent Nr. 619 254

4 ELEMENTE

| 1 | 2 |
| 3 | 4 |

Spiegelglas

Handgri

2.50

DAS FENSTERELEMENT
Seitlich verschiebbares SCHIEBEFENSTER

35. The horizontal sash-window of the houses in Stuttgart, horizontal and vertical sections, façade, example of the aggregates of the base element, and the patent number.

arrived at a solution of the window element that would satisfy those conditions that he held as necessary and sufficient for production on an industrial scale.

In traditional architecture the openings constitute a weakening of the walls, which are the support. The framework in reinforced concrete liberates the openings from this structural condition. Between framework and opening there subsists a dimensional relationship, solely but continually important when it fixes a modular coordination between a possibly reduced number of elements in advance. The determination of length is standardized by the window element as its basis in an eloquent exposition of a structural functional analysis: according to Le Corbusier, the measurement of 2.5 meters is the common denominator of size pertaining to three totally different but concurrent conditions: statico-structural, spatial, and anthropometric. In its turn, the choice of the horizontal sliding shutter element is at the head of a comprehensive analysis that has distinguished and defined various functions, such as the compact space and the vulnerability of the window, the view, lighting, and ventilation. In fact, the sliding window avoids the shutters that encroach on the interior. The ventilation surface is thus perfectly graduated and the fact that the largest opening corresponds to half of the lit surface does not create a problem; "if I have 10 in illuminated surface, I only need to have 3 or 4 in ventilation surface."[17]

If this point of view has allowed such a complex of functional and structural requisites to be satisfied with a single element, then it lends itself to generalized use, and, it can be said, to serial industrial production. Le Corbusier: "We architects are calmly satisfied with a fixed module. With this fixed module we compose."[18] In the explanatory graphics of his "*Appel*," Le Corbusier had shown how through the horizontal and vertical juxtaposition of the elements, it is possible to combine a variety of aperture formats. Among the innumerable "components" of the building object, the window was possibly the only established entity (before installation) that allowed the rational prefiguration of industrial short-term production. This was a widely held conviction among architects of the Modern Movement.

So as Le Corbusier had developed it, the window "élément mécanique-type de la maison" satisfies his architectural program by at least two fundamental and closely correlated aspects:

1. the method followed in his innovation owes its intellectual satisfaction to having raised architectural discipline to the level of the most general modern technical and scientific developments;

2. the window element, in Le Corbusier's teleological concession realized *pars pro toto* signaled the final industrialization of housing; and Le Corbusier recognized in the steel industry, rather than the artisan techniques of the carpenter, an altogether different status and future in the modern world.

The patent no. 619.254 given to the window elements designed for Weissenhof is its consecration.[19]

The "Citrohan" type as "système de structures"

The disheartening statement that closes the "Appel aux industriels" is also meant for the window frames in Stuttgart, still executed in wood: "But . . . everything we have had till now has been but the work of a blacksmith and not of a mechanic."[20]

But Weissenhof, in fact, was an "experimental colony . . . for fixing the principles of modern serial construction. *Consequently the Siedlung cannot be presented as a rational method of serial construction but simply as a preparatory model* [my emphasis]."[21]

This specification, it will soon be seen, is of the greatest importance in the understanding of Le Cor-

[17] Le Corbusier, *Almanach*, p.103.
[18] Ibid.
[19] See Alfred Roth, *Zwei Wohnhäuser*, drawing on p. 14.
[20] Le Corbusier, *Almanach*, p.103.
[21] See the document quoted in footnote 4 above.

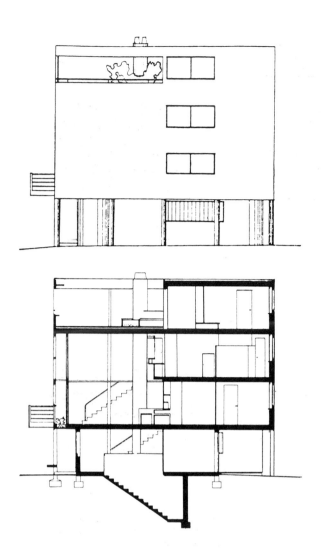

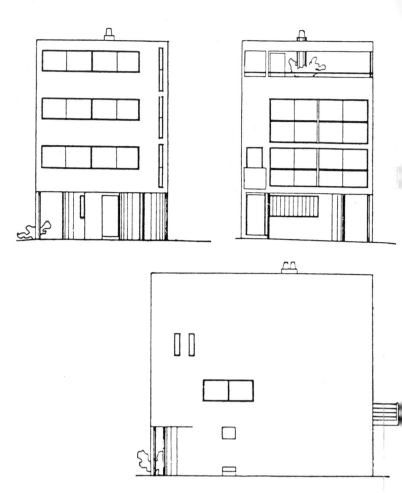

busier's demonstration and the misunderstandings it generated. Anticipating the conclusions with clarity, for Le Corbusier, the production of the work at Weissenhof counted less than the staging of its signs.

"Avec ce module, *nous composerons*"

If all of the four perspectives of the single-family dwelling are considered, the following observations immediately impose themselves:

1. except for some window-slots and the balcony door on the south side, all the frames are of the same type, but

2. at each perspective they are presented in a different configuration, such as:

3. on the western side only one element-type is shown as access to the house toward Bruckmannweg;

4. on the opposite side, toward the east, the same isolated module can be found, but repeated three times and lined up vertically, corresponding to each floor level of the house;

5. on the north side, at each level, two modules are horizontally lined up to form the classic *fenêtre en longueur* that constitutes the fourth of the "5 points d'une architecture nouvelle";

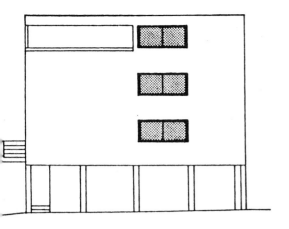
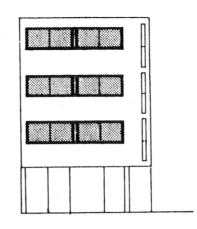
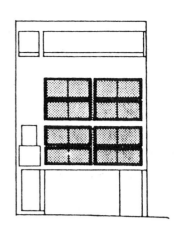

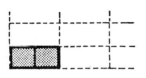
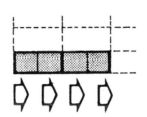
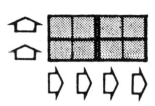

6. finally on the southern perspective, eight combined modules, horizontal as well as vertical, together form that other "word"[22] in Le Corbusier's vocabulary, designated by the term *pan de verre* ". . . a glass surface, that looses the specificity of the window and becomes wall." Le Corbusier, then, takes advantage of the prefabricated walls surrounding the house to demonstrate, as he did in the pages of the publicity folder, the sectional composition of the module base.

But there is more: the correlation established between the four perspectives, and respectively, the four different dispositions of the window modules, shows not only the declensional capacity of the base element, but the latter sends us back to the compositional process itself of "placement and lifting" and therefore, implicitly also to other possible solutions and definitively to the "open" nature of the system. Nevertheless, this formal disposition transcends the conclusive character of the work per se, its unity, and goes against one of the major postulates of the exhibition that lend themselves with more difficulty to visualization: " . . . the mass fabrication of standardized building units and details now allows for the possibility of variation with the greatest respect for the individual."[23] This

36. Single-family dwelling at Weissenhof, southern, eastern, northern, and western façades, and north-south section.
37. Le Corbusier uses the development of the prefabricated wall of the single-family dwelling to present, step by step, the compositional possibilities of the window element.

[22] In *Precisions*, Le Corbusier, after having "demonstrated" that the *fenêtre en longueur* and the *pan de verre* are the logical consequence of a global, technical, and functional rethinking of architecture, states: "The compositional means are so new and truthfully *seem* so reduced, almost to zero, that one is frightened: But where is architecture going?" And then he answers: "The new technologies have given themselves new words . . . ," p. 74.
[23] See the document mentioned in footnote 4 above, p. 5.

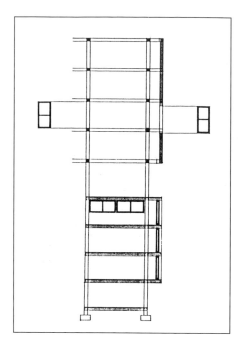

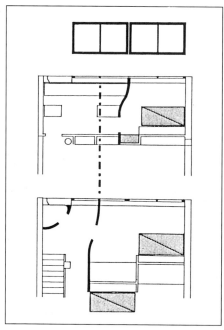

38. The measurement of the supporting structure is the correlate of the window module.
39. The *plan libre*, whose form is determined by the needs of the individual, is subordinate to the industrially-produced window element.
40. The disposition of the openings signals the interior subdivision of space in the "Citrohan" type "through transparency."

individual is always shaken like a scarecrow against any attempt at removing "the house from the clay, from the cave, from the mortar," to consign it "to the factory, to industry, on the carpet of taylorization."[24]

Correlations between openings and the structural module

The measurement of the supporting structure is the correlate of the window module: 2.5 meters of the minor span is $2.5 + 2.5 = 5$ meters of the major span in the direction of the supporting beams. Le Corbusier is not inclined toward the exposure of the framework that Van Doesburg had branded as "architectural naturalism."[25] In a text published in 1926, he saw fit to measure Perret's distances: "[he] wanted to make the structure visible," since "a body doesn't have bones alone. Allow a bone to link the wrist to the ankle and the mind will be delighted."[26] Nevertheless, the correlation between window module and framework is immediately understood: the body of the building supported by the service spaces on the ground floor is liberated. The *pilotis*, the house's volume, the *fenêtres en longueur, pans de verre*, and the window elements of the western façade clearly indicate, "through transparency," that the carrying structure extends to the higher levels also so that—important consequence—the external walls become simple buttresses. But observing the window module from the eastern elevation, it is falsified in relation to the alignments of the supporting structure. Here the didactic intention, if in truth it is such, borders on pedantry because the eastern wall is the only one among the external ones that does not coincide with the reclining level of the pilasters; even that one, in spite of appearances, is only a buttress. The disposition of the window element is liberated from every angle and can therefore adjust itself entirely to the planimetric organization of the house. The exception, then, confirms the rule.

Correlation between openings and *plan libre*

The "élément mécanique-type de la maison" also rules the bedroom floor of the house.

On the terrace floor, the partition that separates the children's room from the hallway proceeds from a straight line; but to join the interior portion of the window element it curves in an almost sinuous trajectory. Analogously, at the mentioned "Wohngeschoss" (service floor)[27] the wall undulates between the kitchen and servant's room: "The two points of departure for

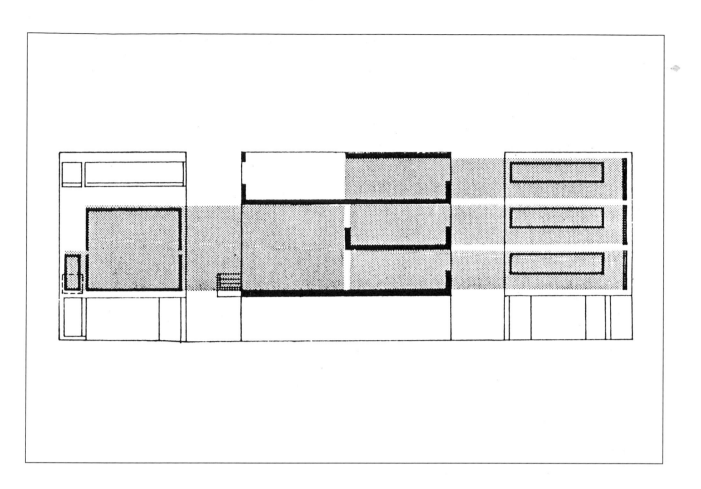

the dividing wall are fixed from the first, on the one hand, by the length of a bed and the minimum width of a closet, and on the other, by the point between two sliding windows. Wall and window frames are joined by sheet metal."[28] Little does their point of departure matter inside the house; the joining partitions on the external enclosing walls *seek* the extremity or the divisions, of the window elements, the width and position of the closet in the servant's room pairing their choices to show that within the *plan libre* of the dwelling determined by individual exigencies and the industrial element there exists a subordinate correlation of the latter over the former.

The openings *declare* the vertical section of the "Maison Citrohan"

To point out the importance that the correlation between objects, phenomena, and various dispositions of the architectural objects assumes in Le Corbusier's work, the openings again offer an example.

It has barely been mentioned that the accidents of the planimetric organization do not cut into nor are even subordinate to the disposition of the window elements.

[24] Le Corbusier and Pierre Jeanneret, "Le problème de la maison minimum," in *L'Architecture Vivante*, Spring–Summer 1930, p.8.
[25] Theo van Doesburg, in the article "Von der neuen Ästhetik zur materiellen Verwirklichung," in *De Stijl* 5, 1923, no. 1; on p. 10 he wrote: "A creative approach reveals the same anatomical attitude belonging to pictorial naturalism." The argument would recur in many other of his writings.
[26] Le Corbusier, "Ce Salon d'Automne," in *L'Esprit Nouveau*, no. 28, January 1925, pp. 2333–34.
[27] For Le Corbusier the modern house begins over the *pilotis* level, which corresponds to the traditional ground floor. This issue manifests itself in Le Corbusier's denomination of the various levels of the home, which often produces confusion. For clarity I have reproduced the various denominations in the following chart:

traditional	Le Corbusier	Alfred Roth
third floor	terrasse	Terrassengeschoss
second floor	soupente	Zwischengeschoss
first floor	rez-de-chausée	Wohngeschoss
ground floor	pilotis	Erdgeschoss

[28] Alfred Roth, *Zwei Wohnhäuser*, p. 15.

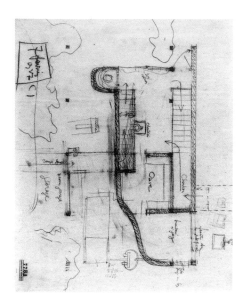

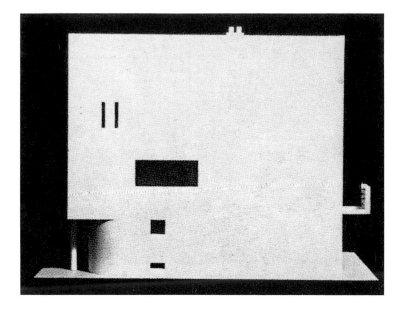

41. Sketch of the ground floor, dated February 7, 1927. In this phase the *pilotis* of the north-west corner are still incorporated in the exterior wall of the ground floor, the structural relations between stair landing and supporting framework are not yet recognizable (FLC 7784).

42. Single-family dwelling at the Weissenhof, model, west façade: the wall curves at the bottom on the left to form the "apse" of the storeroom of the ground floor. This formal devise shows that the stair landing is external to the supporting framework and, at least in principle, suspended from it.

[29] "Le Corbusier und Pierre Jeanneret, "Fünf Pünkte zu einer neuen Architektur," in Alfred Roth, *Zwei Wohnhäuser*, pp. 5–7.
[30] Le Corbusier, "Où en est l'architecture?" in *L'Architecture Vivante*, Autumn–Winter 1927, pp. 23–24.
[31] According to Umberto Eco (*Trattato di semiotica generale*, pp. 294ff.) the way a sign is produced is through "display," when "a given object or event, produced by nature or human action (intentionally or unintentionally), exists as a fact in a world of facts, is selected by someone and is *shown* as the expression of the class of objects to which it belongs."
[32] On abduction as the hypothetical creative moment of inference, see the fundamental contribution of Charles S. Pierce (1839–1914), founder of Pragmatism and Semiotics. For recent arguments, see Charles S. Pierce, *Le leggi dell'ipotesi—antologia dai Collected Papers*, Milan, 1984, and monographic pamphlet in *Versus*, no. 34, 1983.

All the same, the composition of the openings in the elevations inform the vertical section of the dwelling in an authoritative and unequivocal manner, becoming the distinctive mark of the Maison Citrohan: on the southern perspective the *pan de verre* commands the double height of the living room and the opening of the balcony functions as scale recalling through light the height of the normal floor level. Its exposed elevation to the east and north, the vertical alignment of the three window elements, and the *fenêtres en longueur* clearly distinguish three normal levels from the one at double height in this part of the house.

Finally, on the northern elevation, the three steel-framed windows along the left corner not only denote the three floor levels but also the lucidity of the space and width of the floors. Never mind the glaring signs, the message is delivered.

The figures of the *façade libre*

In the fifth of the "5 points d'une architecture nouvelle," Le Corbusier defines the *façade libre*: it is "the fact of extending the floor in relation to the pilasters in the manner of a balcony surrounding the building, shifted around the entire façade beyond the supporting structure. The façade looses, in this way, its supporting specificity . . ."[29] Now, the two buildings at Weissenhof satisfy the preliminary conditions of the *façade libre* in a less than satisfactory manner. Again in the double house, the principle is intact on the main western front, where the *pilotis*, withdrawn in relation to the façade and merging with the terrace level, and the nine modules of the *fenêtre en longueur* do not recreate an effective synecdoche; but in the single-family house the principle of the *façade libre* pays tribute to the original characteristics of the Maison Citrohan: the pilasters have not yet "left the angle of the rooms."[30] As the reduced volume of the service spaces on the ground floor leaves the *pilotis* in view, the coincidence between supporting structure and façade is immediately visible.

Nevertheless, even at the Maison Citrohan, a façade cannot coincide, and in fact does not coincide, with the alignment of the pilasters: the façade bears the staircase, which comes out externally on the supporting ledge so as not to conflict with the floors. In the single-family house nothing conforms anymore to the icon of a carrying wall on the western façade, closed and massive from the ground to the top of the building—this at least is the effect of the ensemble. In the north-west corner on the ground floor this wall bends and describes the semicircular *abside* (apse) of the pantry, leaving the last *pilotis* exposed and closely aligned between building and staircase. In such a way—this is essential—in the north-west corner the staircase is also perceptibly outside of the reinforced concrete frame and is suspended from it. More precisely, the staircase is supported by the floors, because the three sliding windows on the norther side signal the floors.

To summarize: the exposure of the *pilotis* mirrors the supporting structure; consequent are the extended staircase and sliding windows. The three operatives together, "are generated, in a unifying relation, as they respond to an intent that becomes evident."

If the "coupe symbole de l'architecture moderne"— it is worth mentioning the "Dom-ino" principle with extended floors and *façade libre*—is ostensibly manifest[31] here in the double house, in the single-family dwelling the *manner of sign production* remains above all circumstantial, especially because the same theme is atypically applied: the message is entrusted to the not entirely unified signs and distributed over a non-homogeneous ensemble of *objects* in such a way that their decoding requires making inferences[32] based on architectural competence: "the collection that is thus constituted of elective images" and "of the interpretive collaboration" of the consignee: "to measure, to confront one's own spirit, to look."

The process analyzed just now lets us understand more than it shows us, and hence it slows us down, rendering difficult a reading of the work; but with all the benefits of consciousness, it reveals a singular affinity with the logical figures that Fontanier had grouped together in the category of "figures of expression for reflection" and defined in the following terms: "To

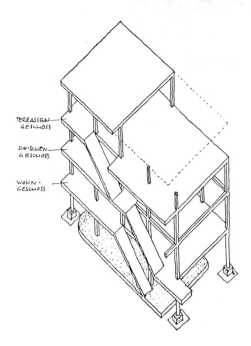

TERRASSEN GESCHOSS

ZWISCHEN GESCHOSS

WOHN- GESCHOSS

43. Axonometric representation of the construction method. It can be observed that the staircase leans on a ledge external to the supporting structure.

44. Drawing of the shelves hung on the level of the boudoir, visually dividing the dining room from the living room.
45. The signs of the *plan libre*: the free disposition of the chest-high dividing walls separating bath, bedroom, and boudoir from the loft floor.

charm the other's spirit again while exercising it, we will present thought only indirectly, with an air of mystery; rather than speak it we will let it be understood or guessed at through the relation of ideas that are articulated with those that are not and those which provoke thought at least, at the same time awakening memory."[33] Interlocutory process, indirectly showing, through a *rotation of signs*, that it has its rhetorical place among the figures of "reticense" and "metalepsia."[34]

Mies *versus* Le Corbusier

The biting, not to mention ferocious, comments of the press and of the general public obliged Le Corbusier to take the defensive. He thus published the instructive text on "L'aménagement intérieur de nos maisons du Weissenhof."[35]

Disorientation and incomprehension are evident in the discordant opinions expressed by his allies and soon by the most hostile observers.[36] But disorientation and incomprehension seem expiated if the ensemble of objectives that Le Corbusier's demonstration was planned to attain are taken into account—the notions of the *plan libre* and the correlative objective of the modern dwelling in particular.

If the *plan libre* is the immediate correlative in the distinction between supporting and non-supporting elements, the walls which stop at 1.6 meters from the pavement, for example, between the boudoir and the master bedroom,[37] between it and the bathroom—reinforce the spatial continuity that generated the building: "the net division of the W.C. is an incongruity in the application of the idea of continuous space."[38] They are the icons of the principle confirmed in "Le problème de la maison minimum" (1929): "the partitions that limit the series of *services* necessary for domestic use don't have any direct relation to the walls; they are subtle isolating membranes or less."

Le Corbusier is obviously not the only architect who profits from the distinction between supporting and non-supporting elements. With Le Corbusier such a distinction is considered one of the logical consequences on the instrumental level of a reflection that in the architectural existence of the object has recognized a generative, intrinsic, and conflictive double determination. An inherent double determination in his *being in the world*, whether as artifact endowed with its own subsistence agenda (material, constructive, productive), or as instrument subjected to a complex, practical, and cognitive agenda (in relation to use, affect,

Bruno Reichlin

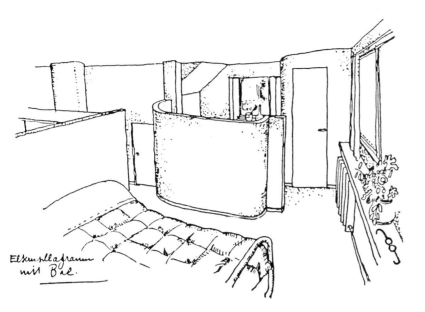

Elternschlafraum
mit Bad.

[33] Pierre Fontanier, *Les figures du discours*, Paris, 1968, with an introduction by Gérard Genette (first published 1821, and in 1830), p. 123.

[34] Fontanier enumerates seven "figures of expression by reflexion." Because it seems to me to be the closest to the process just analyzed, I am presenting the definitions of "reticence," or "metalepsy." "*Reticence* consists in the sudden interruption and closing in the course of a sentence giving to understand little of what is said with the concurrence of circumstances when it pretends to say nothing and frequently also much more" (p. 135). "*Metalepsy* . . . consists in the substitution of an *indirect* expression for a *direct* expression, that is, it explains one thing through another that precedes it, follows it, or accompanies it; nor is it an addition, or just any circumstance; it either connects with it or refers to it in a way that brings it to mind immediately" (pp. 127–28).

[35] Le Corbusier, "L'aménagement intérieur de nos maisons du Weissenhof", in *L'Architecture Vivante*, Spring–Summer 1928, pp. 33–36.

[36] See for example the long commentary written by Rudolf Pfister for the magazine *Der Baumeister*, 1928, no. 2, pp. 33–72; the paragraph "Das Schriftum—Difficile est satiram non scribere," pp. 61–63.

[37] This disposition had left the public very perplexed, the more so as the execution had suppressed—or forgotten?—the screen with sliding panels on the boudoir's parapet. Le Corbusier: "I must confess that at the execution, an important operation was quite simply omitted: on the parapet of the boudoir, which gives onto the living room, there should have been some sliding screens that would have completely closed off the bedroom area from the bath and the dressing room. In the Pavilion of L'Esprit Nouveau, 1925, we had already indicated this type of closure; and if our plans referring to this omitted organ are to be carefully looked at, it will be noticed that all this is not a small matter." From "La signification de la cité-jardin du Weissenhof à Stuttgart," in *L'Architecture Vivante*, 1928, p. 14.

[38] Rudolf Pfister, op. cit., p. 65.

symbolic dimensions, aesthetics, etc.). However, each part, element, or function of the architectural object must be conceived and analyzed starting from this double determination and its inherent conflicts. Even if not formulated in explicit terms, this conviction— this theoretic and/or metaphysical issue—is clearly distinguished among the rules of "general considerations" that introduce the notable text of 1929 dedicated to "Le problème de la maison minimum." Le Corbusier would write: "the dwelling is a biological phenomenon. Moreover, the vases, the sites, the spaces that comprise it, are limited by an envelope that obeys a static order. Biological event, static event, are two different orders of things. They are functions that are independent one from the other. The spirit that is applied to the solution of one or the other of these questions follows different paths. Poverty, inadequacy of traditional techniques, provoked a confusion of powers, a forced combination of functions that are independent one from the other . . . If two independent events are not classified: *to structure the house* on the one hand, and *to build the house* on the other; if two kinds of functions are not distinguished one from the other: *an organized system* on the one hand, and *building the house* on the other; if traditional methods are maintained due to which *the two functions are combined and made to depend on each other*, we will remain frozen in our own immobility . . ." After which Le Corbusier proceeds: "Domestic use consists in a regular succession of precise functions. The regular sequence of these functions constitutes a phenomenon of circulation . . . The succession of these functions is established according to a logic that is of a

[39] Le Corbusier and Pierre Jeanneret, "Le problème de la *maison minimum*," pp. 5–6.

[40] *Le Corbusier et Pierre Jeanneret—Oeuvre complète 1910–29*, p.193; Le Corbusier, *Précisions*, p. 155.

[41] Adolf Behne, in his *Der moderne Zweckbau*, written in 1923, but published three years later, was probably the first critic to distinguish among the tendencies in the bosom of the Modern Movement—the one "rational" and the other "functionalist"; the latter represented principally by Hugo Häring and Hans Scharoun.

[42] A term often used by Walter Gropius to designate the various functions of the home, described in diagrams of trajectories and frequency.

[43] See Henry-Russell Hitchcock and Philip Johnson, *The International Style*: theme of the famous exposition organized by the Museum of Modern Art of New York in 1932, and title of the anonymous book that appeared that same year also in New York. For a critique of the rudimentary definition of style proposed by the authors see B. Reichlin, "The International Style," in *Werk, Bauen+Wohnen*, 1984, no. 5, pp. 48–53.

[44] Le Corbusier, *La signification*, p. 10.

[45] Ibid., p. 12.

biological rather than a geometric order. The scheme of these functions can be established along a continuous line. The play of the necessary surfaces and their contiguity can then be clearly read. It will be appreciated that these surfaces, in their concatenation, don't have much in common with the more or less arbitrary forms and surfaces of traditional rooms."[39]

The dividing wall that follows the curve of the bathtub in the "Zwischengeschoss," the curving walls between corridor and children's room on the "Terrassengeschoss," between servants' room and the kitchen in the "Wohngeschoss," as well as the sinuous walls that elegantly dodge a pilaster and serve as invitation to the living room, etc. . . . . These are the signs of the biological order circulating in the living spaces of the dwelling space. These articulate the fundamental alterity between spaces that are instrumental to man, anthropometrically determined, and spaces that are subject to the material, statico-constructional regime, standardized by the architectural artifact and geometrically determined.

The same theme is also staged on the outside, in the juxtaposition between the formation of the *pilotis* and the mixtilinear perimeter, sinuous from the service spaces on the ground floor (very close to the outline in the first volume of the *Oeuvre complète* and in *Précisions* illustrating the third of the four types of composition developed by Le Corbusier in the 1920s).[40]

The home defined as "a biological phenomenon," the term "vase" used synonymously with locale, the importance attributed to domestic "traffic," but above all the architectural forms that come together there, suggest an otherwise unsuspected *family ambiance* with "functionalist"[41] concerns. Concerns that were challenged, in the name of *flexibility* of the home, by Mies van der Rohe.

With Mies and Le Corbusier the same postulate that proclaims the distinction between supporting and nonsupporting elements is put to the service of two diametrically opposed concessions:

—Mies foresees the *flexibility*, better yet, the *variability* of the home. The dividing walls that organize the various rooms inside of a space that remains the same in its surface and disposition of its foundation and openings, proclaim the *open* character, the generative potential of the measures adopted in his building, but also the indefinite quality, the non-specificity of the singular solution.

—Le Corbusier, instead, pursues the specialization of the home. Each "Lebensablauf"[42] has its instrument made to measure—even the order of personal effects:

"to define functions that are as diverse as sitting down, working, eating at table, I respond: a precise house responds to precise functions, the function is produced *regularly* in a precise place. *Precise places expect precise houses.*" Nobody prevented the construction of "houses" in reinforced concrete. For Le Corbusier, the distinction between supporting and non-supporting elements and the *plan libre* are therefore two structural operations correlated by a system conceived as a function of the specialization of the home.

Two opposing concepts of *type*

The fact that "Weissenhof" was proposed and received as a manifesto of modern architecture, forerunner of a presumed "International Style,"[43] seems to have impeded the full appreciation of the profound differences that separate the architects who took part in it. Among these the notion of "type" is a fundamental watershed.

Le Corbusier's declared subjection of his own audience to the defense of his contribution at Weissenhof ("La signification de la cité-jardin du Weissenhof a Stuttgart," is in fact a pure and simple disavowal of the quest his building types provoked among the "thick" of the modern and less modern architects: " . . . here is the affirmation that I am allowing myself to submit to your judgement: it is not a matter of standardizing houses, small houses, larger houses, or enormous houses; it is a matter of standardizing a structural system . . . I am saying, then, that one shouldn't try to bring industrial progress into the field of the new houses, *but a new structural system very rich in consequences* able to determine an infinite variety of floors, to respond to a multiplicity of ways of life, to respond to a great diversity of life's concessions, to respond to small, medium, or large programs. TO CREATE A STRUCTURAL SYSTEM!"[44]

Le Corbusier's interest therefore is not with the types of building, but with the "*element* types of the house (the alphabet letters) that allow the construction of ensembles, of the houses (words made with letters) that among them share a fundamental unity, and consequently, a common style."[45]

"Les 5 points d'une architecture nouvelle": a synergetic concession of the architectural object?

But the five points and their application to the single-family and double houses demonstrate that they are something other than a simple "Lego box"; they do not simply define five elements nor are they the modern

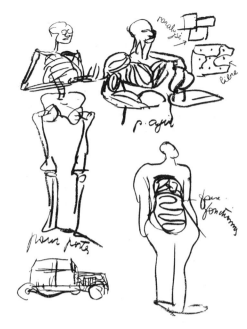

46. The different functions of the human body suggest, by analogy, that the architectural object distinguishes various functions and creates adequate "organs" for each function. These different "functions" are the internal distribution and environment, the supporting structure, the plastic composition, etc. (*Précisions*).

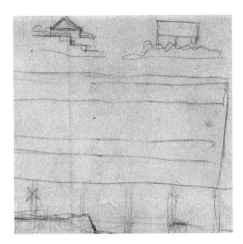

47. Sketches, also probably by Le Corbusier, that show the placement of the double house on the site. This detail shows at left the scheme of the integration of the surrounding towns in the hilly environs of Stuttgart. In *Précisions* it is pointed out that such a siting entails a large expenditure for terracing and earth removal, and compromises the architectural figuration of the building. At the right is shown the principle of the house on *pilotis* (FLC 7716).

equivalent of Vignola's five orders. The number five seems rather the result of an extrinsic, propagandist choice.[46]

The five points—and herein lies the innovative, anti-Vignolesque aspect—propose a comprehension of the architectural object in structural terms: objects, elements, and phenomena pertaining to its production—material, statico-constructional, functional, spatial, plastic, symbolic— and the means of production, are cultivated in their structural relationships, like a system *où tout se tient*. It is typical of this structuralist concession not to have the supporting framework—even if it was the logical antecedent to the *plan libre*—figure in the first of the five points, but defined only after the first three points: the first one we know consists of a plot of vertical punctiforms, the third point goes over the entire building and supports the levels, and finally, in the fifth point, these levels in the mode of balconies come out of alignment from the plinths all around the building.

If Le Corbusier has not been entirely explicit in his proposition, it is to this structuralist concession of the architectural object that the phrase "structural system" must refer to. In 1927 that was practically a new type: no longer an invariant or formal plan, but a structural invariant.

From the point of theory or the design method and its results, the notion of type proposes a regrouping that is unsuspected at first: from the gardens on flat roofs, to the immaculate volumes with stripped outlines, without cornices and decorations, Oud, Stam, Gropius, Hilberseimer, and company are more related to Alexander Klein, Heinrich Tessenow, Paul Schmitthenner than to Le Corbusier.

Gilbert Simondon would give the following synthesizing definition of the mode of existence of technical objects: "the technical object proceeds by internal redistribution of functions in unified compatibility, substituting chance or the antagonism of primitive division; specialization does not come about *function by function*, but *synergy by synergy*; it is the synergetic group of the functions, and not function alone, which constitutes the true underpinnings of the technical object. It is because of this search for synergy that the concrete technical object can be translated with some simplification; the concrete technical object is one that is no longer fighting against itself, one in which no secondary effect harms the functioning of the whole or is left out of this functioning."[47]

Is it too risky to state that the "structural system" subtended by the *five points* is an excellent example of

[46] Le Corbusier settles accounts with Vignola and his distant contemporary descendants in *Précisions*, pp. 67 – 69. Among other things, Le Corbusier writes amusingly of a professor at the Ecole des Beaux-Arts who discovered unexpected affinities with his approach to architecture. The professor held that "he also practiced the discipline" beginning with teaching of the "Orders": first the "doric" because it was the easiest, then . . . the misunderstanding may have been caused by the famous "five points."

[47] Gilbert Simondon, *Du mode d'existence des objets techniques*, Paris, 1969, p. 34

the synergetic redistribution of functions? Structural function on the one hand, covering function on the other, where the latter is no longer conditioned by the former in that they are not co-occurrent, allows them to be organized in turn by sub-systems and functional synergetic groups: isolating functions and/or functions of mobility and/or ventilation, and/or lighting, etc.

In the "structural system" the will to choose among houses as spatial and structural objects, framework and cover, the structural and functional relations, is averted: inclusive and exclusive, subordinate or independent co-ocurrences. To organize them and distribute them in a compatible unity with synergetic functions, in order to exclude or reduce antagonisms, mutual obstacles, waste. Not only are data of the elements given, but also the rules of implementation that assure the plans to be realized without obstacles or a manipulation in performance.

In this concession—available to the theoretical as well as the practical production of the plan—Le Corbusier manifests, as perhaps no other architect of the Modern Movement, the determination to think of architecture in terms that adequately conform to the modern technical object.

In the single-family house in Stuttgart, the "structural system" has not only found its application, but it is the *subject* itself of the demonstration. In fact:
—the window element type exhibits not only the combinatory modalities, but also the modular relations between the foundation elements and framework, and the subordinate role of the *plan libre*.
—But the openings also reveal the vertical distribution of the house's space,
—and the openings concur in indicating the supporting framework *beneath the cover*, and in particular
—the static function of the floors as shelves on the western side of the building, and, consequently, the function of this wall as simple buttress.
—It corroborates the understanding, with full effect, that the *abside* of the store-room on the ground floor obeys the regime of the *plan libre* as well.
—The internal separations of the house manifest in various ways that they are not supporting but backing up the "Lebensabläufe" in the way of "guide forms."

This subtle play of disjunctive or conjunctive correlations among the elements and/or the various operations of the architectural object, reveals how these "forms" "are generated, in which relation reunited, how they respond to an intention that becomes evident" etc.

In other terms, the work draws attention to the

48. Sketches by Paul Schmitthenner, from *Baugestaltung, 1. Folge: Das deutsche Wohnhaus*, Stuttgart, 1932: the five drawings show different ways of placing a building on a hilly site. Schmitthenner hoped that the natural profiles of the hills would be considered and criticizes the systematization of terraces, indicated in drawing no. 4, as it negates "the peculiarity of the houses on a slant."

48 Le Corbusier, *Précisions*, p. 46.

immanent "structural system" and unfolds it: one operation leads to another and vice versa.

"Les 5 points d'une architecture nouvelle": architectural language as institution and structure

The "5 points d'une architecture nouvelle," nevertheless, are not instructions for the making of an architecture congruent with the cultural order and the technological achievements of the machine civilization, as it was naively intended: they are also a finite number, a minimum of elements that make up an easily recognizable system, that allow the formulation, from construction to construction, of always varying messages. Le Corbusier recognizes that the work to be carried out, must acquire meaning and produce knowledge as long as the system of modern architecture assumes the identity of an institution: technical, social, cultural, and artistic. As such it should itself be an identifiable and sufficiently conventionalized order. Moreover, it should define its own place in relation to the notions acquired and is therefore related to tradition. This explains why in the theoretico-methodological tracts Le Corbusier measures efficiency and utility of the constructional, distributive, spatial, and other innovations proposed, comparing them to already observed dispositions, customary solutions as is the case in the diagrams, as opposed to the graphics that illustrate *Précisions*. "I have learned the lesson . . . of things in passing. Why all events and all objects are *in relation to* . . ."[48] And in a text of 1938, written as a commentary to *L'oeuvre plastique*, Le Corbusier immerses himself in considerations that would delight a semiologist: "The work of art is 'a game' for which the author has created the rules. The author—the painter—has created the rules of his game and the rules should be apparent to those who wish to play. It [the work of art] is made of sufficiently intelligible signs. It would not be able to make use of new, unpublished, unexpected, unknown objects; nobody would recognize them. He needs experimental, obsolete, used objects, ground down by habit, recognizable as a base to a simple design." Such a concession explains why Le Corbusier constructs modern architecture's new vocabulary out of a "kind of subtle inversion" of traditional architecture. Bernard Huet in his *Anachroniques d'Architecture* notes in fact that Le Corbusier "speaks of the house thanks to five negative principles that are, point by point, the opposite of what people think when they think *house*. Where one thinks *anchorage on the ground, underground, cellar, basement*, he proposes *pilotis*.

Bruno Reichlin

Where one thinks of *entrance*, he proposes *no entrance*. Where one thinks *walls*, he proposes *plan libre*. Where one thinks *window* he proposes horizontal glass."[49]

But there is more: even the contemporary critics adverse to Le Corbusier have become aware, first, that the will of the form—the distinctive, or if you will, stylistic traits—of modern architecture manifest themselves also by negation. Writing in a 1928 issue of the magazine *Der Baumeister*, Rudolf Pfister thus defines the "Neuen Stil": "The *cubic* shape of the building mass, the missing roof, the strong dissolution of the wall by the glass openings, the lack of plastic subdivision or color and any *decoration*, the renunciation of symmetry and proportions in the constructional order of elements. Therefore, from the above entirely negative point of view of architectural aesthetics, valid until now, there seem to be suppressions rather than innovations here."[50]

As to the aesthetic cultural program—in the understanding that modern anthropology gives the term culture—there are no doubts as to Le Corbusier's systematically subversive intent:

—the *toit-jardin* is the negation of the traditional pitched roof. On the margins of a drawing for Stuttgart there is a sketch, probably by him, that illustrates the double opposition, *foundation-terracing* vs. *pilotis*, and traditional roof vs. *toit-jardin*. In his *Précisions* Le Corbusier would dismantle the argument for the rooting of the building itself in the ground by starting with the central example of his two houses for Stuttgart.

—Around the *plan libre* there unravels the general subversion which Le Corbusier had defined as "the ancestral plan of the house";[51]

—*fenêtre en longueur* and *pan de verre* are finally the oppositional terms of the traditional vertical window, also called the window "*à la française*": the *trou dans le mur* window, considered the inheritance of constructive techniques now exhausted and against which Le Corbusier had fiercely polemicized with Auguste Perret.

"Basement," "traditional roof," "vertical window," on one side, "*pilotis*," "*toit-jardin*," "*fenêtre en longueur*", and "*pan de verre*" on the other, are then oppositional copies "of that collection of elective images of which they were made": the paradigmatic copies according to which selection results,[52] according to which these forms "become classified" in the "measurement, the confrontation of one's own spirit."

The "5 points d'une architecture nouvelle" are the "sufficiently intelligible signs" of modern architecture.*

[49] Quoted J. C. Garcias, J. J. Treuttel, "L'ancrage au sol Taupinière et soubassement", in *Les cahiers de la recherche architecturale*, n. 14, 1984, pp. 67-68.

[50] Rudolf Pfister, *op. cit.*, p. 42.

[51] Le Corbusier, *Une maison—un palais*, Paris, 1928, pp. 54–60.

[52] Selections among virtually interchangeable elements, according to the *Zweiachsentheorie der Sprache*.

* This essay is a part of Bruno Reichlin, "Das Einfamilienhaus von Le Corbusier und Pierre Jeanneret auf dem Weissenhof: Eine Strukturanalyse," pp. 150–87, in *Fünf Punkte in der Architekturgeschichte: Festschrift für Adolf Max Vogt* (Geschichte und Theorie der Architektur, vol. 28), edited by Katharina Medici-Mall, Basel, Boston, Stuttgart, Birkhäuser Verlag, 1985. The analytical drawings are by Bruno Reichlin.

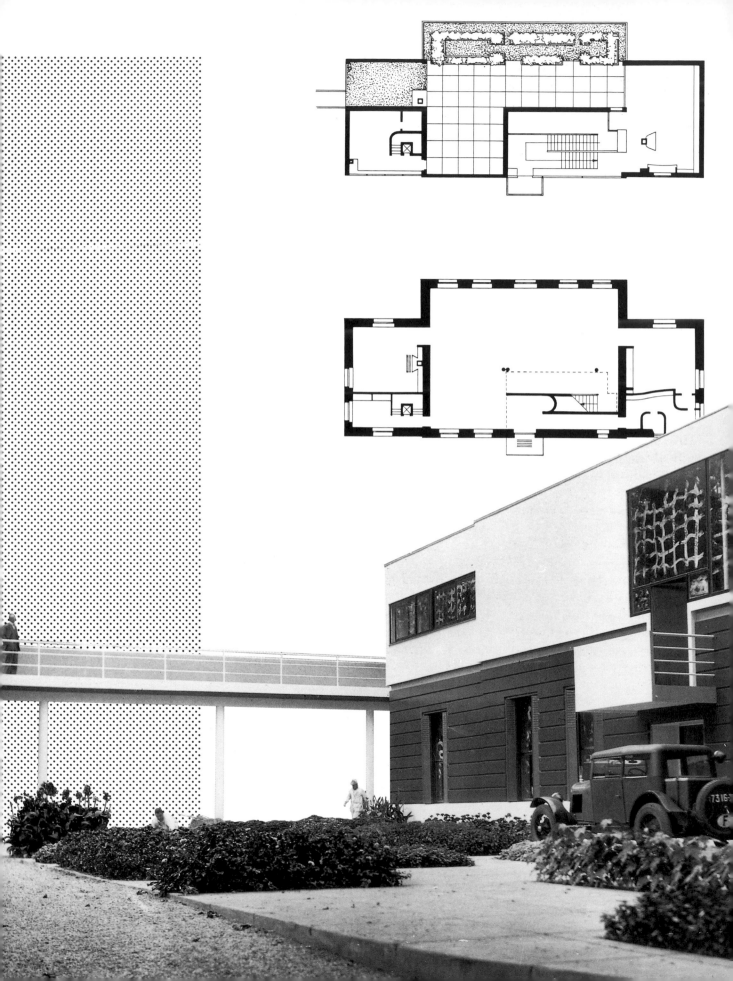

THE PAVILLON CHURCH

Bruno Reichlin

Reference to the tradition of architecture is constant in Le Corbusier's writings. The tradition is at the same time a fountain of certainty and a paradigm against which he measures the validity of his propositions, often returning to diagrammatic comparison drawings.[1]

At Ville d'Avray, the confrontation with traditional architecture takes on a particular concreteness because it is imposed on the job of building itself: the intervention consisted, in fact, in the more or less radical transformation of a preexisting building.

Concerning myself with the music pavilion, I will investigate which relations Le Corbusier established with tradition at the project site.[2]

The task of building

"It concerns the restoration of a beautiful and old property at the Ville d'Avray (M. Church). A villa in the classical style with a new construction annexed to it: on the ground floor the garages, the servants' bedrooms, and entrance hall; on the first floor, guest rooms with every comfort, a dining room, a living room with loft, library, and direct access to the *toit-jardin*.

The pavilion is the transformation of an old house. On the ground floor a large entrance hall was organized with vast closets, toilets, kitchen, etc. The first floor comprises a reception room, library, game room, and bar; from here there is direct access to a hanging garden."[3]

Further details come from an article that was published anonymously, but written by Le Corbusier, in the magazine *Art et Industrie* in the January 1929 issue and from the pamphlet *Ville d'Avray et son histoire* of 1970.[4]

The holdings of Messieurs Church resulted in the merging of two properties: one, more elevated, was

[1] Le Corbusier referred to these *pièces à conviction* above all in his lectures, sketching quickly with charcoal and colored chalks on large sheets of cardboard. Not by chance the most outstanding drawings illustrate *Précisions*, a written account of the lectures held in various parts of South America; for example, one could see the confrontation of the sections of the traditional and modern houses, between the *plan paralysé* and the *plan libre*, on pages 53 and 58 respectively, of the *Précisions* (Le Corbusier, *Précisions sur un état présent de l'Architecture et de l'Urbanisme*, Paris, 1930; reissued, Paris, 1960). For Le Corbusier these conceptual drawings are cognitive instruments: ". . . when one draws with useful words . . . one risks creating something . . . All of my theory, my introspection, and retrospection on the phenomenon of architecture and urbanism come from these improvised and illustrated conferences." (From an interview held three months before his death, now in *Spazio e società*, vol. 2, no. 8, December 1979).

[2] It hasn't been ascertained when Le Corbusier met Henry Church, but his commission of the restructuring of his property at Ville d'Avray takes concrete form in the spring of 1927; letter of April 21, 1927 (FLC, dossier "Church"). Priority would be given to the guest house built on the foundations of the old stables. From the registration of the plans of the atelier conserved by the Fondation Le Corbusier, it turns out that the majority of the elaborate drawings that can be attributed to the pavilion, designated only as "bâtiment B," were edited in the second half of 1927. Except for details, in December 1928, the pavilion was finished, and on the 19th, Le Corbusier wrote the commentary that would appear anonymously in the magazine, *Art et Industrie* (copy of the manuscript in the FLC, dossier "Church").

[3] *Le Corbusier et Pierre Jeanneret—Oeuvre complète 1910–29*, edited by W. Boesiger and O. Stonorov, Zürich, Girsberger, 1929, p. 201.

[4] *Art et Industrie*, January 1929, pp. 5–9.

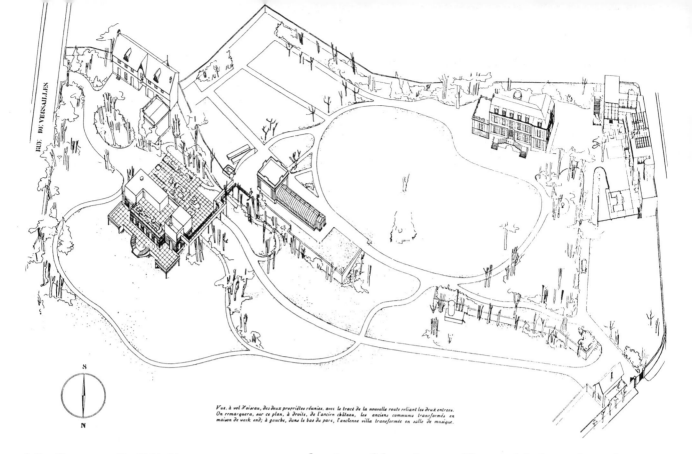

RUE DE VERSAILLES

S

N

Vue. à vol d'oiseau, des deux propriétés réunies, avec le tracé de la nouvelle route reliant les deux entrées.
On remarquera, sur ce plan, à droite, de l'ancien château, les anciens communs transformés en
maison de week end; à gauche, dans le bas du parc, l'ancienne villa transformée en salle de musique.

[5] See *Oeuvre complète 1910–29*, p. 201.
[6] The guest house and the pavilion are published in the January 1929 issue of the magazine *Art et Industrie* (see note 4). The photographs attest that the buildings and the work of the external organization had already been completed for some time. On the 8th of May, 1929, Le Corbusier sent Church the map in *L'Architecture Vivante*, second series, Spring–Summer 1929, with ample photographs on the works executed (see letter by Le Corbusier to Church, FLC dossier "Church").
[7] In the index of the tables of *L'Architecture Vivante*, p. 48, is written: "42. General view of the house situated on the lower part of the plot [referring to the pavilion], addition to a construction of the 18th century."
[8] Le Corbusier, *Art et Industrie*, pp. 6–7.
[9] The "Recapitulation of the estimated and descriptive budget—for the modification and the addition of a building on the property of Monsieur Church at Ville d'Avray" sent by the engineer-contractor G. Sommer to the architects on September 15, 1927 mentioning demolition and reconstruction that retains only the ground floor, in accordance to which Le Corbusier writes in the article quoted in *Art et Industrie*. Of the documents pertaining to a break that occurred in a ceiling of the pavilion in 1935, it turns out that another architect, a certain Leveque, competed for the first reworking of this building. It is not out of the question that in the process of this work the upper levels were removed.
[10] See the "recapitulation" mentioned in the preceding note.

dominated by a large villa; and below, the other one was separated by high walls, terraces, and a thick vegetation, out of which rose the ruins of the old house that was to be adapted as a pavilion for music and entertainments.[5]

The whole operation occupied the architects for approximately four years: from 1927 to the beginning of 1931, not taking into account the usual setbacks (honoraria not received, unexpected mistakes, etc.).

The guest house comes out of the foundations of the old stable along the Rue Bourlon-Clauzel, and the pavilion was already finished in 1928.[6] The relative scarcity of documents available and the fact that the property underwent a radical reconstruction in the 1960s, moreover, do not allow a comprehensive picture of the situation created by the architectcs.

The information doesn't even allow the precise historical placement of the ruined building. The publication in *L'Architecture Vivante* laconically points out that the pavilion was built over an eighteenth-century construction. To judge from the photographs of the pavilion, the horizontal, flat grooved rustication and the way it stops at the openings is very similar, as much as can be observed, to the main façade of the parochial church of the Ville d'Avray, built in 1789–92. Finally, trusting in the rather vague indications in the brief monograph on the Ville d'Avray, the ruins could correspond to the building "Les Tourelles" (The Towers),

60   Bruno Reichlin

built by Eugène Chabrier after the acquisition, in 1835, of the property called "Colombier," that in 1927 would constitute the lowest part of the Church properties.[7] In view of our intent here, this indeterminacy is of little importance; in Le Corbusier's theoretical corpus the concept of "tradition" is sufficiently and deliberately generic for making at least subtle stylistic distinctions, above all at the site of the project. In each case the indication "18th century" meant the Neoclassical French tradition par excellence and as such was a qualified point of reference.

Of much greater interest would be documentation on the state of the ruin at the beginning of the construction work, but because there are missing data in this case, we must trust the indications provided by Le Corbusier himself when he describes the entire intervention:

"The old ground floor remains, as well as an old rotten floor. A *toit-jardin* has been built in cement at the top of the music house; the old internal walls that divided the space have been removed, and better to indicate them, the old parts of the house have been painted dark green, contrasting sharply with the brilliant white of the new parts of the construction."[8]

We are not told how many floors the original building had, but various documents that have come our way[9] confirm that there remained only the ruins of the ground floor.

The "reconstruction in gesso of the plaster of the façades of the ground floor," point nine of the "Recapitulation of the estimated and descriptive budget"[10]

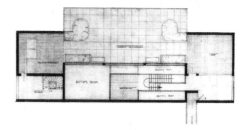

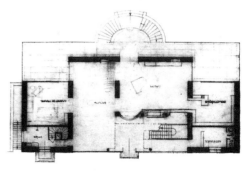

49. Church property at Ville-d'Avray:
—top, the existing villa;
—upper right, the guest apartments that were built on the foundations of the old stables along the Bourlon-Clauzel street;
—at left, the pavilion of Villa Church.
50. The pavilion of Villa Church, first plan, addition of the first floor, around July 27, 1927 (FLC 8161).
51. First plan, ground floor, around July 27, 1927. The preexisting walls were dismantled in strips. The staircase that comes out of the living room joins the first floor in three ramps (FLC 8168).
52. The pavilion of Villa Church at the Ville d'Avray (FLC).

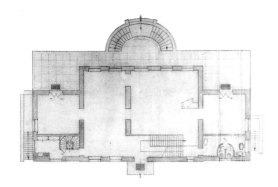

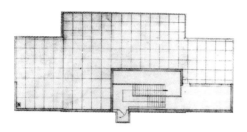

[11] Le Corbusier, *Art et Industrie*, pp. 5–6.
[12] Ibid., p. 6.
[13] Ibid., p. 7.
[14] Ibid.
[15] The actual garden of the castle at Villandry is the minute reconstruction of the original garden "*alla francese*" of the sixteenth century, completed in the preceding century by Docteur Carvalho, founder of the "*Demeure Historique*." Because of its garden, the castle at Villandry is known as "Castle of gardens in the garden of France."
[16] See, for example, drawing FLC 8168.

from the contractor to the architects, perhaps already furnishes a first indication for understanding Le Corbusier's intentions in this *restoration*: however run down, the external aspect of the old rusticated building is re-established in the original conditions.

The rapport with the site: double subversion of the traditional architectural layout

Presenting the transformations of the Church property, Le Corbusier began with some general considerations on the origins and the historical trajectory of the houses on the margins of Parisian bourgeoisie, concluding that the exigencies of modern man require inevitable adjustments.

"More than one hundred years ago, the petit-bourgeoisie built simple and decorative houses in the environs of Paris, and they surrounded them by parks in which they delighted in planting every kind of tree. These properties became magnificent parks and the modest residences of an era, receiving persons of refined taste: at the gates of the giant city, they were sumptuous oases. But the house, in spite of successive internal re-organizations, was not able to adapt to the exigencies of modern comfort: it was too small; so, eventually, a dependence on that same style was created. The purity of these ensembles became questionable. And the vast stables? Henceforth they would be useless. To the absurd this can be added: it is held that following a heat wave, under Louis XV, the tradition of orienting the house toward the north began.

Undoubtedly the heat wave has passed! More exactly, it is the cold wave that now prevails.

Finally the 'crisis of styles' is at its end. The healthy spirits thought it strange, if not grotesque, to build the *new* in the *old* style. It is also admitted (and it was time) that modern man conceives of existence, and therefore also the house, in different ways."[11]

More than logical, in this perspective the "henceforth useless" stables have given way to an entirely new building, with the guestrooms and—from the point of view of circulation an obvious choice, but none the less meaningful—the garages.

As to the pavilion, the disposition *on the living corpus of tradition* subverts the traditional architectural layout that Le Corbusier held to be the ineluctable landing place of his quest. By leaving the foundation of the original construction almost intact, the relation with the surroundings underwent an almost double upheaval:

—proceeding from the highest part of the property,

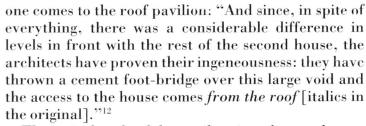

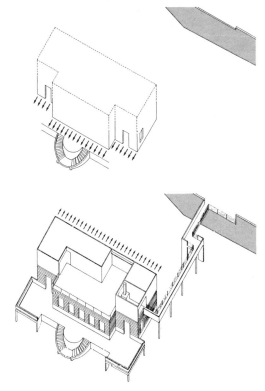

one comes to the roof pavilion: "And since, in spite of everything, there was a considerable difference in levels in front with the rest of the second house, the architects have proven their ingeneousness: they have thrown a cement foot-bridge over this large void and the access to the house comes *from the roof* [italics in the original]."[12]

—The main façade of the pavilion is no longer the one facing the park with the double staircase; the transformation has corrected the *contradiction* of the northwestern exposure, designating the opposite southwestern façade as the new principal one, facing the vast geometric garden and turned toward the new entryway: "Building the foot-bridge, allowed the view over the entire second property; also over the large flower beds (in the manner of embroidery) planted in the *south* [italics in original], there where the back of the house formerly was."[13]

Not all the measures taken, however, are in one direction. The regular and decorative forms of the garden, this "flower bed in geometric style in bright colors and having the most felicitous effect"[14] are unequivocable reminiscences in miniature of the classic French garden; for example, the flowery basrelief of the flower bed of Villandry,[15] predisposed to a sweeping view as in our case. The garden remains, then, *on the side of* tradition, iconographically tying in with the old structure of the pavilion; to this end, it will be noticed, in the first rudimentary drawings of the garden, the composition of the flower beds assumed a more or less symmetrical configuration.[16]

53. "Petit Projet," ground floor, probably September 1927 (FLC 8159).
54. "Petit Projet," first floor, probably September 1927. The southwest façade is defined in good part by a simple mural wing turned on its side (FLC 8158).
55. State of the project on September 21, 1927. First floor; the openings of the library on the southwest façade are still missing, its place is probably taken by a wall closet. The round skylight is subsequently installed (FLC 8219).
56. The back of the October 1927 version. Blueprint of the first floor toward the end of September—beginning of October 1927. The corrections concerning the dimensions of the balcony, the fireplace and the opening-square on the southwest façade of the library foreshadowing the definitive version (FLC 8162).
57. The geometric garden seen from the foot-bridge (FLC).
58. Double subversion of the original architectural layout:
—original main access and orientation;
—access and orientation after the transformation.

[17] In the theory of poetic discourse, certain authors use the term "isotopics" to designate a basic operative device for the production and understanding of a text. Used where the text doesn't necessarily designate an exclusively literary fact, thus, for example, Umberto Eco proposes this term also for events of an architectural, plastic, pictorial, cinematographic, etc., nature. (U. Eco, *Trattato di semiotica generale*, Milan, 1975, see for example p. 7, p. 324, etc.)
By the allowable extension of the application of the concept of isotopics to architecture, it designates those properties common to an ensemble (albeit minimal) of "objects" (or elements: windows, doors, and/or their stylistic-iconographic qualifications, mural conformances, etc.) and/or the configurations that the architectural work exhibits when it is subjected to rules of interpretive coherence. As will be demonstrated, in the case of the music pavilion, some elements and their composition are attributable to architectural tradition; this common property is therefore redundant, reiterative, and it constitutes a coherence of meaning, and it is this that is understood as the isotopics of traditional architecture.
[18] Umberto Eco, *Lector in fabula—la cooperazione interpretativa nei testi narrativi*, Milan, 1979, p. 93.
[19] Without giving too much importance to that which was probably the fortuitous result of a coincidence, however, it is worth pointing out that the planimetric foundation of the traditional *plan paralysé*, which Le Corbusier juxtaposes to the *plan libre* of Modern construction in *Précisions*, p. 58 (and in the second South American lecture: see drawing FLC 32089), takes up, if only in schematic form, the plan of the pavilion: a central body that is staggered in relation to the wings.
[20] In his "Petite contribution à l'étude d'une fenêtre moderne" (*Almanach d'Architecture Moderne*, Paris, 1926, pp. 95ff.), polemicizing, Le Corbusier, writes that Auguste Perret "makes himself the champion of the vertical window that died with Haussmann and with fatal consequences to construction in stone." Explaining the role of the regulatory lines in the southern façade of the pavilion, he specifies that the old windows on the ground floor "are of a totally different type" from those new ones on the first floor (Le Corbusier, "Tracés régulateurs," in *L'Architecture Vivante*, p. 23).
[21] "Arrangement. Solution/dominant character/a façade characterized by a rhythmic composition," from *Principes d'analyse scientifique—Architecture—méthode et vocabulaire*, Paris, 1972, p. 34.
[22] See drawings FLC 8157, 8158, 8159.
[23] See the southern façade of the pavilion inscribed with the complex plot of the regulatory lines, reproduced in *L'Architecture Vivante*, p. 24. The explanations of Le Corbusier are referred to in note 28.

The main façade: tradition and innovation in confrontation

In the façade facing toward the courtyard, the old and the new parts can clearly be distinguished. Proceeding from a description of the elements that comprise it and their configuration, it is possible to subdivide them into kinds of affinities, using as criteria whether or not they belong to traditional architecture; after which the mutual relations can be analyzed from the point of view of this distinction.

In the theory of political discourse, the term isotopic,[17] close to its more generic beginnings, designates those "various semiotic phenomena generically definable as the coherence during the process of a reading at different textual levels."[18] In architecture this could correspond to the ensemble of formal facts and/or the meaning between their coherence through a determinate appearance at least. It is in this sense, in the case of the pavilion, that he wishes to distinguish between an isotopics of traditional architecture and an isotopics of the new architecture.

The elements and the configurations that form the conserved structure of the pre-existent building belong to traditional architecture. It can be said:
—the broad but barely hinted at symmetrical volumetric composition with central support;[19]
—the symmetrical disposition of the external openings of the ground floor and the entrance on the building's axis;
—the rusticated wall;
—the openings on the ground floor of the *vertical window* type, that Le Corbusier assigned to the historical past in the evolution of openings;[20] the two windows on the left side of the central support constitute, finally, what could be defined as a minimal fragment of *ordonnance* (arrangement).[21]

As for the new addition, it was necessary to design elements and configurations that conformed to the norms of traditional architecture, specifying the mode of their adaptation, distinguishing them from those that represented, instead, an innovation and as such concurred to define the system of modern architecture in the process of becoming.

Among the new and the old structures, the following correspondences can be found:
—the new addition traces the perimeter of the ground floor and takes on the entire main façade. This is anything but specific, in that the proportion of the walls without openings of the central support is only one-fifth as high as the wall of an entire floor separating

Bruno Reichlin

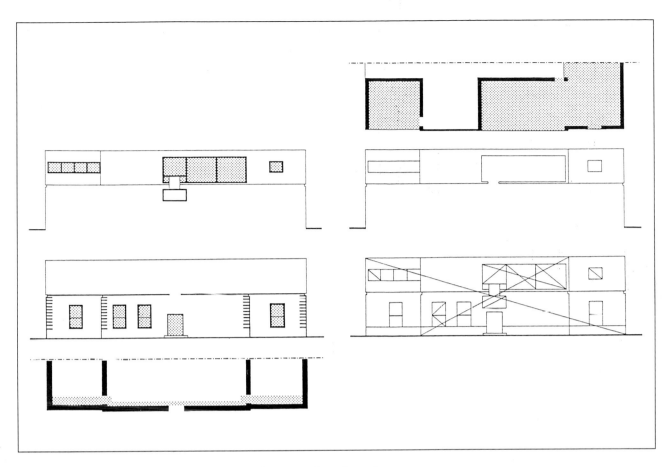

two external spaces. In the intermediate and reduced version, aptly called *petit projet*,[22] the wall section took up almost half of the main façade and turned the corner just barely suggesting the image of a modern addition that takes on the entire main façade. Functional considerations aside (the greatest amount of privacy for the terrace that is on top of the wall, for example), it seems possible to admit that to the architects it was important to counterbalance the old parts in this manner;

—the balcony, new plastic element of the façade, underscores the symmetrical foundation of the building. This balcony is the focal point of the main façade in several respects: from the exterior it shows the platform for the orchestra that straddles both levels of the pavilion; in the definitive version the frontal parapet of the balcony becomes massive, assuming the same proportions as the central projection.[23]

The new elements:

—The first floor has three openings, each one a different type; from left to right and, using the terminology coined by Le Corbusier, a *fenêtre en longueur*, a *pan de verre*, and a *trou dans le mur*.

Together, these three types of openings constitute the basic repertory developed and researched by Le Corbusier during those years. Nevertheless, a distinc-

59. Preexisting elements, new elements and their mutual relations;
—preexisting elements of the building that belong to architectural tradition: rusticated ground floor with central projection;
—new elements: the *fenêtre en longueur*, the axial balcony, the *pan de verre*, the opening of the library;
—relations between preexistent and new elements: the lateral openings are symmetrical in relation to the wings; the symmetry of the preexisting foundation is underscored by the axial balcony; the additional floor traces the perimeter of the ground floor over the entire main façade, hiding the terrace on the first floor.
—the *tracés régulateurs* harmonize the preexistent and new parts.

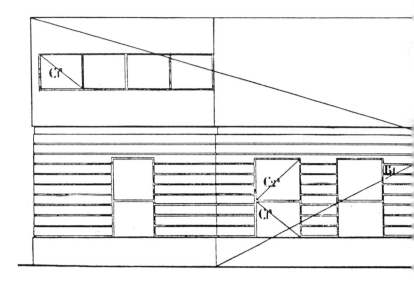

60. The *tracés régulateurs* (*L'Architecture Vivante*, Spring/Summer, 1929).

[24] Le Corbusier would insist many times on this aspect of the modern building, considered the cornerstone of a veritable mutation in architecture. Among the texts in which Le Corbusier most fully develops this argument, he will recall the lecture given at the Sorbonne on June 12, 1924 and reproduced in *Almanach*, under the title "L'Esprit Nouveau en Architecture" and the second lecture delivered at the "Amis des Arts" of Buenos Aires, October 5, 1929, then taken up again in *Précisions* under the title "The technologies are the order itself of lyricism—they are opening a new cycle in architecture." The graphics that synthetically illustrate the preachings of the new building technologies would be defined by Le Corbusier himself as "the cutting symbol of the contemporary architectural revolution" (*Précisions*, p. 56).

[25] The '"Appel aux industriels" is reproduced in Le Corbusier, *Almanach*, pp. 102–3.

[26] In *Précisions*, p. 69 and reproduction on p. 68: "Mr. Vignola does not concern himself with the window, but rather with the 'intra-windows' (pilasters, columns). I interpret him as saying: architecture means light only.
I want to demonstrate this with a series of small drawings [on page 68] representing the story of architecture over the ages, through that of the window."

[27] Le Corbusier, *Précisions*, p. 70.

[28] The stylistic and formal heterogeneity of the elements in the façade created a problem; as in the explanation provided by Le Corbusier himself, the "regulatory lines" essentially had the function of linking pre-existing elements belonging to the isotopics of tradition, to the new parts: "Here is. . .a layout that has allowed the sufficient harmonizing of the new floor of a building (at Ville D'Avray) that has been raised over the pre-existing ground floor."
And referring to the façade, he specifies: "Layout A-1. —That determines the dimensions of the total construction, furnishes the exact dimension of the large window that occupies the center of the composition.
Layout B-1. —Associates the dimensions of the

tion is necessary: in Le Corbusier's understanding, *fenêtre en longueur* and a *pan de verre* are architectural solutions made possible by the new technologies that have liberated spatial elements from static-constructional functions;[24] the third window, instead, has a double isotopic status belonging to two systems: on the one hand, it is Le Corbusier's version of the traditional *trou dans le mur*, on the other, it is the basic unit of a system of composition (proposed by Le Corbusier at the end of his "Appel aux industriels"[25]) that renders the other types as additions.

In the main façade of the pavilion, then, the openings are inventoried and confrontationally placed in a sinuous representation, documenting the "révolution architecturale contemporaine" theorized by Le Corbusier in those years, telling "l'histoire de l'architecture par celle de la fenêtre" (the history of architecture through that of the window).[26] Inserted into the type of wall that unequivocally belongs to tradition, the vertical windows on the ground floor are the *ante quem* terms of this revolution. The fragments of *ordonnance* hinted at by the two paired openings at the left of the central support, figuratively reinforce the isotopic "traditional architecture," not only because it reinforces the system, but because it ostensibly designates, *pars pro toto*, those "regularly perforated surfaces of those closely placed holes as much as possible" that for Le Corbusier represented the quintessence of traditional stone architecture: "Consider once more the appearance of Luigi's or Haussmann's façades in stone, the aspect of the façade through which architecture has come to a stop: it is a surface regularly perforated by holes placed as close as possible one to the other. The design seems prosaic: *but this*

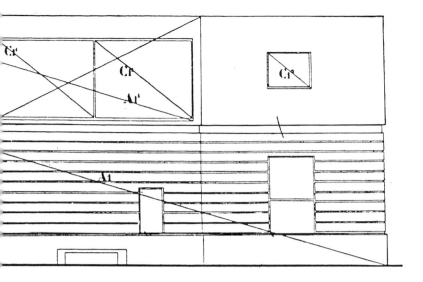

is the true architecture in stone, the expression of a pure system of construction" [italics in original].[27]

The new architecture has absorbed the old

Considering the composition of the main façade on the south in its ensemble, we will now investigate the confrontation between the new and the old architectural systems and how it was orchestrated. The role already assigned to the *tracés régulateurs* (regulating or coordinating lines) in harmonizing an ensemble composed of heterogeneous elements, furnishes precise specifications as to their use, and Le Corbusier himself, explaining their implementation in this particular case and in others that can be easily referred to, gives further suggestions for a reading of the façade that conforms to his understanding, according to a procedure that privileges by turn different constellations of parts.[28]

Painting the rest of the old villa dark green,[29] Le Corbusier intended to accentuate the confrontation: ". . . better to indicate them, the old parts of the house have been painted dark green, which contrasts sharply with the brilliant white of the new construction."[30] This color doesn't completely cover the entire ground floor, but it stops at the window sill line, so that the new parts painted in white and the old ones painted green appear as approximately identical surfaces: this symmetrical correspondence between above and below highlights their difference.

On the ground floor, the two vertical windows of the central projection to the left of the entrance don't have a symmetrical equivalent on the right, visually contradicting a basic principle of traditional composition.[31]

central pavilion to those of the central balcony. Layouts C-1., C-2. —The layouts C-1 and C-2 that derive from the large central window, dictate on the one hand the dimensions of the lateral small windows of the new construction and on the other allow the old windows of the ground floor (which are of a totally different type) to relate to the new ones of the third floor" (Le Corbusier, "Tracés régulateurs," in *L'Architecture Vivante*, p. 23).

As to a reading of the façade proposed in this study, it unfolds according to a procedure that privileges different constellations of parts in turn (for example, the central projection and then the wings) and the elements, finding its support in considerations on ways that Le Corbusier's vision was sustained in terms of a work that wasn't better specified, but easily identified in the Villa Schwob of la Chaux-de-Fonds: considerations that make such a good case for the pavilion and that pose the question whether the example quoted doesn't overshadow the recent experience of the Church pavilion. Le Corbusier makes this reference: "I allow myself to confess a personal experience to help clarify things: I have spent at least fifteen years since then, having on my design table the façades of a house in which the solids and voids were disposed according to the requirements of the layout plan, I felt as if I were in front of a cacophonous ensemble; seeking to put order in the disposition of solids and voids, only my sensibility guided me. I then had the sharpest inkling that the relation among the various elements of the same family should be stabilized. More particularly between those that the eye grasps first: the contour of a pavilion; and that which it then measures: the door opening and the space that it determines on the left and the right; the window hole and the full walls that surround it, etc. An ordering layout was called for: the one of a diagonal that allows the expression, with a single line, of the individuality of a surface. Then tracing the diagonal from the façade to the jutting pavilion, the one from the door and the full surface that emerges with clarity from the composition, I measured to see if these diagonals were parallel among themselves or if they cut into each other at a right angle; if the diverse surfaces that they represented were of the same family and therefore would be reconciled. And if it wasn't like that, I was doing the impossible to obtain this result" (Le Corbusier, *L'Architecture Vivante*, pp. 13–14).

[29] On July 9, 1928, Church had challenged the first samples in black, proposing that the entire pavilion be painted white. He would also disagree with the polychromy of the exterior used by the architects on the guest houses (FLC, dossier "Church").

[30] Le Corbusier, *Art et Industrie*, p. 7.

[31] The documents accessible at FLC do not allow clarification on this rather singular fact, that is, to find out if the symmetry was already present in the old villa, or rather, if it is part of the architect's modifications; which, even when leaving out the considerations that follow, could have good reasons for plugging up openings that conflicted with the principal staircase. Unfortunately the elevation of the preexistent building is missing, assuming that it had been drawn up in the first place.

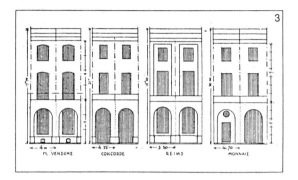

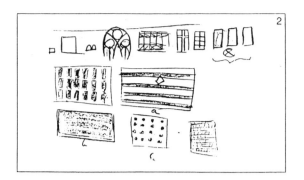

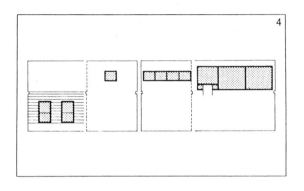

[32] Georges Gromort, *Essais sur la théorie de l'architecture*, Paris, 1946, 2d ed., p. 59. The expression is used by Gromort to characterize bilateral symmetry referring to the human body, symmetrical in relation to the axis that runs through the torso. Gromort was a professor at the Ecole des Beaux-Arts of Paris and the *Essais*, which received a prize from the Académie, summarize the course he gave between 1937 and 1940; moreover, they contain a pertinent paradigm for a synchronic confrontation between architectural tradition and innovation. Going into conjecture, it can be supposed that the systematics, competence, and logic of Le Corbusier's arguments have as an unrenounceable presupposition the imposing theoretical, methodological, and ideological corpus developed at the Beaux-Arts and in Gromort's publications. Le Corbusier deconstructs a solidly established system; when he says "tradition," he means "Beaux-Arts."

[33] The expression "solids and voids" adequately explains Le Corbusier's compositional preoccupations; he himself uses it on different occasions. See for example his "Traces regulateurs," op. cit., pp. 12ff.

[34] See J. Dubois, in AA. VV., *Rhétorique générale*, Paris, 1970, p. 82: "The *chiasmo* traditionally designates the symmetry of a cross." In the text, *chiasmo* is produced when "within a period, it happens that a first order is given that finds itself diammetrically contradicted in its development."

On the first floor the *pan de verre*, instead, takes up the entire half on the right of the central projection, leaving intact the left one.

In the genealogical tree that Le Corbusier himself delineated, the two types of openings occupying an extreme position—the vertical window and the *pan de verre*, respectively—are then put into direct confrontation in the central projection according to a diagonal composition that pivots at the balcony. Grafted directly onto the traditional compositional principle of bilateral symmetry, and using its disjunctions, the new asserts itself displacing the old order: "the unity of things that come in pairs"[32] is succeeded by the accumulation of solids and voids[33] on either side of the building's axis; and according to the order given on the ground floor, with the void at the left and the solid on the right, the first floor can be seen as symmetrically opposed. He designated this cross formation with the term *chiasmo* because of the structural similarity with that term in rhetoric.[34]

Even though anything but infrequent in the projects of Le Corbusier and the Modern Movement in general, the relation of elements organized on the diagonals of the building contradicts the iconographic *topos* of the horizontal stratification of the floors. A figure in

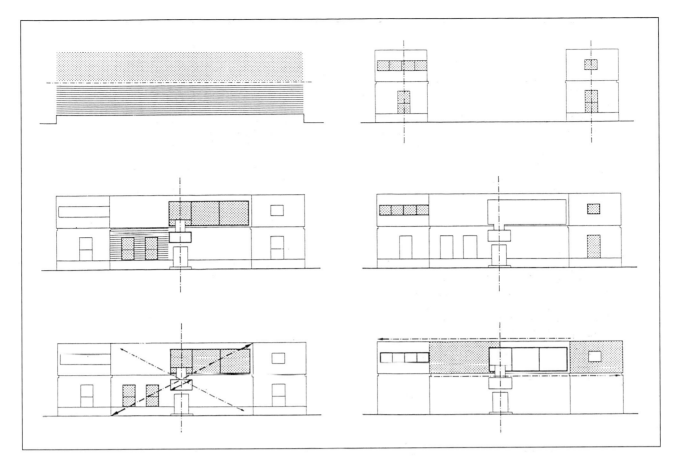

chiasmo determines even the composition of the solid and empty spaces on the first floor: its flank at the void of the window is at the viewer's left, and the solid of the wall with the aperture of the window is at the right; while in the central projection, as has been mentioned, the distribution of the solids and voids is symmetrically inverse.

According to a bilaterally symmetrical façade in the case of the *chiasmo*, the equilibrium of the composition is configured in different ways: this is no longer entrusted to correspondences from point to point among identical elements, even if the complex adjustment of diverse elements that correspond to each other are organized in a cross formation. In other words: the ensemble alone is symmetrical and only from the point of view of distribution of the elements in the space of the façade, but not in their structure. It will be noted, finally, that the middle terms of the genealogy delineated by Le Corbusier, the *fenêtre en longueur* is the basic element of the type *trou dans le mur*, occupying the blank spaces of the building. In this case the juxtaposition is at the horizontal second level, and the fact that the two openings occupy the otherwise identical wings of the building, gives a particular contrast to the comparison.

61. The history of the window:
1) The role of openings in the architectural concessions of Le Corbusier: "The window has always been an obstacle. Its evolution through time signals the perfectioning of its usage";
2) Le Corbusier: "the history of architecture through the window's" (*Précisions*);
3) examples of "*Ordonnances*, more or less perforated" (Gromort);
4) inventory of the aperture types that participate in the composition of the southwest façade: traditional vertical window, window *trou dans le mur*, *fenêtre en longueur*, *pan de verre*.
62. The new architecture has absorbed the old:
—the use of color determines a symmetrical correspondence between the preexisting ground floor, painted in dark green, and the addition painted in white;
—the wings are in themselves symmetrical;
—vertical windows and *pan de verre*, extreme elements in the chronology of openings established by Le Corbusier, occupy the central projection and oppose each other according to a diagonal arrangement;
—*fenêtre en longueur* and *trou dans le mur*, median elements in the chronology of openings established by Le Corbusier, occupy the wings of the building;
—in the central projection the "solids and voids" correspond to each other according to a *chiasmo* arrangement that pivots on the building's axis.

63. The final touches on the pavilion of the Villa Church (FLC).

The nature of the intervention itself—the addition to the remains of an old building—has triggered the architectural theme of the main side of the pavilion.

This theme consists in the confrontation and in the composition of elements and their configuration belonging to *architectural tradition*—understood as a system of standards and distributional, constructional, stylistic-formalist, iconographic, etc. customs—and, respectively, to the new architecture in the case in point: the architectural poetics of Le Corbusier.

Different types of openings, but also diverse wall formations are the *materials* placed in confrontation; Le Corbusier tests and illustrates figurative properties and possibilites of his repertory of openings. The confrontation is directed, it has an outcome: the main side of the pavilion allegorically stages the advent of a new architectural poetics that annexes to, englobes the elements—relics—of tradition in its system.

Bruno Reichlin

Le Corbusier creates the distance between the new and traditional architecture through *antithesis*—"figure of style by confrontation."[35]

In the context of the analyzed façade, the role of *chiasmo* and symmetry is a double one. On the one side there are the configurations—the compositional operations—that give shape to the antithesis between innovation and tradition, and from this point of view have an auxiliary function. Borrowing concepts and names that until now have been used above all in literary rhetoric, one could say that it is a matter of architectural figures of expression of the syntactic type, predisposed to transmit meaning; precisely while making the support a figure having antithesis as its content.[36] On the other hand, bilateral symmetry and *chiasmo*, in so far as they allow themselves to be subsumed respectively, one by tradition and the other by innovation, themselves form an *antithesis* such as the one that has just been uncovered.*

[35] In the pavilion, the stylistic paradigm tradition vs. new divides elements and configurations of the southern façade into two ensembles of opposite meaning. It seems, moreover, permissible to consider the confrontation of two ensembles as an exemplar of architectural antithesis.

[36] In the classification established by AA. VV., *Rhétorique générale*, p.49, the antithesis is catalogued between the *métalogismes* (basis for logic), that is, between the *métaboles* of the content "that modify the logic value of the sentence," p. 34; symmetry and *chiasmo* are listed instead between *métataxse*, that is, the *métaboles* of the expressions that intervene on the syntax: "acting on the structure of the sentence" (p. 33).

* This essay was first published with the title "L'ancien et le nouveau—Le Corbusier, le Pavillon de la Villa Church," in *AMC*, no. 1, May 1983, pp. 100–111; an expanded version, translated here, appeared in *Parametro*, no. 121, November 1983, pp. 12–25, 64–65. The analytical drawings are by B. Reichlin.

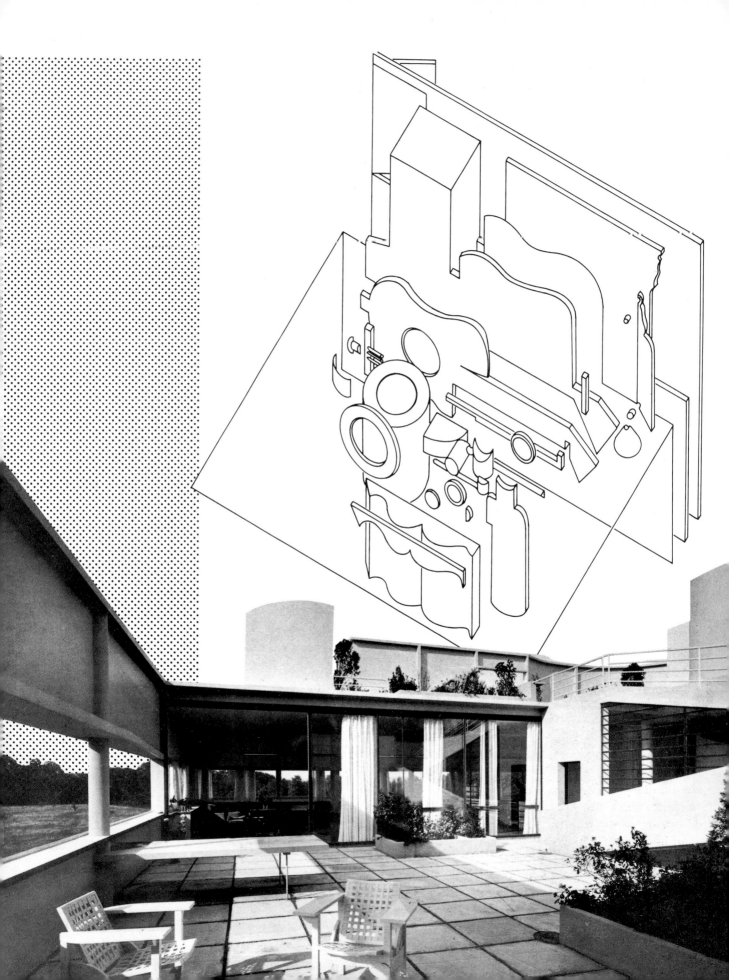

THE VILLA SAVOYE
REVISITED

Alvaro Siza Vieira

Picasso said that it takes ten years to learn how to draw, and another ten to learn how to draw like a child.

These last ten years seem to be missing from an apprenticeship in architecture today.

The charm of a visit to the Villa Savoye comes from the encounter with a kind of ingenuity and with the continual transformation of each idea: with a continual inventiveness.

Each step alters the Order, which is always present, inverts the hierarchy of the elements. These can be banal per se: they surround any inhabitant unobtrusively whether they have been assimilated or not. Each invention generates another. The possibilities of discovery are endless: to the right, to the left, high or low, obliquely, orthogonally. The direct and almost crude expression of the details has nothing forced or primitive about it; it has to do with a second spontaneity, laboriously acquired and at the same time spontaneously found, of an exercise accelerated to the point of a synchretism of the critical hypotheses in an approximation of the essential.

Unlike Chareau, whose ingeneous discoveries and applications of new materials Le Corbusier seems to always have observed, Le Corbusier did not have a fixed clientele, nor a team of great artisans. He pursued an idea in depth and to its extreme; rigorous but undetailed plans, open to conformism or to adventure, furrowed with doubts, intuitions, and influences, at the waining of a world in which designer and artisan understood each other directly, as in Chareau's case, but without any competitiveness.

In his readings he could have been influenced by the ideas of Alexandre Vaneyre,[1] so that in an event as important as the trip to the Orient, he reported back to Switzerland—land of confluence and indecision—the plastic whiteness of the Mediterranean. He was not satisfied with the invented national style, a mixture of

[1] Jacques Gubler, *Nationalisme et Internationalisme dans l'Architecture Moderne de la Suisse*, Lausanne, 1975.

[2] Paul V. Turner, *La formation de Le Corbusier—Idéalisme et Mouvement Moderne*, Paris, Editions MACULA, 1987.

alpine architecture and the Middle Ages, for which the Turinese "burg" of Alfredo d'Andrade was a valid model.[2]

The practice of painting, in the encounter with Ozenfant, was oriented toward the linear association of common objects—the bottle, the guitar, the pipe, the common drinking glass—stripped forms whose straight and curved lines, forming a muddle without head or code, become the inner potential of a type: the presuppositions of the terrace at Poissy, from which they burst forth to the sky.

This exercise in associations and expansion keeps branching out its roots and extending its mane; it advances from the plateaus of La Chaux-de-Fonds toward the very distant horizons of Chandigarh, passing through the small lots of Paris, by the vast cities of South America—apartments in series of 144 x 144 or large platforms among colossal rocks.

Linear and curving structures are vertiginously insinuated among the mountains of Algiers or Rio de Janeiro, making use of the gorges and overhangs

Alvaro Siza Vieira

above the sea; compact cells are articulated in the interstices of the apartments and fragmented in the Maison du Salut.

In the 3 x 3 studio of the Rue de Sèvres, in which not even the central light of the Hospital of Venice is of any use, Paris has just been leveled by the advent of an *Esprit Nouveau*. The search isn't always a patient one.

But Poissy appears as the encounter between research and some liberty: client and open space.

It could be an object from the other side of the world; at first sight it would seem to be that. It could be built out of iron and aluminium: *à sec*.

But on the contrary, the plaster renders continuous the syncopated forms and fissures that emerge daily denouncing technological indecisions and the hands that have realized the design.

Close to the street, half-covered by a wall, the custodian's house announces in a precise way the language of the villa that is not yet visible. A skillfully calculated distance articulates the two constructions related in this perfect and complete manner, almost like a small Parisian lot. Le Corbusier occupies the space completely, and the house is a particularity in such a space.

The powerful forms contained in a parallelepiped rising from the *pilotis*, appear here and there, across a continuous, horizontal split, on the pavement or on the terrace. The peripheral *pilotis* almost coincide

64. "... half-covered by a wall, the custodian's house announces in a precise way the language of the villa that is not yet visible."
65. Villa Savoye, south and west façades.

The Villa Savoye   **75**

Alvaro Siza Vieira

66. ". . . the appearance of the house creates a feeling of hardness; the *pilotis* merge with the wall of the first floor."
67. ". . . a wall balanced by the opposite side with a built-in table and a mass-produced sink, two lamps symmetrically placed near the door."

with the limits of the construction. The capitals have vanished, the encounter with the horizontal floor is uncertain, withdrawn from the wall by a few centimeters. The house form could fall tumbling off the *pilotis*; it is not enough to elevate the expansive forms of the terrace, so taut and close to breaking, prefigured by the narrow architrave of an opening.

The appearance of the house creates a feeling of hardness, the *pilotis* melt into the wall of the first floor. It is necessary to walk around it; in the remaining three façades the independent structure delimits a covered portico. A curve with a calculated radius renders the other *pilotis* external; it indicates the access to garage. Some overhanging beams keep any softening at a remove.

The entrance door occupies a central position on the curving wall, coinciding with the axis of the structural link of the four intercolumns.

Inside, the structure is doubled, framing the door and the entryway, signaled by the double-loop ramp.

This framing is reinforced with an incredible economy: a wall balanced on the opposite side by a built-in table and mass-produced sink, two lamps symmetrically placed near the door.

The Villa Savoye

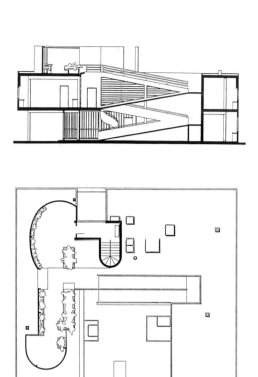

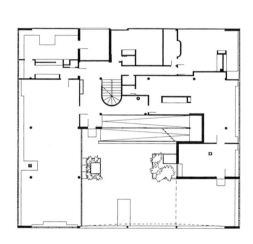

This simple order is constantly subverted: sculptural staircase, triangular opening onto the patio, the symmetry of the ramp itself, light, twists of the walls.

The second floor is developed around a patio that illuminates it perfectly. The asymmetry is controlled by the axial ramp that continues on the outside of the terrace; the abruptness of this path is contained in an embrace by the sinuous curves of the wall.

Mysteriously it is calm, however saturated with tension. The ample development of the living room dominates diagonals that are multiplied and that are reflected on the mosaic pavement of the atrium; the way to the main room—another U—creates a sensation of depth, as in an old house, and again yields a view of the patio and the clearing.

Each element has an autonomous life, it blurs immediately, as in a city of which we have everyday knowledge. The combination of elements is not absolutely perfect. The baseboards protrude like obstacles, as do the water pipes; there is a lack of rigor from the doorjambs, to the curve of the staircase or the bathroom wall. Nothing is systematic. There are obvious errors in the design and the way it is carried out, mutual indecisions reinforce each other yet each error generates poetry, teaching transformation.

What is impressive in this particular work of Le Corbusier, and runs through all of his work, written or designed, is the disconcerting refutation of the already affirmed, a kind of candor, a restlessness that his capacity for analysis and synthesis and convictions did not destroy, a certain insecurity, the repudiation of self-sufficiency under an apparent arrogance.

The hugging of a worker in front of a supposed mistake in a wall.

Much of the charm of the Villa Savoye—of Architecture—originates in a subtension, a precarious complicity among those who realize it: customer, builders, plan. Its continuous breakdown reflects the impossibility of maintaining this magical equilibrium, but also of looking for it again. We do not know which Gods inhabit it. Like a Japanese temple, it was first made out of its decomposition. Gold under white evokes youth, health, cleanliness, boxing—*the noble art*. An inexhaustible and everflowing research inhabits the meadowlands of Chandigarh planned from the sky, sculptures modeled by correspondence, portraits of Josephine, a smile of Eve in Paradise.*

* The analytical drawings are by Alvaro Siza Vieira.

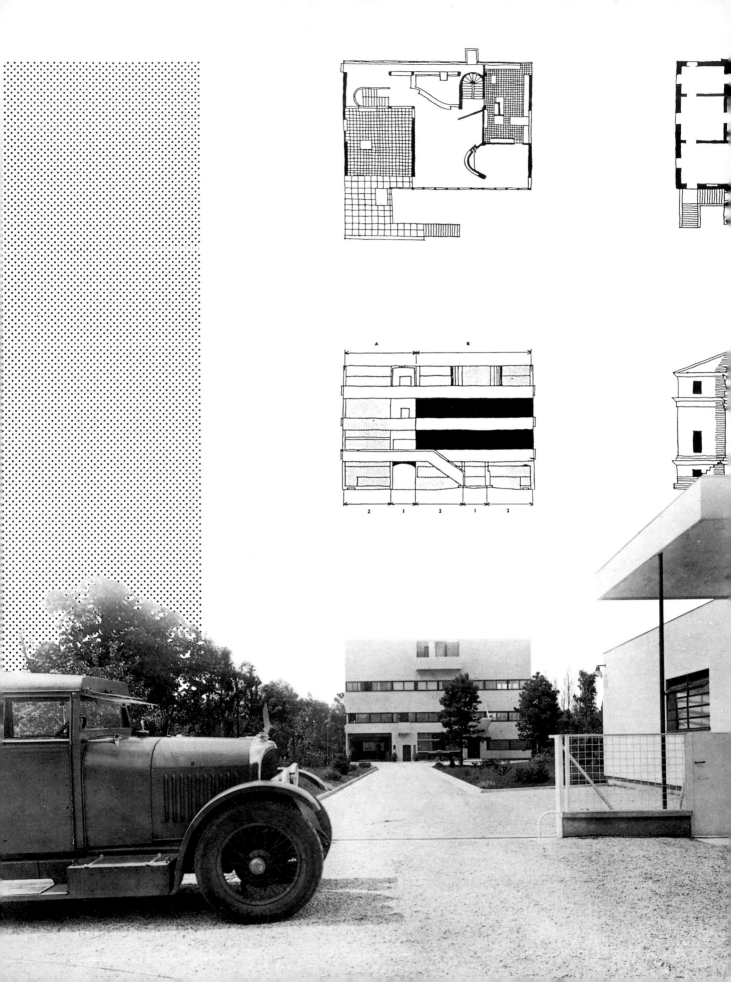

GARCHES
TO JAOUL

James Stirling

Villa Garches, recently reoccupied, and the two houses for Mr. Jaoul and his son, now nearing completion, are possibly the most significant buildings by Le Corbusier to be seen in Paris today, for they represent the extremes of his vocabulary: the former, rational, urbane, programmatic, the latter, personal and anti-mechanistic. If style is the crystallization of an attitude, then these buildings, so different even at the most superficial level of comparison, may, on examination, reveal something of a philosophical change of attitude on the part of their author.

Garches, built at the culmination of Cubism and canonizing the theories in "Towards a New Architecture," has since its inception been a standard by which Le Corbusier's genius is measured against that of the other great architects of this century. Inhabited, again by Americans, after 15 years' splendid isolation, it has been painted in a manner more "de Stijl" than the original: walls white inside and out, all structural members black and single planes of primary colour on areas of lesser consequence. It is never possible to see more than one coloured plane from any single viewpoint. On the principal façade, the underside of the entrance canopy is painted sky blue as the underside of the slab over the terrace. Inside, one wall of the living area is painted yellow, etc.

As with the still deserted Poissy, the deterioration at Garches was only skin-deep; paint decay, broken glass and slight cracks in the rendering; there has been no deterioration to the structure nor any waterproofing failures. Though the landscape has thickened considerably to the rear of the house, trees have not yet grown close against the main façades; where this has happened, at La Roche, Cook and Pleinex, the balanced asymmetry of the elevations, as total compositions, has been grossly disfigured. The one instance among the Paris buildings where trees are sympathetic is the Pavillon Suisse where they have

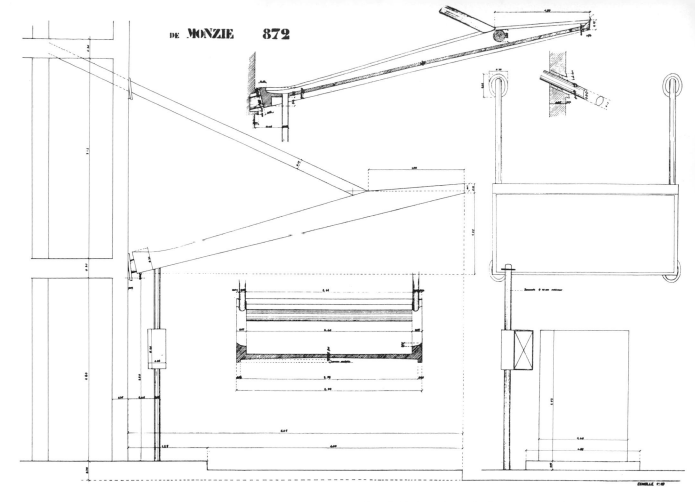

70. Villa Stein at Garches, execution drawing of the porch entrance.

grown the full height of the south elevation, significantly one of the most repetitive façades that Le Corbusier has produced. In more extreme examples of additive elevations, as in many American buildings, the presence of trees, naturalistic incidents, might almost be considered essential. The disembowelled machine parts of the Armée du Salut outbuildings have a similar juxtaposition to the neutral backdrop of the slab.

If Garches appears urban, sophisticated and essentially in keeping with 'l'esprit parisien', then the Jaoul houses seem primitive in character, recalling the Provençal farmhouse community; they seem out of tune with their Parisian environment. Their pyramidal massing is reminiscent of traditional Indian architecture and they were in fact designed after Le Corbusier's first visit to that country. Frequently accused of being 'internationalist', Le Corbusier is actually the most regional of architects. The difference between the cities of Paris and Marseilles is precisely the difference between the Pavillon Suisse and the Unité, and at Chandigarh the centre buildings are indebted to the history and traditions of a native Indian culture; even a project for the Palace of the Soviets makes considerable reference to Russian

James Stirling

constructivism. Therefore, it is perhaps disturbing to encounter the Jaoul houses within half a mile of the Champs Elysées.

Assuming that the observer has become familiar with the architecture of Le Corbusier through the medium of the glossy books, then the first impression registered on arriving at the Jaoul houses is unique for they are of the scale and size expected, possibly because of the expressed floor beams. Usually, the scale is either greater or smaller than anticipated, that of Garches being unexpectedly heroic.

Differing from the point structure and therefore free plan of Garches, the structure of Jaoul is of load-bearing, brick cross-walls, cellular in planning by implication. It would, however, be a mistake to think of these buildings as models for cross-wall architecture as this aspect is visually subordinated to the massive, concrete, Catalan vaults occurring at each floor level. These vaults are to be covered with soil and grass to resist thermal expansion and the timber shutter-boards have been set to leave a carefully contrived pattern. Internally one-inch solid steel tiles are positioned at approximately fifteen-foot centres to resist diagonal thrust into the brick walls. At the external centre point of these vaults, bird-nesting boxes are formed, and occasionally concrete rainwater heads are projected from the side-beams,

71. Maison Jaoul, detail of the vaulting.

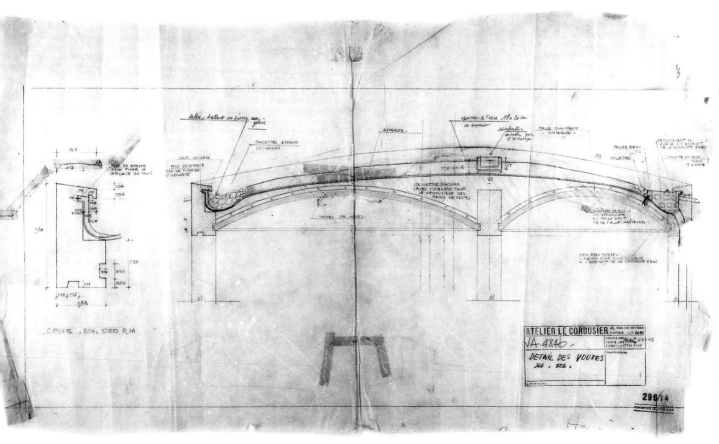

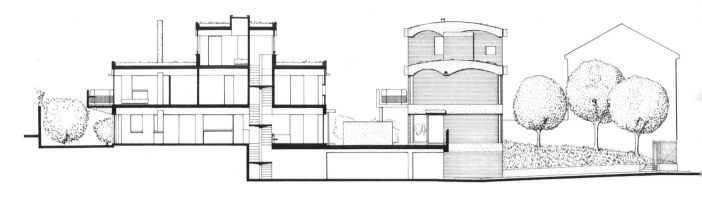

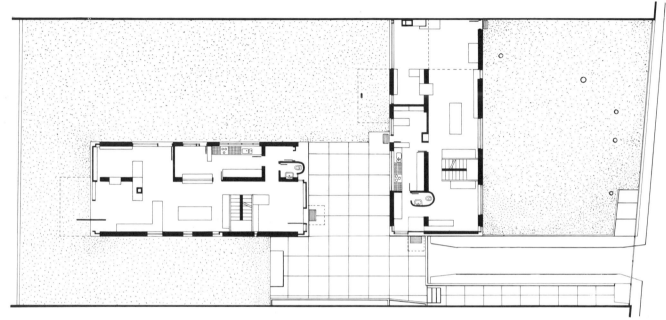

72. Maison Jaoul, section and plan of the ground floor.

though the pipes drop internally. Rising from the underground garage through to the top of each house are dog-leg stairs, cast in situ; they are a development of the Marseilles fire-escape stair, with the treads cantilevered either side of the vertical concrete slab. By English standards, the brickwork is poor, but then the wall is considered as a surface and not a pattern. Masonry, rubble, or, perhaps more rationally in view of the vault construction, mass concrete walls could be substituted without difference to the principle of design.

Perhaps the only factor that Garches and Jaoul have in common is the considerable influence of the site on both. All Le Corbusier's buildings tend to fall into one of two categories: those in which the peculiarities of the site are a paramount factor in conception—most notably the Armée du Salut—and those where the site is of little consequence, being subordinated to a preconception or archetype, e.g., the Unité. To some extent this may account for the lack of inevitability, sometimes felt with buildings of this latter category,

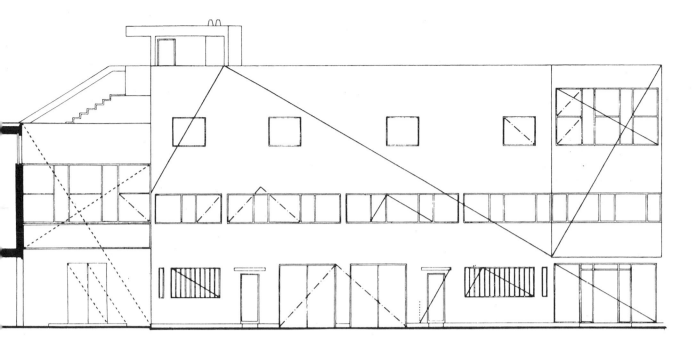

most particularly the Pavillon Suisse where, except as
an archetype per se, there seems little justification for
raising the building above ground, there being no
circulation or view through. If the entrance hall, approachable from any direction, had been under and
not to the rear of the slab, the raising of the block
would not appear so arbitrary. None the less, the
town-planning ideas which generated this form retain
their urgent validity.

The exact relationship and planning of the two
Jaoul houses have been motivated by the nature of the
site. The circulation is on two levels and of two kinds.
Cars drive straight off the road into the garage, a large
underground cavern from which separate stairs rise
through to each house. Walking circulation is above
this garage on what appears to be natural ground level
but which is actually a made-up terrace on which the
houses stand. This level is linked to the road by a
ramp. The differentiation of circulation on superimposed levels and the free movement around the
houses are reminiscent in another medium of the suspended routes into the Armée du Salut.

At Maison Jaoul the only entire elevation that can be
seen from a single viewpoint is to the rear and has to be
observed over the garden wall of the adjoining private
property. Owing to the narrowness of the plot, all
other façades have to be viewed either episodically
through the trees or close up at an oblique angle. The
solid-void relationship of the exterior does not appear
to follow any easily apparent scheme. This is a development from Le Corbusier's earlier work where at La
Roche the drawing board elevation also cannot be seen
at right angles and the studied balance of window to

73. Maison La Roche-Jeanneret, *tracés régulateurs.*
74. Maison La Roche-Jeanneret, view of the
entrance.

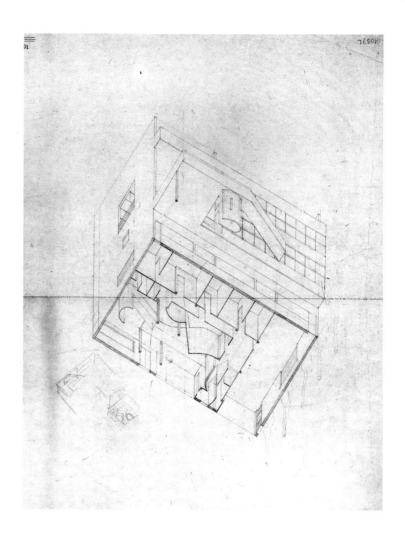

wall is destroyed. This is due not only to the trees
which have grown since but especially to the necessity
of viewing the elevation at a sharp angle.

The hierarchic presentation of external elements
occurs also in the work of Frank Lloyd Wright, where
the most important feature is the corner, and this may
account for much of the undergrowth against the
façades proper. It may be argued that the only exterior which can maintain interest, as the eye moves at
an equal distance around the corner, is the cage or
box. The most notable example of this is the Lake
Shore Apartments where it would be inappropriate to
suggest a 'principal façade.' Poissy almost comes into
the category of the box but only on three sides; the
fourth, receiving no undercut, becomes a vertical
plane differing from the dynamic horizontality of the
others. At Garches there is no point in moving around
the corner for there is a very definite axis and the side
elevations are of little consequence, their window
openings positioned functionally make no attempt to
arrive at a formal composition. The site boundary

lines, defined by tall, closely planted trees, are about six feet from each of these side elevations, making it almost impossible to see them. The long façades, on the contrary, may be seen head on from a considerable distance by the approaching visitor and their balanced asymmetry is masterfully exploited.

Internally, space departs radically from the structure; an explosion in terms of Cubist space is contained within the four peripheral walls which externally give little evidence of this phenomenon, contained except where it escapes and rushes out along the direction of the terrace, to be finally dissipated in the heavy landscape. However, space is not contrived for the sake of effect only, it invariably has a psychological as well as a functional context. For instance, on passing through the front door, the immediate double height and the presence of a stair indicate that the main floor is above. Similarly, the diagonal spatial stress across the first floor suggests the route through the house.

The main living areas are flooded with an even intensity of light, but, where accommodation and circulation are of lesser consequence, natural lighting becomes more restricted and as one moves through the house a continuous contrast in definition is attained. 'The elements of architecture are light and shade, walls and space.' The natural light which penetrates to the interior of the Jaoul houses is consistently subdued and not dissimilar to that found inside many Frank Lloyd Wright buildings.

Eventually somebody will have to consider the numerous similarities between Le Corbusier and Wright, and their common differences from the work of Mies van der Rohe. For instance, the pattern of circulation, repetitive on all floors as in the Pavillon Suisse and many of Le Corbusier's larger buildings, becomes in some of his and Wright's domestic works a route so complex and involved, as at Pleinex, that it is with the greatest difficulty that the stranger finds his way out. To a lesser extent, this applies at Jaoul and again, similar to Wright, the spatial effects, though exciting, are unexpected, encountered suddenly on turning a corner or glimpsed on passing a slit in the wall. Where double height does occur in one of the living rooms it appears as a dead area, having no secondary use such as the vertical height of the Unité flats which lights and ventilates the bedroom. If the space inside Garches can be considered dynamic, then here it is static; there is certainly no question of being able to stand inside and comprehend at a glance the limits of the house, as at Garches.

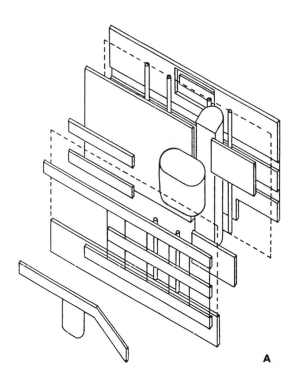

A

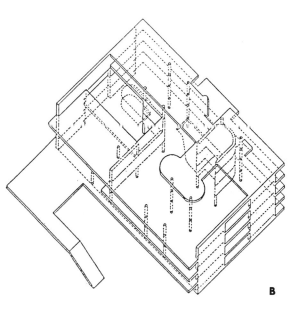

B

76. Villa Stein, Garches:
a) the sequence of vertical planes of the walls;
b) the sequence of horizontal planes of the floors.

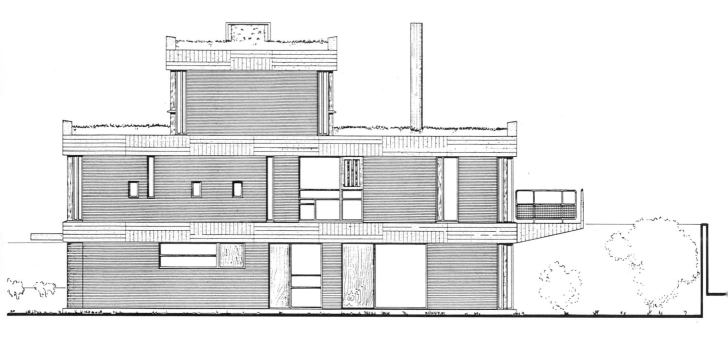

77. Maison Jaoul, south elevation of House B.

Implicit in the structural system, rooms tend to be small boxes with the living areas more generous. The internal finishes have a greater variety and richness of surface than at Garches, where, with the exception of the floor, the materials, though not the form, of the walls and ceilings are neutralized. Inside Jaoul, concrete is left shutter-marked, walls are plastered or brick fair-faced, floors are tiled and there is a considerable variety and quantity of timber and, most significantly, the ceiling or underside of the vaults is frequently finished in a dark clay tile which cannot be expected to amplify 'the magnificent play of light on form.' The 'fourth wall'—the incorporation of shelving and opaque materials into the window opening—is symptomatic of Le Corbusier's recent attitude to surface depth. Windows are no longer to be looked through but looked at. The eye finding interest in every part of the surface impasto, does not, as at Garches, seek relief from the hard textureless finish by examining the contours and form of the plane.

Maison Jaoul is no doubt dimensioned according to 'Le Modulor', a development from the application of the golden section by regulating lines as at Garches, where it is possible to read off the inter-relations of squares and sections as the eye traverses the façade and where, internally, every element is positioned according to an exact geometrical hierarchy. In fact, Garches must be considered the masterpiece of Neo-

Palladianism in modern architecture, conceived in plan, section, elevation from two proportions which, owing to their particular inter-relationship, achieve an organic or harmonic whole as distinct from an additive total. The variety of dimensions available from 'Le Modulor' are considerable and as Bodiansky (the structural engineer for the Marseilles Unité) has said 'there is always a figure near at hand to adjust to.' This considerable flexibility may create a visually non-apparent geometry, as at Jaoul, but here the restrictions of the site already mentioned must be remenbered when considering whether this is a valid criticism.

Garches is an excellent example of Le Corbusier's particular interpretation of the machine aesthetic. The body of the house, built by quite conventional methods for its time, has skin-walls of concrete block rendered to a monolithic, poured or sprayed effect; an aesthetic for a structural system not yet in being. Yet while Garches is not the product of any high-powered mechanization, the whole spirit of the building expresses the essence of machine power. To be on the first floor is to witness the Mumfordian end product of twentieth-century technology, 'the silent, staffless power-house.' The incorporation of rail-road and steamship fabrication is decidedly technocrat and the integration of architecture to specialist requirements extremely considered as the boiler-house disposed like

78. Villa Stein at Garches, garage with boiler.

an industrial engine-room or the timber-strip flooring obviously laid by ship's carpenters. The type of detailing in synthetic materials here and at the Armée du Salut is almost the last of the steam-age period; crude maybe, it is nevertheless powerful. After this date, the number of synthetic materials per building increases, and, as at the Pavillon Suisse, the detailing becomes more refined but somehow less memorable. There is no reference to any aspect of the machine at Jaoul either in construction or aesthetic. These houses, total cost £30,000, are being built by Algerian labourers equipped with ladders, hammers and nails, and with the exception of glass no synthetic materials are being used; technologically, they make no advance on medieval building. The timber window-wall units may be prefabricated but as with technology one suspects that prefabrication must begin with the structure.

To imply that these houses will be anything less than magnificent art would be incorrect. Their sheer plastic virtuosity is beyond emulation. Nevertheless, on analysis, it is disturbing to find little reference to the rational principles which are the basis of the modern movement, and it is difficult to avoid assessing these buildings except in terms of 'art for art's sake.' More so than any other architect of this century, Le Corbusier's buildings present a continuous architectural development which, however, has not recently been supplemented by programmatic theory.

As homes the Jaoul houses are almost cosy and could be inhabited by any civilized family, urban or rural. They are built by and intended for the status quo. Conversely, it is difficult to imagine Garches being lived in spontaneously except by such as the Sitwells, with never less than half a dozen brilliant, and permanent, guests. Utopian, it anticipates, and participates in, the progress of twentieth-century emancipation. A monument, not to an age which is dead, but to a way of life which has not generally arrived, and a continuous reminder of the quality to which all architects must aspire if modern architecture is to retain its vitality.[*]

[*] This essay first appeared as "Garches to Jaoul: Le Corbusier as domestic architect in 1927 and 1953," in *Architectural Review*, no. 118, September 1955, pp. 145–51.

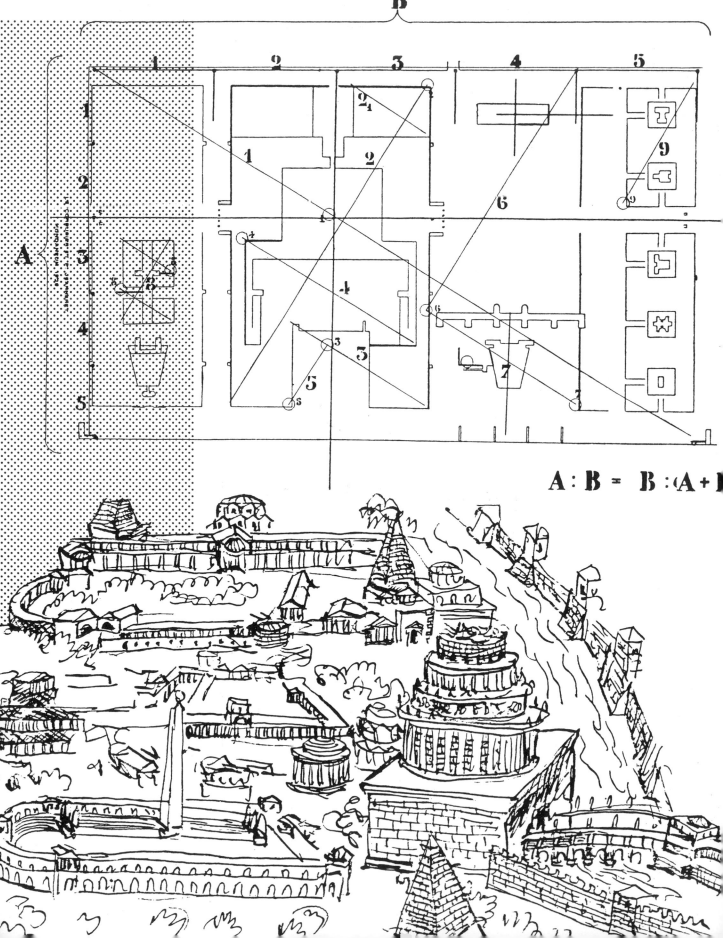

T H E MUNDANEUM P L A N

Giuliano Gresleri

During the first months of 1928, the Union of International Associations of Brussels came into contact with the work of Le Corbusier and Pierre Jeanneret in Paris through the Belgian philosopher, Paul Otlet (1868–1944), an officer of the International Bibliographical Institute.

The proposal that the Union intended to make the architects consisted of a commission for the project for a "museum of knowledge" to be built in Geneva: The Mundaneum, administered by an Association of "Friends" with seats in various European capitals, to be articulated in a "library, museum, scientific societies, universities, and institutes," which Otlet himself and Hébrard had formulated from the beginning of the century in their famous hypothesis of the World City.

The unique relation (in intensity rather than duration) that was established between the intellectuals and the architects soon resulted in a correspondence of more than 400 letters and various documents that accompany a project whose intellectual ambition, ideological motivations, and diplomatic intrigues were interwoven among the various organizations for many years in Switzerland, France, the U.S.A., and Italy.

The research I conducted on this material at the Fondation Le Corbusier in Paris between 1980 and 1982, alternatively with Dario Matteoni, allowed the "critical" reconstruction of one of the most interesting and most obscure chapters of the *Oeuvre complète*, throwing into relief a singular and little investigated moment in the history of contemporary architecture. The intellectual complexity that is evident in the ideological contents of the Mundaneum, and the international interests that remain at the basis of Le Corbusier's urban ideology, explain the complex genealogy of the plan for the World City at the center of which the Mundaneum was to be born around the nucleus of the Society of Nations.

Otlet and Le Corbusier

The planning of the Mundaneum took place during 1928 and 1929 surrounded by a complex network of connected events. In order to accurately run through the course by which the plan achieved its definitive formulation and to evaluate its significance, we will divide Le Corbusier's work into two phases.

The first phase goes from March to September 1928 and includes the publication of a brochure, edited by Otlet and published by the International Association of Brussels, dedicated to the promotion of the idea and containing a detailed description of the architectural plan written by Le Corbusier.

The second phase goes from the end of September in 1928 to August 1929. It took an entire year for the plan to undergo a general revision and slowly expand into the one for a new World City. Otlet's internationalist idea, the interest he solicited, and the reason it was linked to a political vision that was brought into play only at the end of 1928, constrained Le Corbusier to a planning effort of particular intensity that accompanied the certainty of having definitively lost the bid for the Palace of the Society of Nations.

When Otlet met Le Corbusier for the project, at the end of March 1928, the choice of Geneva as the seat of the future Mundaneum was motivated by political issues, by the fact that the capital city of the canton was preparing to become one of the great centers in world politics. Geneva had already welcomed many international associations; above all, close to the city was a site destined for the new seat of the SdN where the building of the International Bureau of Labor already existed. Along with it was the park of Ariana, with its Neoclassical villa as the museum.

After preliminary contacts, in contrast to the client's only approximate knowledge and description of the site, Le Corbusier took his bearings with self-confidence: during the preparatory phase of the plan for the SdN in 1926, he had researched the entire coastal area in depth, from the park of Mon Repos where his building should have been built, pushing himself to sketch the highest site on the plateau of Morillon beneath the village of Saconnex, exactly on the terrain of the future Mundaneum.

After the commission letter with which Otlet enjoined Le Corbusier and Pierre Jeanneret to accept his proposal, we have no documents that certify a suitable site inspection of Geneva for a re-examination of the terrain destined for the project; nor do the sketches drawn up for the occasion bear dates of

Giuliano Gresleri

[1] H.C. Andersen, *Création d'un Centre mondial de Communication*, Paris, 1913.

reference. It is probable that Le Corbusier had worked "from memory" his photograph and layout design for the environmental control of the project of the National Palace, and that some of these sketches with summary notes for the first hypotheses were executed directly with Otlet there.

The latter, during a meeting in Brussels, consigned Le Corbusier and Pierre Jeanneret, who accompanied him, the documentation collected during the long years of work with the architect Hébrard on the same subject and also the correspondence on the various proposals for Andersen's "World Center," collected in the long book written by him in 1912: "I have brought you up to date on the status of the studies and negotiations . . ."[1]

Otlet soon after told the two architects that the possibilities of realizing the work were rather reduced, but taking the "risk" of such a project they would have to work with him "to transform possibility into reality" and should consider themselves "responsible for definitively concluding the project in time."

Otlet synthesized the program of operation concerning the actual plan as well as the meaning and ideology of the work; with clarity he revealed the role that the intellectual and the architect respectively assigned each other.

Le Corbusier was called upon to give form to an articulated and definitive plan to which Otlet would successively add his own architectural notations in agreement with an understanding of the collaboration by which the plan would find its definitive configuration, passing from a first stage (the construction of the museum—Mundaneum) to a second stage (the realization of the World City destined to contain it).

For Otlet the "institution" of the Mundaneum would not have been able to find its place in an anonymous building: better an immense empty space with curtain walls "than a project conditioned by decorative intentions." The institutions that comprised the ensemble and that Le Corbusier was called upon to give form to, in fact required a large museum, the "library," the seat of an association of international universities; in addition, a large natural park with athletic facilities, a residential center, train stations and airports were to be studied, exactly as in the preceding project by Andersen and Hébrard. But Otlet pushed beyond a simple list of functional requisites and advanced architectural suggestions in tune with the universalist ideology of the institution itself.

He wrote, in fact, regarding the contribution of architecture to the overall idea that "The Mundaneum

[2] This thesis was presented at the convention for studies on Le Corbusier at Lugano in September 1980 on the occasion of the retrospective, "The Patient Search," the catalogue for which also included a section on the Mundaneum. See G. Gresleri and D. Matteoni, "La Cité Mondiale e la costruzione della Nuova Babilonia," in B. Reichlin and S. Pagnamenta, Le Corbusier—la ricerca paziente, Lugano, 1980, pp. 79–86.

[3] A. Ozenfant and Ch. E. Jeanneret, "Sur la plastique, examen des conditions primordiales," in L'Esprit Nouveau, no. 1, p. 38.

thus defined in its essential features needs the concurrence of architecture considered as: 1) the art of ordering, delimiting, bounding of the spaces; 2) the art of arranging these spaces with installations that render their use more efficient; 3) the art of creating in the building an ambience favorable to work, to the activities that take place there, even the art of making of the buildings and everything that contributes to them the symbol (expression-representation) of the idea and the institution itself . . ."

The drawings with which Otlet accompanied the notes to Le Corbusier are mainly emblematic. They pertain to a kind of synoptic chart that he calls "*plan formes*" (fig. 81), that was to direct Le Corbusier himself—perhaps—in the choice of model to develop and that we, on another occasion, have thought to be close to the oriental philosophical treatises on which the philosopher was an expert.[2]

The represented forms easily lead to figures of the circle, square, and the triangle, and to their combinations in a grid, ordered within different squares, making one consider the "type" of each possible construction with a geometric image that summarizes the meaning of precise functions within, through the primary forms of square, triangle, and circle.

In the case of the chart in question, the origin of the abacus would seem to contain more than any simple or logical indications of organization read into the idea of collective building. Le Corbusier and Pierre Jeanneret would then have been able to direct themselves in turn toward one scheme rather than another one secondary to the architectural object that was to take shape. Perhaps such combinations of "assembly hall," "hall with converging corridors," of "spiral development," etc. were already a part of the organization of the rooms in the old Palace of the Fiftieth where the international associations and the museum of Brussels were situated and that Otlet had studied. It is interesting to note, nevertheless, how these elementary forms are substantially the same as the ones that Le Corbusier and Ozenfant mention in the essay "Sur la Plastique," which appeared in the first issue of L'Esprit Nouveau, and were already indicated as "primary elements whose plastic operation" and whose "association drives the emanation of symphonic sensations."[3] As carriers of geometric constants they become the key to the architectural composition. Cylinder, pyramid, cube, and sphere are the three-dimensional transpositions to the degree that they manifest the symbolic contents of the flat forms that generated them. It is also very likely that Otlet had intended to indicate a standard iconography corresponding to the precise contents of one or more parts of the building. The fourth series of the lower figures corresponds in fact to the forms that could lead to very individuated parts of the architectural plan—the Mundaneum included—or at least schematic allusions to the same, such as a hall with a central plan, an open hall, bays converging in a single point, a building in cubic form, a plan in comb and cross formation.

It hasn't been possible to trace direct references to the supposed procedure in the correspondence between Le Corbusier and Otlet during this period. Nevertheless, it is certain that Le Corbusier and Pierre Jeanneret must have been rather struck by Otlet's typological and formal program that, moreover, coincided in a surprising way with their own design vision.

Concluding their first meetings, architects and committee had the certainty of having in front of them a rather vast but already well articulated program to which Hébrard had already given important solutions that were impossible to ignore.

The ensemble brought together, more or less, a verification of assigned dimensions; the parts out of which it would be composed are securely known and Le Corbusier doesn't even mention alternatives for the choices made. Moreover, the placement of the whole in Geneva cannot be left out of consideration. The new urban landscape was to be integrated into a "constructed" environment where the large buildings of the BIT and the Ariana were present, and where the future Palace of the Nations would rise. But there were also several hard realities—small centers like Saconnex, Pregny, and Morillon—as well as a natural landscape of great beauty, against which it would be measured. It is from this moment that talks of the "international city" would begin. The "new Geneva" was destined to concretize that dream of the enlightened bourgeoisie—the construction of a place that would gather the entire world of knowledge, symbol of all humanity. It would conserve in its "center of centers" the world's memory, but the memory of a world that was, in spite of the progressivist utopia in which the intellectuals and the architects believe, still completely "western" and that governed the rest of humanity through brutal mechanisms of colonial exploitation. The "symbol for the necessary unity to uphold the organizational efforts of humanity and of life become universal" must nevertheless have appeared to Le Corbusier, in spite of all the why's and how's, more important than any other opportunity.

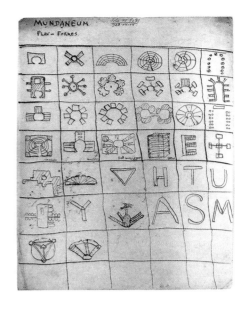

81. Paul Otlet, *Mundaneum, Plan-Formes*, April 4, 1928 (FLC 24611).

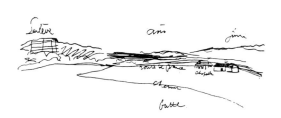

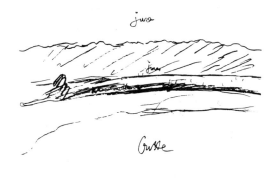

The synthesis of the design work conducted toward that goal and finally become "city" was already partially thought about, already projected and imagined in the first volume of the *Oeuvre complète*, which was about to be published at the time, awaiting possible revisions.

It is not casually that this project is thus linked to the preparations of the first CIAM of La Sarraz and to the formulations of this program.

Genesis of the idea: the tower and the pyramid

The land on which Mundaneum was to have risen faced the lake of Geneva across the heights of Petit Saconnex, Grand Saconnex, and Pregny, and was approachable by the road of Faucille that goes to the French border, or the Quai Wilson, taking on the left the first site destined for the palace of the SdN, then going over the railroad tracks, again in the direction of Grand Saconnex. It is a plateau that slopes toward the lake, facing approximately two kilometers in the direction of Jura-Mont Blanc and Geneva-Lausanne.

There are five "topographical notes" written by Le Corbusier. Three of these layouts turn their back to the lake and look over the Jura mountains, and two in the opposite direction face Mont Blanc. Another small sketch simply indicates the geographic connections: the coast with the BIT palace and the one of the SdN, the road that goes out toward Saconnex, the park of the Ariana with its villa, and the area indicated as "zone for the project of the international city" (figs. 82–85).

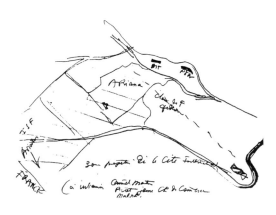

The horizon is closed wherever natural formations appear, and Le Corbusier limits himself to making a note of those that are important to the future project: the back of the Belair ("butte"), the Chapelle de la Croix, the central depression, and probably soon after, without any apparent relation to Otlet's recommendations, he lays out a first architectural idea: a rectangular platform supported by *pilotis* from which three towers arise in cross formation of the type already present in the proposal for the City of three million inhabitants (fig. 87).

The spatial complexity and articulation that Otlet wanted for the Mundaneum seem reduced to a pure sign in space. The three gigantic architectural constructions face Mont Blanc in the background and with the radio antennae from the transmitting station as its fulcrum—as in Hébrard's project—it would transmit new ideas throughout the world. Evidently the proposal had no rapport whatsoever with Otlet's "desiderata": as often happens in Le Corbusier's design process, the first intuition almost never addresses the problem, it tends thus to take off in an "excessive" manner. It is during the stages that follow that dimensions are calculated, calibrated, and contracted "to bring order." A small sketch done soon after, in fact, shows skyscrapers reduced to two, and the support base that comes out of a hemicycle form is better specified: the stadium required by the program and mentioned also in the preceding note (fig. 86). Among the materials that Otlet had consigned to Le Corbusier "as a study dossier," there is a "metaprojectural"

82. The *route de France* seen from the site of the Mundaneum, March (?) 1928 (FLC 24613).
83. The site of the Mudaneum against the background of the Saléve facing Geneva. From the notes of March (?) 1928 (FLC 24631).
84. The Jura ridge, toward the Col de la Faucille, March (?) 1928 (FLC 24631).
85. The sites of the international city behind the road that comes from the train station of Cornavin at Sacconex. At the bottom Le Corbusier's notes indicate: Camille Martin/Pictet/Chamber of Commerce/Malsch (FLC 24611).
86. Mundaneum, first hypothesis: the cruciform skyscrapers rest against a suspended slab at the center of the site. In front toward the lake the stadium's ellipsis can be glimpsed; March–April 1928 (FLC 24611)
87. Mundaneum: antennae of the TSF, stadium, large suspended plaza, cruciform skyscrapers; March (?) 1928 (FLC 24613).

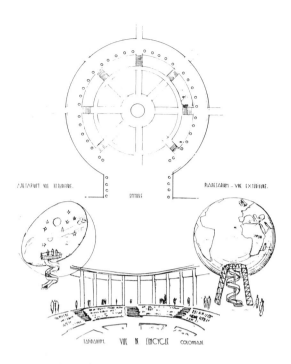

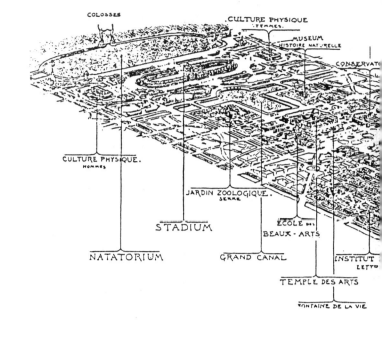

88. Paul Otlet, sketches for the planetarium.
89. Andersen and Hébrard, World City, schematic view with indications of the main buildings and international zone.
90. Sketch for the building organized around a vast circular court; the same building with central plan fully defined; cross section of the cupola shaped building with floors shown over the central void.

[4] See L. Van del Swaelmen, *Préliminaires d'art civique*, Amsterdam, 1915, p. 113, now reissued by CIAUD, Brussels, 1980. See also P. Otlet and Le Corbusier, *Mundaneum*, Brussels, Lebèque et Cie., Union des associations internationales, 1928, p. 29.
[5] Otlet's scheme, for example, singles out eight parts for the Mundaneum: 1. museum (scientific, historical, national section); 2. Library (reading room, bibliography and index, archives, world encyclopedia); 3. societies (offices for the international associations, theater, and auditorium); 4. nations (offices and headquarters for the delegations); 5. university (auditorium, club, and university residences); 6. arts (permanent and temporary exhibitions, theater, music, cinema, panorama); 7. stadium; 8. sacrarium; 9. varies. The 9th point (varies) gathers a sereis of voices. It concerns 9.1 Miscellaneous, divided into 9.1.2. the earth globe and planetarium, 9.1.3. Centrum, 9.1.4. Radio; 9.2 Nature: 9.2.1. Minerals, 9.2.2 Botany, 9.2.3 Zoology; 9.3 Urbanism: pavilion of the city; 9.4 Institute: various autonomous institutes; 9.5 Scholarium: center for

table that allows the understanding of the mechanism through which the said project had subsequently taken form. One can also read with a certain precision the until then only supposed relation between Le Corbusier's plan and the World City of Hébrard, which remains at the basis of the organizational hypotheses to the end of the experience (fig. 89).

A system of reduced complexities in the operational organization were traditionally applied to the studies of the international union of cities in Brussels. The writing used for the schemes of the Union is not just casually analogous to Otlet's.[4] It has substantially to do with organization charts that reveal a very strong capacity for synthesis and that clearly establish the "functional" relations among the single components of the reality described.[5]

Otlet's is a substantially conceptual image that pivots on the figure of a terrestrial globe seen as planetarium (fig. 88). Around this center is developed a hemicycle divided into museum on the one side (containing the whole history of civilization), and three sections on the other, dedicated to society, man, and nature. Along the central axis that crosses the ensemble, in connection with the globe, a "centrum" is found first, closely linked to the "national associations," then a median zone, closed on two sides by the gallery of fine arts and the library, and in the third side, the outstanding element of the building of "peace" and "progress" that would hold sessions of the SdN and the international associations. The heart of this ensemble is individuated in the "sacrarium,"

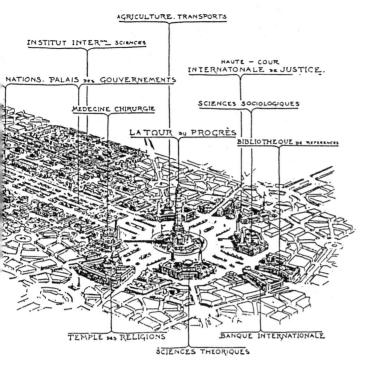

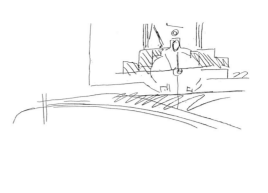

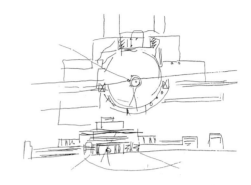

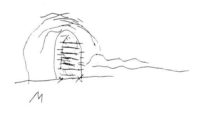

consisting of very few elements, the most significant ones of man's adventure, symbolized by a circular and radiating form (fig. 90). Besides the ensemble, at the head of the whole, the transmitting stations, primed by the force of words and ideas, and the natural park containing the places and pavilions of the city and zoological, mineral, and botanical sections of the park itself. At the angles of the diagram, the site for the arts, and for the cinema, is the circular element of a large "diorama." Five sections around the hemicycle complete the scheme for a national museum that would collect significant works from Europe, Asia, America, Africa, and Oceanea. At the exterior of this scheme a "center of schools" (which are not mentioned in Le Corbusier's project) and a business center are then isolated.

However precise the indications that Le Corbusier disposed of, he did not immediately abandon the idea of a tall building. His motives could have been of a double nature: the suggestion of finally being able to realize a taller and perfect building of reinforced concrete of the American type in steel (for which he also consulted Freyssinet),[6] and the idea of responding to the complexity of Otlet's proposal with the greatest simplification and concentration. Pierre Jeanneret left some very precise notes on the moment when the idea of the cruciform skyscraper gave way to new hypotheses. Particularly interesting to the proposal is a sketch (fig. 91) in which are clearly noted the thoughts that accompanied the passage of the idea of the tower to the one of the pyramid generated, how-

schools; 9.6 Business: centre for business. This classification analogously comprises Andersen's terminology and hypotheses and is at the base of Hébrard's urban planning, corresponding with minor variations also to Le Corbusier's parts of the urban plan that he incorporates and follows, as we shall see, according to the given specifications.

[6] See Le Corbusier's letter to Freyssinet, March 6, 1925, FLC, now in G. Gresleri, "L'Esprit Nouveau" costruzione e ricostruzione di un prototipo dell'architettura moderna, Milan, 1978, p. 120. Let us also recall, as recounted by José Oubrerie, that during the first site inspection in Venice in 1965 for the construction of the new hospital, Le Corbusier terrorized the bystanders by proposing the resolution to the problem with a high building of the "Cartesian skyscraper" type and only afterward, returning to his own drawings executed in 1915 at the Bibliothèque Nationale and published several times, and completing the morphological analysis of the environs, returned to a horizontal grid that was then adopted.

91. First studies for the pyramid and the cruciform plan, March–April 1928 (FLC 24610).
92. First studies of the relations between form and function; "construction that should allow expansion or extensible construction?" March–April 1928 (FLC 24610).
93. Fragments of the plan and their relations; nations, societies, university, stadium; March–April 1928 (FLC 24612).

ever, from the same cruciform base, surrounded by elements added in a sunburst pattern. In the successive passage (fig. 92) the desiderata that are similar to those in Otlet's already mentioned chart, are listed in order under the entry *Mudaneum* (museum, sacrarium, pavilion of the city, etc.) while the question at the top of the sketch reveals what could have been the motive that pushed the two architects toward the new solution: "a building that can be enlarged, or a non-extensible building?"

Further below, the cruciform plan reassembles the scientific, historical, national, and other organizations in its four arms, while other passages introduce new forms taken directly from the plans for the design of the palace of the SdN and have been added to the cruciform plan. When Le Corbusier intervenes (fig. 93) the discourse is further improved. He organizes a series of forms to which he assigns certain purposes, exactly as Otlet had done. The forms are sparse on paper, possibly casual fragments from the preceding design of the Society of Nations, and do not seem to be generated out of any logical progression but can immediately be connected when we read the notes: "2. library with longitudinal grid and two-way street; 3. associations with longitudinal façade + semicircumference; 4. nations with longitudinal façade; 5. university with circumference; 7. stadium in elliptical form." Le Corbusier seems scrupulous in staying with Otlet's indications so that the process of correspondence between meaningful form and functional end has been researched from the first design

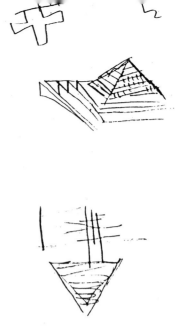

hypotheses.

The Mundaneum, therefore, has come to coincide with the image of the "conical pyramid," or of a "pyramid with circular base," and of an helicoid development, according to the traditional, classical image that the temple of heaven and the mountain of the world (sacred mountain and ziggurat) had assumed in ancient iconography. A last sketch explicitly underlines the ideal of the mountain as real and present. Le Corbusier, in fact, draws a peak on the side of the architectural figure identical to the one that portrays Mont Blanc in the same section, and seems ultimately to confirm the concept of Mundaneum-mons-magnun (fig. 94). The spiral, in fact, resolves the question written by Pierre Jeanneret: "construction that can be enlarged or non-extensible construction?" Conceptually, it is an unresolvable question involving both time and space in a single stroke; otherwise "it means," as Otlet wanted, something that goes on endlessly, like history, without solution.

In this phase the most complicated moment seems to have been that passage from the spiral to the pyramid. It is Pierre who returns to the square plan traversed by orthogonal axes joining together cross and square once again (fig. 95). But it is Le Corbusier who works out a synthesis (fig. 96). In folio 24610, four elements have been chosen: 1. pyramid, 2. and 3. tall buildings, 4. low building or hemicyclical form. Soon after, Pierre attempted a first composition in the direction indicated by Le Corbusier: on the site of the Jura chain in the background is the road that comes from

94. Notes on the idea of the conical spiral and, at right, the figure of an alpine peak; March–April 1928 (FLC 24612).
95. The pyramid of the World Museum across the axis of the cruciform plan; March–April 1928 (FLC 24610).
96. The pyramid, the tower and the low building. Other illegible notes are also on the page; March–April 1928 (FLC 24610).

97. Mundaneum, first hypothesis on the enclosure. On the right can be distinguished the amphitheater and the wedge of the university, a tower building in the background, at the center the pyramid of the World Museum, at the extreme left the building of the International Associations. The whole turns laterally on the highway axis that links the city to the lake; March–April 1928 (FLC 24611).

the lake turning off for Pregny. The primitive platform has been transformed into a large enclosure in front of which the ellipsis of the stadium opens (fig. 97).

A rough, square, stepped pyramid is placed at its center; at an angle to the right, a tower building, while in front two buildings similar to the assembly halls of the design for the new seat of the SdN palace are annexed to the auditorium.

The Mundaneum

The group of notes and drawings written in May 1928 for the organizational definition of the enclosure and of the main buildings of the Mundaneum, is a document of rare interest for its completeness and organic unity, and helpful in the difficult work of reaching what would be the definitive solution on the following July.

To compose the ensemble Le Corbusier fixed some parameters for the enclosure (henceforth confirmed at 1200 x 700 meters), the pyramid (approximately 200 meters on the side), and the surrounding buildings (that seem to come from a dismantling of the plan for the palace of the SdN and therefore have assigned dimensions).

The passage from the fragmentary and uncertain schematization preceding the resolved composition already comes from the table 24585 (fig. 98). On the right side of a road axis—the one going from the lake to Grand Saconnex—is located the enclosure with the large pyramid of the museum in the center, having two axes that come together to divide the rectangle into four quarters. At the center, the pyramid rises from a circular piazza inscribed in a square: pyramid, circle, and square obey the same compositional logic that is at the base of Boulée's "museum plan," while the surrounding buildings are now placed in symmetrical positions. Outside of the enclosure, toward the lake, the stadium is a precise indication for the hotel city envisioned by Otlet but which neither Le Corbusier nor Pierre Jeanneret had considered.

Recalling Otlet's scheme, it is now easy to understand why, in his suggestion to Le Corbusier, he did not limit himself to an architectural solution that would be applicable within the tradition of the preceding studies. Otlet proposes a "finite" scheme that the architect picks up without any difficulty because to the singular parts of the organization chart correspond precise design elements. In substance, Otlet wants a "functional city," exactly in Hébrard's tradition, whose methodology he still seems to be connected to and aware of. A "rationality" that to be concretized awaits the intervention of the architect-patron of art "to order, delimit, and define spaces."

"A city," he writes, in fact, "is not an accumulation of constructions some of which have an architectural character. It is a rational and harmonious distribution of buildings according to their functions and affinities, with an appropriate distribution of constructed and free spaces with a varied elevation plan in their reciprocal rapport, and with a cunning that assures them connections with the neighboring centers from other regions."[7]

Otlet thus demonstrates having been always present at the "plan" that had just been drawn up elsewhere and had very clear ideas on the city-monument and site for the collective memory; he always returns to the progressive world of functionalist and rationalist technology. The mark that the foundation of the city should leave in space is indeed the classic sign of the "*mise en ordre*," of the taking into possession of the entire universe, of the cross that divides space into measurable quarters, but is also a material fact linked to the concrete laws that regulate the communication systems of functionalist relations between the different areas discovered by modern urbanism. One of Le Corbusier's notes is meaningful because the preceding scheme is extended to the scale of the terrain. Traced in thick pencil, the axis that connects the northwest direction (the large urban highway, that is, with the one in back of the site) makes a "locus" of the future Mundaneum. It is not only an "accumulation" of buildings, but a complete urban fact that relates to its surroundings according to a definite and precise logic

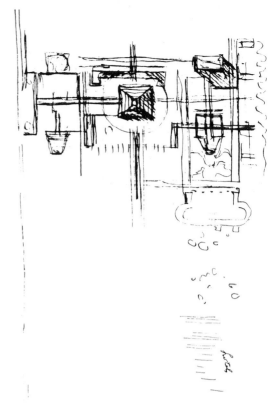

98. Mundaneum: the elements of an urban composition and their annexation. At center: in the circular plaza, the pyramid of the World Museum. On the back: the halls of modern times. At right: the wedge-shaped block of the university and in back the building of the international library. At left: the building of the Interantional Associations and in back a block for undetermined use. Before the enclosure the stadium and the grid of the hotel city; March–April 1928 (FLC 24585).

[7] P. Otlet, "Sur la Cité internationale et les moyens de la realiser," typescript n. 5750, October 19, 1928, FLC, p. 3.

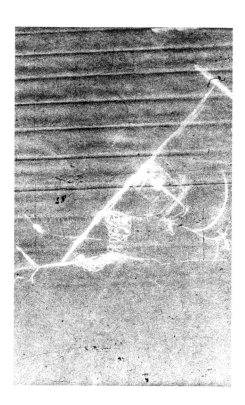

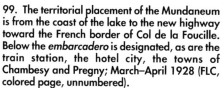

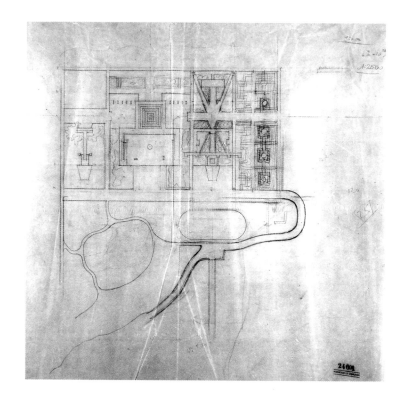

99. The territorial placement of the Mundaneum is from the coast of the lake to the new highway toward the French border of Col de la Foucille. Below the *embarcadero* is designated, as are the train station, the hotel city, the towns of Chambesy and Pregny; March–April 1928 (FLC, colored page, unnumbered).
100. Pierre Jeanneret and Le Corbusier. First geometric study of the enclosure of the Mundaneum; March–April 1928 (FLC 24601).
101. Pierre Jeanneret and Le Corbusier. Study for the proportions in height of the World Museum; May–June 1928 (FLC 24581).
102. The pyramid of the Mundaneum, schematic cross-section of the spiral form.

(fig. 99).

The informative scheme is thus articulated on the functional as well as on the symbolic scale of meaning, in an exercise of researched integration among natural elements and architectural forms analogous to the work for the project of the Society of Nations.

On table 24601 (fig. 100) Le Corbusier intervenes three times: he resolves the problem of the pavilions of the continents and nations left in suspense on the extreme right; he corrects the drawing of the park between the university and the international libray; and with a curve that categorically interferes with the highway system, he confronts the problem of the preexistent Pregny that at this point enters as part of the composition, as one of the fundamental elements of the whole, and will be found rather emphasized in the large perspective for the "diorama" of the following year. But also the pyramid is defined: Pierre clearly designs the seven steps and the ramps that connect with the platform that rises from it. Otlet's program is finally taken up fully: at the center of the esplanade is the terrestrial globe that was to contain the planetarium while in the successive table all the annotations translated by the collaborator are ultimately defined, adjusted, and calibrated.

Above all Le Corbusier insists on the node represented by the problem of the Pregny agglomeration and of the grafting of the stadium to the highway.

Before turning to Saconnex, the boulevard that comes from the lake leads to a large cylindrical memorial in rotary form, a Vendôme column in the middle of the country side, that points out, as in the classical tradition but also as in the "City of three million inhabitants" or the layout of Washington, D.C. by L'Enfant, an urban site reduced to a single residential function and charged with "diverse" meanings.

This is also the moment in which Le Corbusier goes further into the study of the pyramid: the most general problem of the ensemble, the architectural object is formally and structurally researched on some variant profiles of 50 to 90 meters in height (fig. 101). His attention becomes fixed mainly on one of these, and for the first time, he gives an indication of the function of the spiral distributed in three naves that were to receive, as Otlet had suggested, objects, places, and times (fig. 102).[8]

The image of the pyramid, definitively appropriated by the project, had not yet been studied as an architectural structure, as a foreign element in the large typological family of modern architeture. While it is true that it was Otlet to whom Le Corbusier presented the expressionist dream of the "enchanted mountain," he doesn't seem to admit the objective limitations of an architecture based on the unreal (*Eisenbeton, Glas, Edelmetalle unter Glasbögen*) as in Hablik's dream. The image that they propose is closer

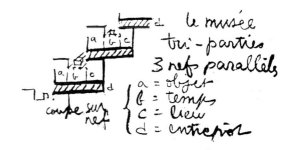

[8] "The visitor enters the museum from above. Three parallel naves turn, flank to flank, without any separate closure." *Le Corbusier et Pierre Jeanneret—Oeuvre complète 1910–29*, Zurich, Girsberger, 1929, p. 193.

[9] L. Boullée, *Architecture, essai sur l'art*, Paris, 1968, p. 47.
[10] Le Corbusier, *Précisions sur un état présent de l'architecture et de l'urbanisme*, Paris, Crès (coll. Esprit Nouveau), 1930; reissued Paris, Vincent Fréal, 1960, p. 219.

to Boullée's rational one: ". . . yes, I believe our buildings, above all the public buildings, should be poems in some way. The images offered to our eyes should arouse feelings in us that correspond to the use for which they have been destined. It has seemed to me that to confer this poetry of enchantment on architecture, to which it is susceptible, I would have had to do research on the theory of bodies, analyze them, try to learn their properties, their power over our senses."[9]

Reference is made here to a "poetry of enchantment" (*poésie enchanteresse*) that can be found in syntony with Le Corbusier's lyrical descriptions. "The floor levels of the World City are true machines along with their buildings, carriers of a certain magnificence . . . But from my point of view this quality of harmony comes from something other than the simple response to a well-established utilitarian problem; I attribute it purely and simply to a certain state of lyricism."[10]

The many things that are revealed in investigating and confronting the materials and the possible relations with other things, are still reduced by Le Corbusier to the flowing image of the *état de lyrisme*. The *espace indicible* (ineffable space) does not allow mere description, but involves the spectator in a dialogue that dazzles, made of mute words, written with stones. The drawing of the plan, in fact, possibly also speaks more of necessity, and this design, at the moment in which Le Corbusier immerses himself in the structural study of the pyramid, becomes removed, sent to a future time. The longitudinal section behind Saconnex shows itself to be such a desert site upon which it rises. Between the obelisk of the esplanade and the building joining it to the halls of modern times, the prism weighs upon the ground, supported by a forest of columns around the central pit of the lapidarium; the sacrarium that Otlet had imagined containing stone sculptures and memorial stones engraved with the greates pronouncements and names of human intelligence. Here the seven levels of the sections can be adjoined through a horizontal tunnel coming from the connections with the halls of modern times, with no façade on the outside except the exit door on the terrace of the first circle (fig. 103). The visitor who reaches this point above ground, has already walked on the ramps and has lost all contact with external reality. The tunnel and the ramp that took him to the highest level of the building in a few minutes, coincides with the first sector of the museum in which the origins of history would be placed. It begins the long journey of descent along the large

11 P. Otlet and Le Corbusier, *Mundaneum*, p. 36.

spiral (since history itself is long) where space and time coincide, to the end of "the contemporary age" summarized at the sacrarium.

"At the beginning of the spiral," wrote Le Corbusier, "up high, are the prehistoric times and the succinct—and yet expressive—representation that we have on it. Then comes the first age that we call historical. And, descending the spiral, progressively, the entire civilization of the world. History and archeology are always accumulating more documents, while we are always improving our knowledge of how man oriented himself through various organizations, forms, and cultures."[11]

The anthropocentric model of antiquity as paragon is soon manifest; it also proposes to enclose in its circles or levels the totality of the cosmic situation. Square (the foundation of the world museum) and circumference (the large sacrarium contained by the museum), universal symbols of earth and sky, put man at the center of space. In Le Corbusier's pyramid, however, it is the entire universe, transformed by the manual and intellectual activity of man, that opens all around him; it is rational man who controls, measures, orders, recreates.

The helycoid of Babel, through which divinity is said to have descended on earth to find man, is turned upside down in its meaning: it serves to make man aware of his own history or his own role. The person who goes from level to level, from age to age, on the ramp of time and space, enclosed in a silent dialogue with himself, in the illuminated tunnel, is faced everywhere in the same manner and intensity and at each turn (at each loss of height) with the immense, disturbing, interior void at a small balcony under which the space of the prism flows without allowing itself to be measured, hiding, paradoxically, its own base from sight.

To reassure him, to give him a sense of an active role, he should have, as in Leonardo's metaphor, the sense of "passing time." Descending the ramp he voluntarily detaches himself from the void of the large cavity in whose depths he would have understood the idea itself of "cathedral," as in Les Invalides, the moment encompassing the meaning of architecture itself.

The "impossible" descent, in spite of the emotions that Le Corbusier risks transmitting and that would last three-quarters of an hour, was thus removed from any idea of "mystical journey" practiced in the sacred mountains or sacred steps, cherished by the Expressionist tradition, becoming instead a journey of reason

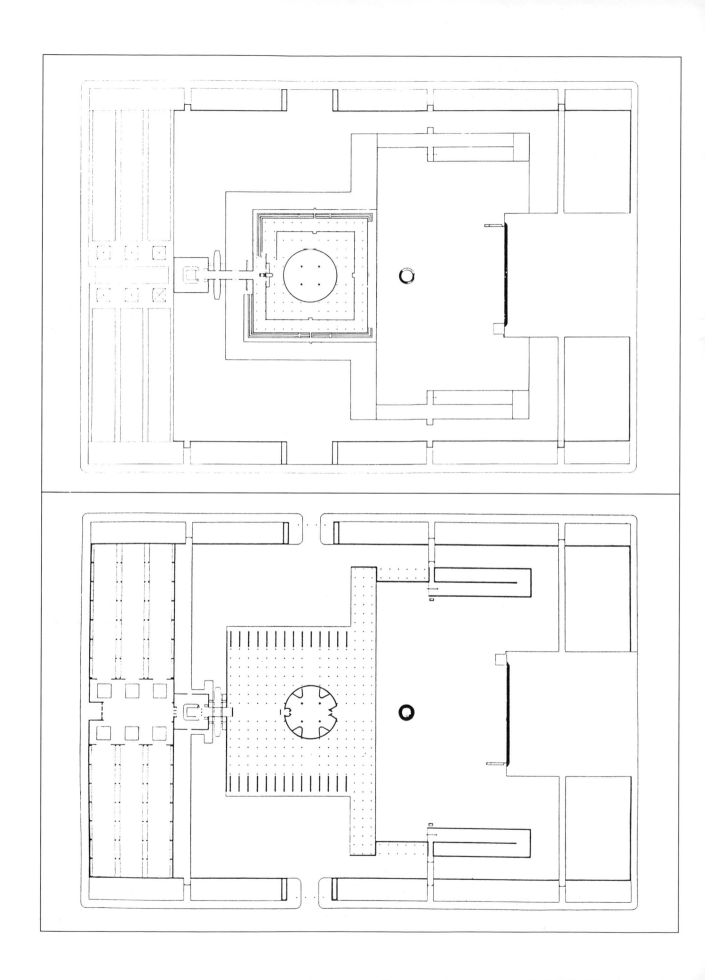

103. Mundaneum, building of the World Museum. Plan of the first turn of the spiral. At the center the hemicycle of the sacrarium. On the esplanade the planetarium and access to underground parking, around it the enclosure wall of the Museum with set access and in back the plan of the halls of modern times.

104. Mundaneum, building of the World Museum. Floor level plan.

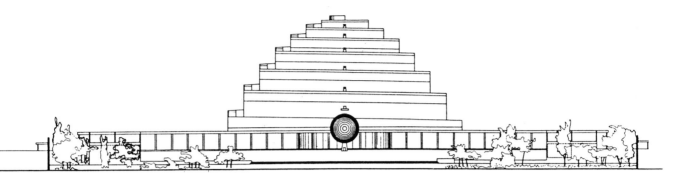

105. World Museum. Main façade on the esplanade.

106. Rear façade seen from the halls of modern times.

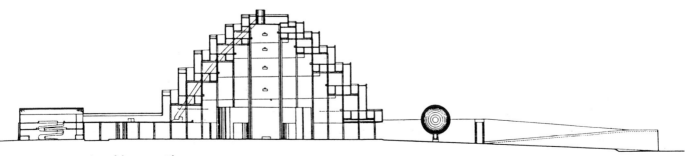

107. Cross-section of the pyramid.

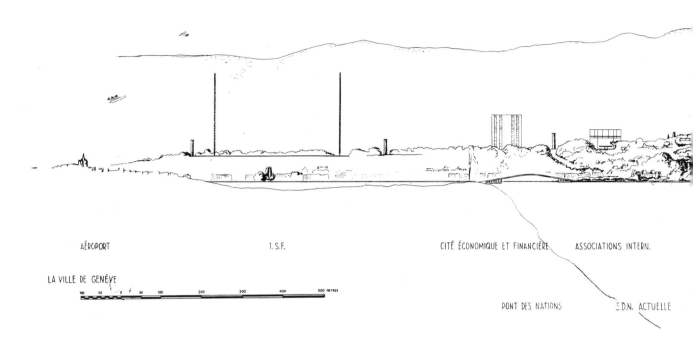

AÉROPORT   T.S.F.   CITÉ ÉCONOMIQUE ET FINANCIÈRE   ASSOCIATIONS INTERN.

LA VILLE DE GENÈVE

100 50 0 f 50 100 200 300 400 500 METRES

PONT DES NATIONS   S.D.N. ACTUELLE

108. Prospect of the World City from the lake.

and knowledge, gathered from the history of man himself.[12]

But the game wasn't over yet; now that everything was functionally organized, it was necessary to give a precise structure to the machine, to see to it that everything would also be functioning technically.

The last plans drawn up showed it 180 meters in length and 85–90 meters in height (figs. 105–106). Four cement pilasters in a cruciform foundation that perplexed the estimates engineer of Zurich[13] were to be pushed to the seventh level to hold the platform of the belvedere and to form a connective node with the entire secondary structure, which remained free for another 70 meters in height at the center of the Sacrarium and the 224 columns erected to support the floors and the descending ramps (fig. 104). On the outside the pyramid is transformed into an aereal mass: removed from the static image, it no longer uses the ground as a point of support (fig. 107). The pilasters—thin in dimensional relation—hold it suspended, creating a shadow void that raises the superimposed walls of glass against which the ramp belts lean in a unique upheaval of any structural logic. Seen from afar, its mass would appear to dissolve against the backdrop of the Juras or the Alps with a surprising levitational effect. It reawakens the memory of the temple observatory of Khorsabad, of the cusp of Hasepsowe and Newton's cenotaph; trees and the rear view of Saconnex would appear beyond the columns

BIBLIOTHÈQUE MONDIALE   SALLES DES EXPOSITIONS
UNIVERSITÉ
STADE   CITÉ HÔTELIÈRE

SECRETARIAT S.D.N.   SALLE DES ASSEMBLÉES S.D.N.
HÈQUE S.D.N.
ESPLANADE DU PALAIS   HALTE STATION C.F.F.
SUR VOIE FERRÉE   B.I.T.   PORT DE PLAISANCE

and under the ramps, while the horizon, open at 180°, would have transmitted an appearance foreign to the world of things built by the moderns, belonging to a superior, classical order.

It is at this point that Le Corbusier could write to Otlet asking him to take part in the Committee of patrons for the congress of La Sarraz: "The project of the Mundaneum will be, I believe, very beautiful. It is progressing well."[14] "The plans . . . have been scrupulously followed and are *not lacking in grandeur while remaining strongly realistic*. The whole can be considered a manifestation of modern architecture."[15]

In the middle of July the first phase of the project was practically finished. In the great assonometry destined for the pages of *Oeuvre complète 1910–29*, the entire urban site is represented as a complex architectural organism. From the project for the palace of the SdN that can be seen facing the lake, to the complicated system of the highway network (that should have received and directed traffic from and to Lausanne in a large spherical building), to the hotel city that invaded the Ariana park, the whole site is organized in the form of a city. The philosopher and the architect made themselves instruments of an autonomous and absolute will that proposed, outside of any logic directing the administration of a city, the construction of a world of images by portraying its intelligence before its real needs.*

[12] On the symbolic aspect of Le Corbusier's architecture see references in our treatise included in the essay by S. Cohen and S. Hurtt, "The Pilgrimage Chapel at Ronchamp: its Architectonic Structure and Typological Antecedents," in *Oppositions*, no. 19–20, 1982, pp. 146–49. See also A. Eardley, "Grandeur is in the Intention," in *Le Corbusier's Firminy Church*, New York, 1982.
[13] Letter from the engineers Terner and Choppard to Le Corbusier, April 3, 1929, FLC.
[14] Letter from Le Corbusier to Otlet, June 12, 1928, FLC.
[15] Letter from Le Corbusier to Otlet, July 7, 1928, FLC.
* The drawings of the Mundaneum that accompany this essay are by G. Gresleri.

THE PROBLEM OF URBAN CONTEXT IN THE
GRANDS TRAVAUX

Alan Colquhoun

Among the illustrations of the Centrosoyus and the Cité de Refuge in the *Oeuvre complète*, there are two which show both projects extended to adjacent sites, to form complexes with the scale and texture of urban fragments. In the case of the Centrosoyus, the extension visualized a new administrative district of which the Centrosoyus building would be an organic part.[1] In the case of the Cité de Refuge, the extension comprised a proposed Cité d'hospitalisation, linked to a new wing of the original building.

At first sight there is nothing particularly surprising in these extensions, given Le Corbusier's tendency to treat each of his projects, not only as the solution to a particular set of problems, but also as a prototypical element in a new urban totality. Yet the more we look at them, the more problematic they become. Firstly, in being dissolved into general urban textures and in thus losing their uniqueness, they seem to suffer a loss of representational power. Secondly, the urban continuum which they imply, though it bears an obvious formal resemblance to such urban projects as the plan for the Porte de St.-Cloud of 1938, would be difficult to locate in them.

Whether or not we interpret these two projects as administrative buildings or as "social condensers" on the model of the Soviet avant-garde, it is difficult to imagine them constituting part of that linear continuum which Le Corbusier reserved exclusively for housing in all his city plans. In the light of these extensions a reinterpretation of the buildings is forced, according to which they become hybrids, hovering uncertainly between the status of *"objets types"* or *"organs"* of the new city, and that of urban texture or ground against which other *objets types* might stand out as figures.

The ambiguity of these extensions seems to invite an investigation of the compositional principles at work in Le Corbusier's "Grands Travaux" of the inter-war

[1] See Jean-Louis Cohen, "Le Corbusier and the Mystique of the U.S.S.R.," *Oppositions* 23 (Winter 1981), pp. 85–121.

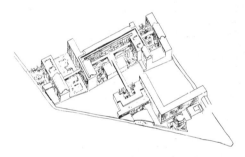

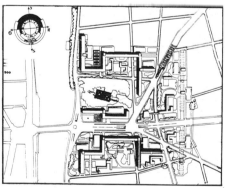

109. Le Corbusier. Project for an extension to the neighboring block of the Centrosoyus, Moscow, 1928.
110. Le Corbusier. Project for a Cité d'hospitalisation, extending to the rear of the Cité de Refuge, Paris, 1932.
111. Le Corbusier. Boulogne-sur-Seine, plan for the Porte de Saint-Cloud, 1938 (FLC 1349).

115

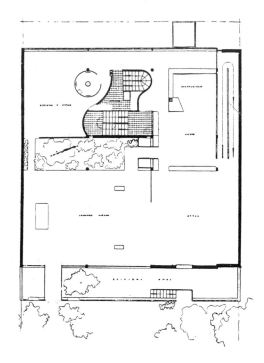

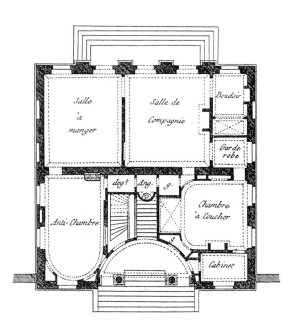

112. Le Corbusier. Project for Villa Meyer, 1925,
interior and plan.
113. Claude-Nicolas Ledoux. La Maison de M.
Tabary (*Architecture de C.-N. Ledoux*, Paris,
1847).

years, in order to discover how these principles were
used to reconcile the disparate and often contradictory needs that he had to satisfy in these buildings.
These can be summarized as follows:
1. The need for the building to adapt to a specific site
within a given urban context.
2. The need to create a building of symbolic presence.
3. The need to establish the building as the representative of a modern type.

The main concept underlying the composition of the
four public buildings to be studied in this essay is that
of *elementarization*. It is this that distinguishes them
from traditional schemes with closed courtyards,
where the programmatic volumes are not clearly distinct from each other. In Le Corbusier's *partis* each
program element is given its own form and is clearly
articulated in relation to its neighbor. The principle
elements are linear bars (containing cellular accommodation) and centroidal masses (containing places of
assembly). The linear bars are coupled to each other
at right angles, to form open courts. Such a principle
of flexible jointing provides for a large number of
permutations in the overall plan, and Le Corbusier's
early sketches show him trying out these permutations.

This arrangement of articulated bars is first found
in the Dom-ino housing projects of 1914 where they
still retain some of the picturesque qualities derived
from the Garden City Movement and Camillo Sitte's
*Der Städtbau nach seinen künstlerischen
Grundsätzen*. In one particularly striking example, U
and L shaped blocks create rectangular spaces
through which a country road meanders in contra-
puntal movement. This counterpoint between static
buildings and free circulation was to achieve its ultimate form in the concept of the *pilotis*, according to
which, thanks to the separation of levels, each could
be developed without interfering with the other.

The articulated bars of Dom-ino were systematized
as continuous bars of housing *à redent* in the Ville
Contemporaine and the Plan Voisin. When Le
Corbusier came to design his major public buildings in
the late 1920s he adapted this compositional procedure to the needs of multi-purpose public buildings
with their linear strings of offices or living cells.

There are strong analogies between this system of
composition and the revolutionary changes in spatial
organization which Le Corbusier had already worked
out for houses and villas. In the houses the solid *poché*
forming the left-over space between the rooms disap-
pears, to be replaced by a free-flowing space inter-

rupted only by the convex, sculptural forms of specialized volumes—bathrooms, closets, and staircases. This complex "hot" arrangement of spaces and volumes is set in dialectical contrast to the "cool" Platonic geometry within which it is contained. Le Corbusier drew attention to the dialectic between outside and inside, pure geometry and free form, when, in describing the villa at Garches, he said, "on affirme à l'exterieur une volunté architecturale, on satisfait à l'interieur tous les besoins functionels."[2]

A similar transformation can be found in the public buildings. But, whereas in the houses the ground for the play of volumes is the enveloping cube, pierced and hollowed out but never totally destroyed, in the public buildings the ground is formed by the linear bars and the play of volumes now takes place externally. The public building is an open-work of slender prisms which define the spatial limits of the ensemble, while at the same time they imply its possible extension. All of Le Corbusier's Grands Travaux of the late 1920s share these general formal characteristics.

[2] Le Corbusier et Pierre Janneret—Oeuvre complète, 1910–29, edited by W. Boesiger and O. Stonorov, Zurich, Girsberger, 1930, p. 189.
[3] Le Corbusier, Urbanisme, Paris, Crès, 1925, p. 158.

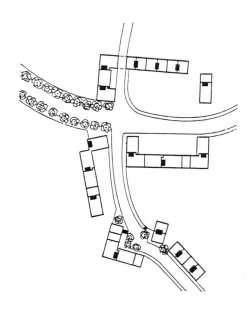

CS

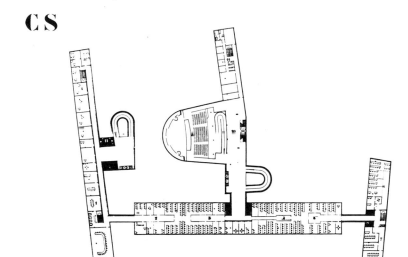

1ᵉ ETAGE

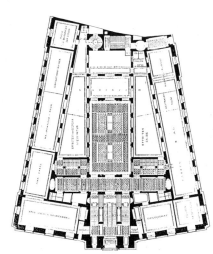

Adaptation to the site

Le Corbusier's city plans assume ideal sites, and in defending them he was careful to point out their intentionally schematic character.[3] In the commissions for public buildings of the late 1920s, on the contrary, the problem was one of accommodation to local conditions. This was not, for Le Corbusier, a purely negative constraint. As the text of Vers une Architecture makes clear, he had absorbed Auguste Choisy's theory of the picturesque, according to which the

114. Le Corbusier. Dom-ino development site plan.
115. Le Corbusier. Centrosoyus, first project plan (FLC 15678).
116. Otto Wagner, Bodenkreditanstalt (Land Credit Association), competition design, 1884, ground plan.

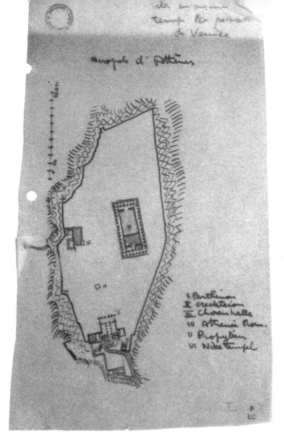

117. Le Corbusier. The buildings on the Acropolis of Athens, after Auguste Choisy, L'*Histoire de l'Architecture* (FLC).

118. Le Corbusier. Palais des Nations, Geneva, 1926–28, axonometric drawing.

accidents of a given site play a constitutive role in the artistic organization of architectural ensembles, resulting, as in the Acropolis in Athens, in compositions of balanced asymmetry which present to the viewer a "succession des tableaux."[4] Even among the houses, where the picturesque "*promenade architecturale*" usually takes place *within* the constraints of the ideal cube, there are several whose external form is determined by the irregularities of their sites or by building regulations. The most celebrated of these is the Maison La Roche—Jeanneret, in describing which Le Corbusier uses the word "pyramidal"—the very word used by Choisy to describe that other irregular building, the Erechthion. These houses remain, however, at least until the 1930s, the exception rather than the rule, whereas in the case of the Grands Travaux, picturesque grouping and asymmetry are normal.

For Le Corbusier, therefore, to be site specific was more than simply to make a building conform to boundary lines and irregularly shaped sites. It was to bring into play a system of forms and masses in relation to a viewer occupying specific positions in space; in short, it was "composition," which means—in the sense given it by Choisy—the artistic resolution of unforeseen exigencies, not the application of a priori rules.

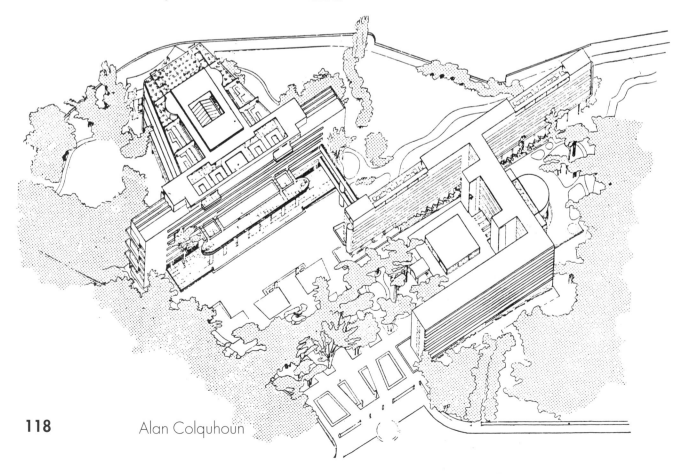

　　Alan Colquhoun

The Palais des Nations

119. Le Corbusier. Palais des Nations, view from the lake (FLC 23169).

The complex of the Palais des Nations consists of two blocks—the assembly and its ancillary accommodation and the Secretariat—linked by a long *passerelle*. The blocks are organized symmetrically about the orthogonal axes, the principle axis being through the block containing the assembly which presents a long frontal surface to the visitor's line of approach. This line is cut by imaginary planes which are prolongations of the wings of the administrative wing and which are reinforced by a system of paths, running parallel to the secondary axis.

Individually, both blocks conform to the species of frontalized buildings reserved by Choisy for propylaea.[5] As a pair, however, these two blocks form a "balanced asymmetry" whose outline follows the shore of the lake, and whose masses offer themselves as picturesque ensembles partly screened by trees. The north side of the imagined symmetrical *parti* is missing. In the third edition of *Vers une Architecture*, Le Corbusier appended a plan of the Palais showing an assumed extension to the north, whose axis is rotated by about 10° to conform to existing building and road alignments, so that even in its final form the building was not conceived of as perfectly symmetrical. The *parti* resembles certain sixteenth and seventeenth century projects in which long narrow galleries are extended from older nuclei, such as the "Manica Lunga" of the Quirinale and the Grande Galerie of the Louvre—especially the latter, with its development of only one side of the central axis, and its subtle shift of angle.

[4] See Auguste Choisy, *L'Histoire de l'Architecture*, Paris, 1899, chap. 11,"Architecture Grecque; La pittoresque dans l'art Grecque." In *Vers une Architecture* Le Corbusier not only printed several engravings from the *Histoire* but also paraphrased much of its picturesque theory, particularly in the chapters "Trois rapelles à messieurs les architectes/III Le plan," e "Architecture/II L'illusion des plans." See also Reyner Banham, *Theory and Design of the First Machine Age*, New York, Praeger, 1960, chap. 2.
[5] A. Choisy, "La pittoresque dans l'art Grecque."

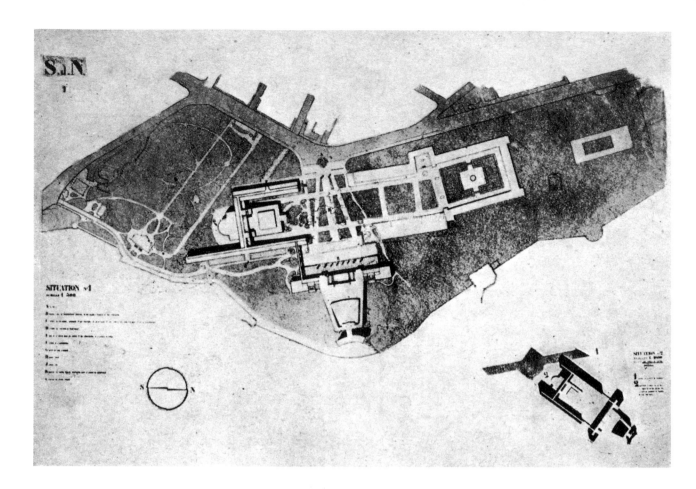

120. Le Corbusier. Palais des Nations, plan of the symmetrical extension of the Secretariat (*Vers une Architecture*).

If we compare the arrangement of bars *à redent* in this plan with those in the Ville Contemporaine or the Plan Voisin, we see that whereas the urban blocks *à redent* are oriented in both directions, those at Geneva have two aspects, one facing the public realm of the entrance court, the other the private realm of the garden. Whereas in Le Corbusier's city plans the bars *à redent* cut through a uniform and undifferentiated spatial continuum, in the Geneva project the bars act as walls dividing the site into two phenomenally different kinds of space.

When talking of context, therefore, we refer not only to the physical context (rural or urban) but also to the temporal, historical context. The Palais des Nations is not only adjusted to the exigencies of the site, it also restates the perennial tradition of architecture in terms of modern life and modern technology. Le Corbusier seems to have wholeheartedly embraced the ceremonial, humanistic implications of the program, and to have attempted to give the building an appropriate character. We shall see later that the same desire to imbue a building with an appropriate character was able, in the case of another project, to lead to diametrically opposite results.

Alan Colquhoun

The Centrosoyus

Unlike the Palais des Nations, the Centrosoyus was assigned to an urban site, and presented Le Corbusier with unprecedented contextual problems. The site was bounded by roads on its three regular sides, and on the fourth side by an irregular boundary cutting across the block. In the earliest solutions he rejected the articulated system of bars which he had used for the Palais de Nations, and based his design on a simple perimeter courtyard block divided into quadrants, with the auditorium at the intersection of a cruciform system of circulation, and with one quadrant omitted to avoid encroaching over the site boundary. There are several extant variants of this early scheme, but in all of them the hermetic and regular quality of the plan configuration is compensated for by irregular (and apparently somewhat arbitrary) elevational profiles, and wide penetrations at street level to gain access to the otherwise land-locked auditorium.

Notwithstanding Le Corbusier's tendency towards elementarism, the courtyard building was a recurrent type in his work. It occurs for the first time in the *immeubles-villas* of 1922 (though these were dropped in his later city plans), and formed the basis of two buildings in the Mundaneum project: the large cloister surrounding the University, and the exhibition buildings based on the themes of continents, nations, and cities. In his later work, the most outstanding example of this type is the monastery at Eveux, in which, as in the early schemes for the Centrosoyus, the interior of the court is opened to the outside at the lower levels and divided into quadrants.

In these early solutions for the Centrosoyus the short south-west side is the principle façade, on axis with the auditorium and facing the Boulevard with its central reservation of trees. During the evolution of the design the main façade migrated to the long frontage facing Miasnitskaia Street. At the same time the courtyard arrangement was transformed and the scheme began to assume its final configuration of articulated bars forming an unequal H, and providing the entrance façade with a shallow forecourt.

In all these transformations we can see a persistent concern for maintaining the street alignments and for frontalized blocks, which it is necessary to penetrate in order to arrive at the "private" interior space. In all the solutions, this interior space is used at ground and first floor level for vast cloak rooms and foyers, which define a pattern of movement that is in counterpoint to the configuration of the blocks above. This contra-

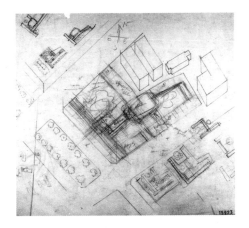

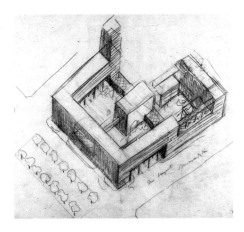

121. Le Corbusier. Centrosoyus, sketch for the first project (FLC 15923), and variation on the first project (16223).

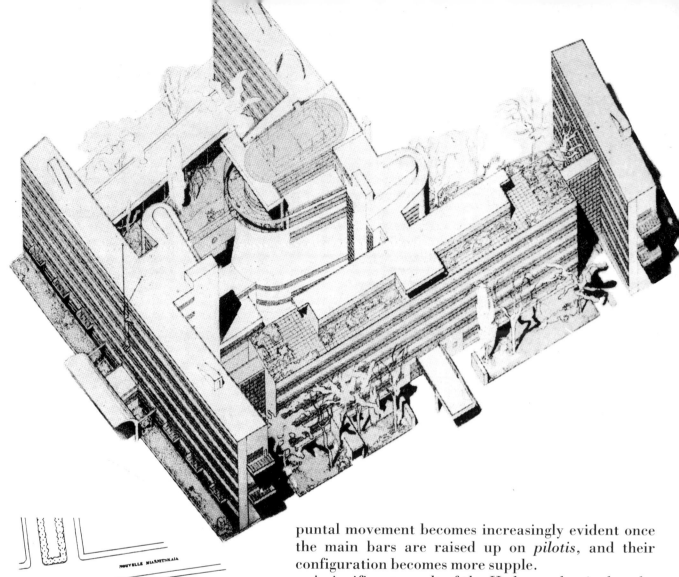

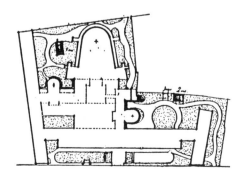

puntal movement becomes increasingly evident once the main bars are raised up on *pilotis*, and their configuration becomes more supple.

A significant result of the H-shape plan is that the tumultuous convex form of the auditorium and the horseshoe ramps become exposed to the northwest frontage, strongly implying public and private sides analogous to those of the Palais des Nations, but seemingly inappropriate to the actual context of regular streets and blocks. At first, even after the courtyard scheme had been abandoned, the northwest frontage was symmetrically framed by two bars, one facing the Boulevard, the other holding the auditorium, and the edge of the street was defined by a low colonade. But when, in a final move, the auditorium was rotated through 90° so that its convex "apse" faced the road, this contextual discipline was lost, and the northwest façade became a "back" relative to the formal, frontalized southwest and southeast façades, suggesting the need for the kind of rural open space with distant views, which was the spatial context of the Palais de Nations, and which would enable the building to be understood as an object in space. Simultaneously the overall plan became unambiguously

    Alan Colquhoun

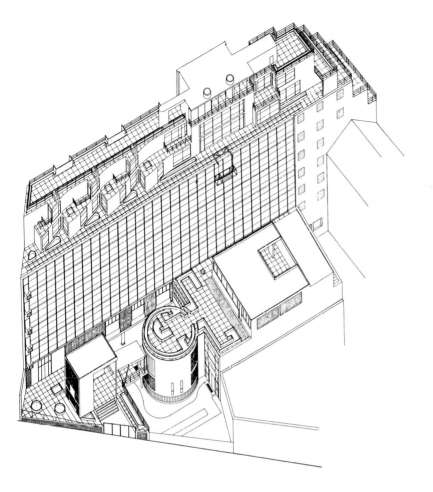

122. Le Corbusier. Centrosoyus, axonometric drawing of the first project.
123. Le Corbusier. Centrosoyus, first project site plan (FLC).
124. Le Corbusier. Centrosoyus, plan of the project as built, 1929 (FLC).
125. Le Corbusier. Cité de Refuge, axonometric drawing of the project as built.

diagonal in organization, losing much of its earlier multivalency and complexity.[6]

In the Centrosoyus one sees the unresolved tension often found in the work of Le Corbusier between the need for the building on the one hand to form part of an existing urban framework, to form street edges, and to consist of frontalized façades, and on the other, to exist as a freestanding object.

The Cité de Refuge

The site of the Cité de Refuge cuts across the center of a triangular block formed by rue Cantagrel and rue de Chevaleret. In the *Oeuvre complète* it is described as follows: "The site was extremely unfavorable: it provided a façade of only 17 meters to the south on rue Cantagrel and another of 9 meters to the east on rue de Chevaleret: everything else was in the middle. If one had built directly on the street, according to custom, all the rooms would have overlooked courtyards and faced north."[7] Although this passage sounds like special pleading, it is certainly true that the site did not lend itself to a perimeter solution, even if this had been desired. What is open to question, however, is

[6] The drawings in the *Oeuvre complète* do not correspond to the scheme as built. The chief differences are that (i) the southwest ramp is rotated through 180° and faces away from the building and (ii) the curved auditorium block is attached to a projecting rectangular slab containing foyer spaces and staircases. The extant drawings of the scheme as built are in a very fragmentary state.
[7] *Le Corbusier, Oeuvre complète 1929–34*, Zurich, Girsberger, 1964, p. 98.

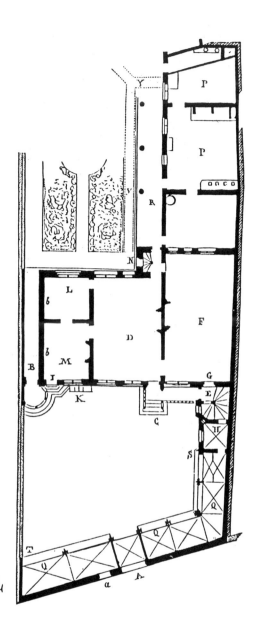

126. Hôtel le Gendre, plan. From Eugene-Emmanuel Viollet-le-Duc, *Dictionnaire raisonné de l'architecture française du XI au XVI siècle*, 6 (1868).

[8] For a detailed analysis of the stages through which the design passed see Brian Brace Taylor, *La Cité de Refuge di Le Corbusier 1929–33*, Rome, Officina, 1979.

Alan Colquhoun

whether Le Corbusier's successive solutions did not, in fact, have recourse to a traditional typology *other* than that of the perimeter block. After all, this was a representational building and not a mere part of the urban tissue. Certainly, for Le Corbusier it had, first and foremost, to represent modernity, but it was also called upon to symbolize a social and moral idea. In these circumstances it would be reasonable to expect the architect to have turned to Parisian precedent in giving the building a symbolic presence and setting it off against its immediate surroundings. And, in fact, the *parti* of both the first and the final schemes have much in common with that of the Parisian *hôtel particulière*. As in the *hôtel*, the *corps de logis* is set back some distance from the street, and consists of a block frontalized to the axis of approach, extending across the full width of the site. As in the *hôtel*, there is a portico *plomb sur la rue* which acts as a sign of the building and also as a controlled point of entry to the site, which thus forms a relatively secluded private realm, walled off from the street.

Initially only the western half of the site was available. One of the earliest sketches shows a cranked single-story passage leading from the entry on rue Cantagrel to a six- or seven-story dormitory block crossing the site from north to south. The east half of the site was developed by adding a second block parallel to the first and connecting them by means of a longitudinal block running west-east, extending to the rue Chevaleret boundary. At the change in direction of the entrance passage there was a rotunda containing the reception hall, which absorbed the axial rotation—a somewhat Beaux-Arts device. Over the rotunda a wedge-shaped lecture theatre was suspended. A *passarelle*, threading through a pavilion (the dispensary) connected the rotunda to the main building. In place of the *cour d'honneur* there was a sunken garden which was extended under the dormitory blocks.

In the final scheme, in one of those violent changes of mind that often characterized Le Corbusier's design process, the building was turned through 90°, and the two north-south bars were now replaced by a single building running east-west along the northern boundary of the site. At first, a single wing projected from the center of this east-west bar, but this was later eliminated.[8] The new arrangement had a radical effect on the entry sequence, which now had to penetrate to the middle of the site before it could be connected to the main building at the point where the main stair and the wall separating men and women occurred. Le

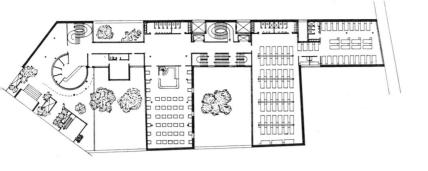

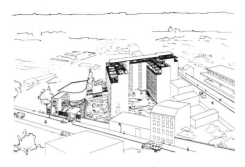

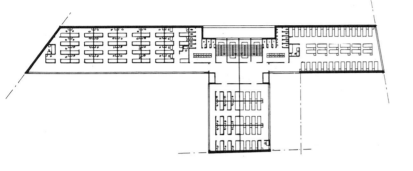

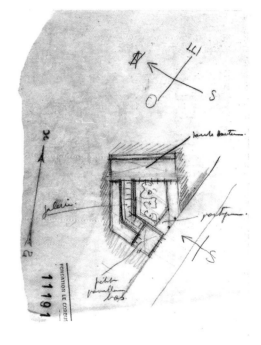

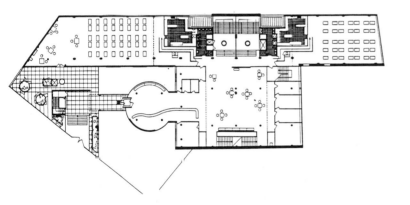

Corbusier, however, hardly altered the elements of this sequence. He simply resited them so that they formed a series of pavilions of various shapes running in front of and parallel to the main building, to which they were now connected by a protruding element containing entrance foyer and lecture theatre.

From the start, therefore, Le Corbusier had visualized an elaborate *promenade architecturale* connecting the point of entry to the site with the main accommodation. Programmatically, the promenade consists of a series of initiatory acts, necessary before entering the inner sanctum of the building, and these acts are symbolized by a series of architectural elements: portico, rotunda, *passarelle*. Yet it is important to note that this solution owes as much to the architectural demands of the site, and their formal implications, as

127. Le Corbusier. Cité de Refuge, plan of the ground floor of the second project: entrance, walkway, dining room, dormitory (FLC 10594).
128. Le Corbusier. Cité de Refuge, plan of the second floor of the fourth project: dormitories for women and for men (FLC 10612).
129. Le Corbusier. Cité de Refuge, plan of the ground floor of the project as built (1931): information office, central hall, office for social workers, dining hall and meeting room for the women, central stair leading to the men's and women's dormitories and the men's dining room (FLC 10667).
130. Le Corbusier. Cité de Refuge, bird's-eye view of the second project.
131. Le Corbusier. Cité de Refuge, planimetric sketch using only half the area, May–June 1929 (FLC 11191).

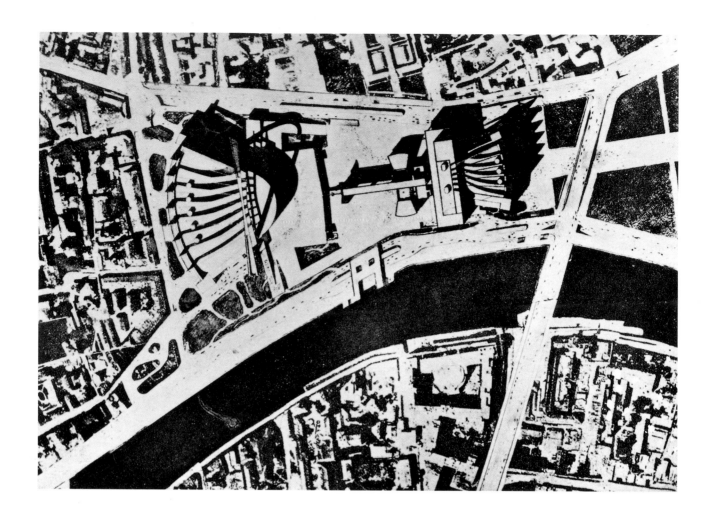

132. Le Corbusier. Palace of the Soviets, photomontage showing building in relation to its urban context (FLC).

it does to the practical and symbolic peculiarities of the program. "This group of buildings" wrote Le Corbusier, "constitutes a kind of *hors d'oeuvre*, disposed in front of the great hostel building; this last serves, in fact, as ground to the very irregular group consisting of the portico and the social service spaces." The reversal of *poché* space found in his houses is repeated here; instead of a series of concave spaces carved out of the building, such as one might have found in a traditional scheme, we are presented with their negative—a small collection of architecture volumes. But now, instead of these objects being disposed within the cube of the building, they are placed in front of it, and the table on which they are displayed is tilted upwards and becomes a vertical plane of reference. It seems impossible to separate the sensuous and intellectual pleasure derived from this arrangement of architectural forms from the site to which it owes its origin, and, as in the Palais de Nations, and the Centrosoyus, the building is the result of a response to accidental circumstances of the kind described by Choisy in his analysis of the Acropolis.

The Palace of the Soviets

This project differs from the three that we have already discussed in respect to its programmatic elements. The administrative content is very small, and the project consists mainly of a series of auditoria of different sizes.

It differs from them also in its relation to the site. In the other projects the buildings are thought of as creating spatial boundaries. Long walls of offices or living cells form frontalized planes the approach to which involves a more or less elaborate preparation. In all these projects there exists at least the suggestion of a *cour d'honneur* and a *corps de logis*, and the centroidal masses of assembly spaces are presented as figures against the surface of "le prism pure."

Despite the absence of accommodation suitable for creation of such frontalized surfaces, the earliest solutions for the Palace of the Soviets did, however, provide an urban space—a huge "forum" overlooking the Moscow river against which the various auditoria are lined up, rather in the manner of the temples in the Forum at Pompei, of which Le Corbusier had published a sketch in *Vers une Architecture*. In this solution it would presumably have been necessary to find some way of establishing the equivalent of a portico which would connect the irregular group of auditoria and unify them in a single grand gesture. In the second solution, an urban space facing the river is still provided, but now the two main auditoria have been moved to the two sides, and the back of the space is defined by a low range of offices raised on columns.

In the final scheme all attempts to create a specifically urban space are abandoned. The complex is now seen as an object organized along a spine on the analogy of a biological organism. The spaces it now offers to the city are the pure epiphenomena of its own internal structure. The complex is symmetrical along a single axis only. On the other axis it consists of objects whose configuration is explosively centrifugal and asymmetrically balanced.[9]

The spine is purely metaphorical since the range of offices, which in the second solution had formed a physical link betwee the two auditoria, is now stopped half-way across the gap, its end supporting the acoustic sounding board of the open-air assembly. The two auditoria only *appear* to be connected.

In thus interpreting the complex as a series of objects in space, Le Corbusier turned it into a constructivist icon whose silhouette was seen as complementing that of the domes of St. Basil and the

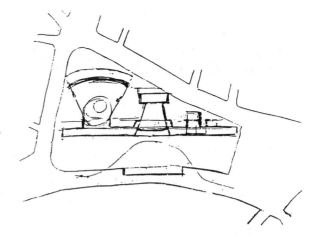

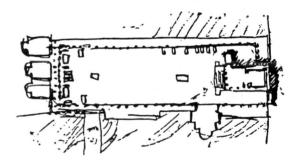

133. Le Corbusier. Palace of the Soviets, second variant of the project (FLC 27562).
134. Le Corbusier. Palace of the Soviets, second variant of the project (FLC 27505).
135. Le Corbusier. Sketch of the forum at Pompeii.

[9] The uniaxiality is also a characteristic of the plan of the Ville Radieuse, which was initiated as a result of Le Corbusier's contacts with Moscow; see Jean-Louis Cohen, "Le Corbusier and the Mystique of the U.S.S.R." The symbolism of biological structure and growth is similar in both cases.

136. Le Corbusier. Palace of the Soviets, panoramic view showing its relation to the Kremlin and the Cathedral of Saint Basil.

Kremlin. The group of auditoria, *très accidenté*, no longer need the backdrop that was necessary in the case of the Cité de Refuge; there is nothing larger on which they can be grounded. The structural, acoustic, and circulatory demands of the complex were used to give expressive form to each element.

Whereas the desire to give it an appropriate character led Le Corbusier to interpret the Palais des Nations in terms of what, failing a better word, we might call "an architecture of humanism," the same desire led him to make the Palais des Soviets into a symbol of mass culture and of the work of art in the age of the machine.

The building versus the city

Our analysis of Le Corbusier's compositional procedures as exhibited in the "Grands Travaux" of the interwar years shows that the need to adapt to the idiosyncracies of particular sites made a positive contribution to the architectural quality of these projects. It cannot be considered as a mere obstacle to the achievement of a "new architecture." The arbitrary urban conditions with which Le Corbusier was faced played a catalytic role comparable to that of "function" in the internal arrangement of his houses.

In having to build in existing urban or rural contexts, no less than in having to give form and character to programs with strongly idealist contents, Le Corbusier was also confronted with the architectural tradition. But these buildings are not a reflection of these factors alone. As in all Le Corbusier's buildings there is a dialectic at work. What they reflect is the tension between the tradition of architecture and the

types of a new and contentious architecture, and, as such, they put into question the very urban contexts on which they depend.

When experienced in the context of the existing urban fabric these buildings do indeed stand out as the types of a new architectural culture. Their ability to be read in this way is at least partly due to the extent to which they accommodate themselves to their context and in so doing expose both their similarity to, and their difference from, traditional representational buildings.

When, however, Le Corbusier shows these buildings as extended they immediately start to play a different role in the urban continuum. The use of flexible joints allows the bars to adapt to adjacent blocks, the use of *pilotis* and bridges enables them to leap across existing streets, or across plots that are not yet available, so that the existing street pattern becomes the equivalent of the pedestrian paths that meander under the *à redent* blocks of the Ville Radieuse. Thus, a new urban pattern starts to emerge, tentacle-like, before the old one has ceased to exist. The original Centrosoyus and Cité de Refuge buildings are each absorbed into this new context. What had by itself been experienced as a whole, with articulated parts that opened up the building to its surroundings but at the same time differentiated it from its neighbors, now becomes part of a greater whole. Before, these buildings were able to act as the synecdochic fragments of an absent city; now they become part of the metonymic series of an actual city fragment.

However, this new urban fragment itself also merely "stands for" the new city and can never become a part of it. Both extensions take the form of a web or matrix,

137. Le Corbusier. Cité de Refuge, principle entrance on rue Cantagrel (FLC).
138. Le Corbusier. Centrosoyus view of the club from Miasnitskaya Street.

and yet their representational purpose resists absorption into such a matrix. It could only be by denying their representational function that they could assume the role of background buildings demanded of them. It is true that the articulation of their elements suggests their possible extension and allows them to become metamorphosed into small cities. But whereas from a purely formal point of view this seems to be an advantage, from the point of view of architectural content or meaning it is a serious disadvantage. For, while it enables Le Corbusier to make an apparently flawless demonstration of architecture in the process of becoming merged with city, and of the consistency of a design strategy that makes such a conversion possible, it also denies those very qualities of discreteness, difference, and *lack* of continuity that would make it possible for these buildings to fulfill their larger signifying ambitions.

To belabor this point is perhaps merely to reiterate what has been said before many times, that the Corbusian city would be alienating and lacking in that quality of multivalency that his buildings possess in the highest degree. Yet an examination of the compositional principles at work in his large public buildings enables one to see this problem from a new point of view. For the real difficulty with the transformation of the representational building into a fragment of urban tissue lies in the fact that Le Corbusier applied the same principles of composition to both, despite their differences of scale and purpose. Because the form of the city blocks consisted of a system of articulations similar to that found in his larger public buildings, neither could act as a satisfactory foil to the other.

In the Corbusian city it is only housing that can legitimately act as the background to representational buildings. If an attempt is made to interpret the linear bars of cellular office space in his public buildings in the same way, these buildings start to disintegrate. All that is left as a possible representation of the public realm is that part of each project that consists of places of public assembly. Only these can project, in their specialized and concentrated forms, the social meanings that the architecture of the city ought to provide. Yet, in the Corbusian scheme, it is only within the individual building that such a meaning can develop— that building whose abstract and neutral ranges of accommodation provide the necessary ground against which, in Le Corbusier's compositional practice, the dynamic figures generated by function can be displayed.

It is in this sense that the Corbusian city seems to lack any technique by which representational buildings could continue to exist. Seen in these terms, the "Grands Travaux" of the late 1920s, with their original and seductive forms and their plenitude of meaning, seem to exist in an ambiguous and metaphorical world half way between the existing city of which they are the critique, and the city of the future in which they would cease to exist.[*]

* This essay, first published as the entry "Strategies," in *Le Corbusier—une encyclopédie*, Centre Georges Pompidou, Paris, 1987, and *Le Corbusier—enciclopedia*, Milan, Electa, 1988, has been revised for publication in this volume.

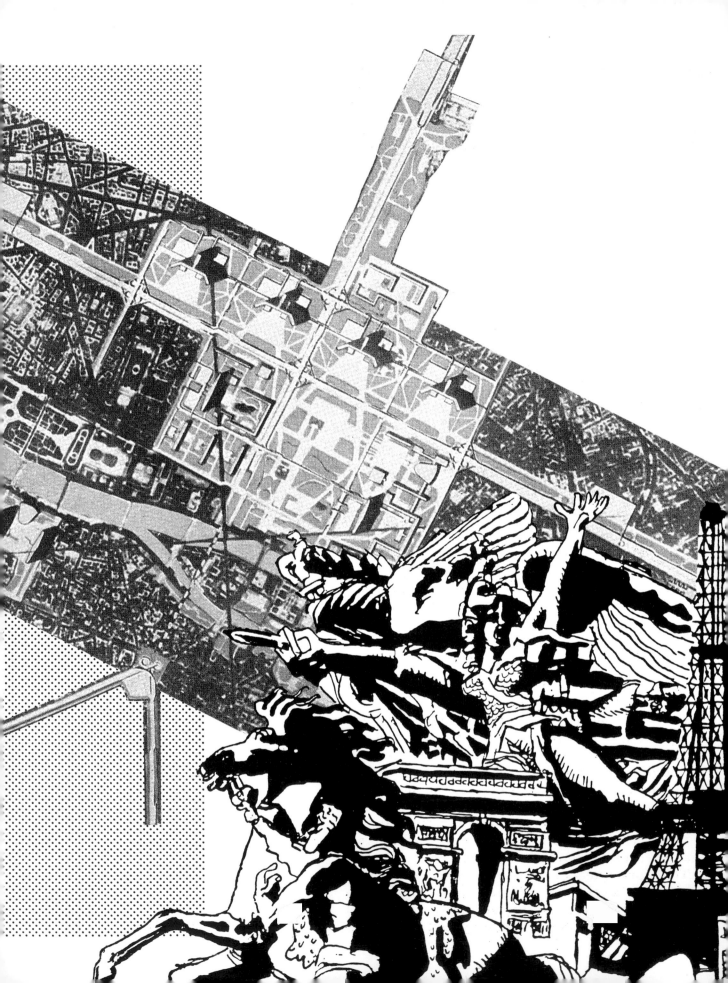

PARIS
1922 – 46

Filippo Messina

sache, par un subtil mensonge,
garder mon aile dans ta main.
Mallarmé

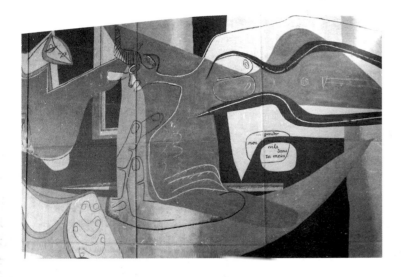

139. Pavillon Suisse at the Cité Universitaire, Paris, 1948, mural painting in the refectory of the ground floor.

[1] M. Foucault, "Un fantastico da biblioteca," in *Scritti letterari*, Milan, 1984, p. 135.

The Plan of Paris was a text that Le Corbusier would write and rewrite many times. This return to one's own work, so frequent in literary and artistic practice, at times assumes a particular import in the poetics of an author. Flaubert rewrote his *Tentation* before making it the dream of his writing; as Foucault observes,[1] Braque and Cézanne painted the same subjects obsessively, Proust wrote his *Remembrance of Things Past* an infinite number of times. Thus, from its very first formulation, without directly assimilating this experience into literary experience, it cannot be denied that the Plan of Paris was a formative experience and an enduring challenge to the urban and architectural theory and practice of Le Corbusier.

This work spans thirty years of activity, and was conceived as a continuous laboratory, itself internal to the much larger laboratory of his research; he doesn't represent it or substitute it entirely, but he securely

133

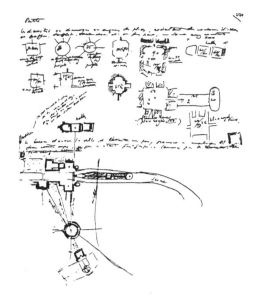

formulates its principal direction and its most salient shifts.

His fundamental versions are singularly connected to the definition of two urban models, the *Ville Contemporaine* and *Ville Radieuse* schemes, representations—expressions—of an abstract urban ideal, notably different one from the other, to which Le Corbusier brings the diversity and specificity of the single urban house. But in the case of Paris, a rapport that he has never repeated in any other project is established between model and city. During the long succession of developments, not only does the plan change in relation to the general theoretical formulation, but the very relation that is established between model and city mutates substantially. If, in fact, at first it was the city that conditioned the model, it would then be the model that influenced the project's solution. A tension is determined in such a way that between ideal and real city its meaning is simply inverted but remains constant and unresolved. It alone can lead back to this project's process of progressive reduction and its contemporaneous articulation.

It is possible to recognize, in the succession of propositions, a shift from the initial prevalent interest in aspects of the constructions or of revision of the discipline to something more concrete and pragmatic and to the expression of autobiography and poetics in the latter. Relating the plan directly to theory, which for a long time had not existed separate from the city itself, or simply connecting the plan to some design "opportunity" would undoubtedly limit our understanding of it. It seems rather more useful to consider these plans in their continuity and specificity, beyond their own conclusion that refers to the significance of other experiences and renders homogeneous the complex of the work according to an outline that Le Corbusier himself delineates in the *Oeuvre complète*: the Plan, that remains with so much embarrassment, like a missed rendezvous with history, has been placed at the center of the search. At its foundation is the profound interweaving between the general and the specific, the permanent and the contingent of which a discernible trace has been left in history, geography, and the topography of each city.

This first work of architectural analysis and synthesis on the urban problem doesn't appear to be as extemporaneous as Le Corbusier would have us believe in *Oeuvre complète*.

The years between 1915 and 1922 span Le Corbusier's studies at the Bibliothèque Nationale and the first Plan of Paris; they are the years in which his

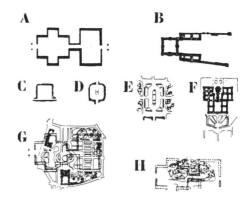

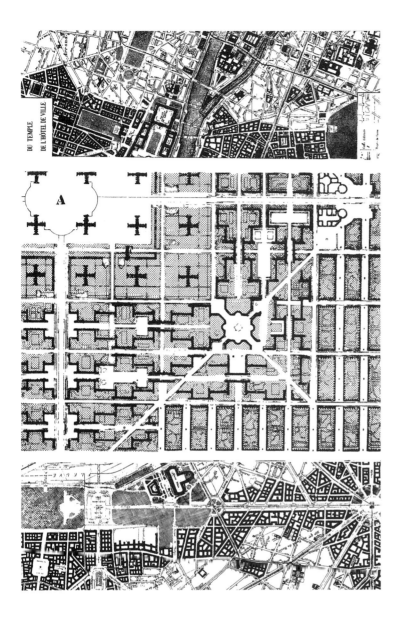

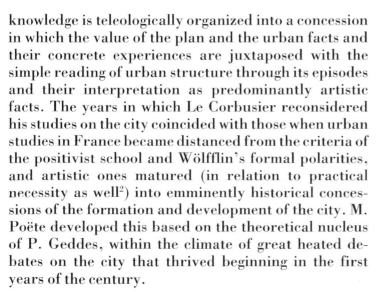

140. Ch. E. Jeanneret, drawing no. 278 at the Bibliothèque Nationale: "According to Patte, I refer to lecture note 279" (FLC).
141. The Luxembourg with the Palais-Royal, the City for 3 million inhabitants and the Tuileries with the Champs Elysées; planimetric drawings on the same scale (*Urbanisme*).
142. "A même échelle" (at the same scale), a *redent* of the ville Radieuse (A), for workers' quarters (1000 inhabitants per hectare) faced by the Louvre (B), Place des Vosges (C), Place Vendôme (D), Place de la Concorde (E), Les Invalides (F), the Luxembourg Gardens (G), Parc Monceau (H).

knowledge is teleologically organized into a concession in which the value of the plan and the urban facts and their concrete experiences are juxtaposed with the simple reading of urban structure through its episodes and their interpretation as predominantly artistic facts. The years in which Le Corbusier reconsidered his studies on the city coincided with those when urban studies in France became distanced from the criteria of the positivist school and Wölfflin's formal polarities, and artistic ones matured (in relation to practical necessity as well[2]) into emminently historical concessions of the formation and development of the city. M. Poëte developed this based on the theoretical nucleus of P. Geddes, within the climate of great heated debates on the city that thrived beginning in the first years of the century.

[2] The laws of 1914 and 1924 that obligated the French city to draw up an expansion and restructuring plan.

[3] Letter to Eplattenier on November 22, 1908, in Le Corbusier, *Il Viaggio d'Oriente*, Faenza, Faenza Editrice, 1974.
[4] Le Corbusier, *Urbanisme*, Paris, Crès (Coll. Esprit Nouveau), 1925, reissued Paris, Vincent Fréal et Cie., 1966; Italian trans. *Urbanistica*, Milan, Il Saggiatore, 1967, p. 14.

Moreover, Paris is the place from which he left on his trip to the Orient: "Arriving in Paris I perceived in myself an enormous void and I said to myself: poor fellow! You still don't know anything . . ."[3]

This allows the most resistant nucleus of Le Corbusier's formative experience, the memory that is solidified in images, to become transferred into urban realities and architectural specifics and the plan itself: "Fifteen years ago, during some long journeys, I had a way of measuring the force of architecture in all its power, but I had to go through difficult stages to find the suitable environment. Architecture, oppressed by an absurd chaos of heritages, only indirectly reached the spirit and made it vibrate only slightly; a well unified architecture would resonate and leave a profound impression. Putting aside the manuals, he realized the presence of an essential factor with certainty: urbanism, designating it with a word that he would come to know only much later."[4]

Paris has the significance of a chosen, an acquired, and deeply felt location within the framework of the European cultural architecture. Paris is Perret as well as Behrens. Paris is the opposite of Vienna, it is the contemporary city that is reborn from itself and by

143. City for 3 million inhabitants, planimetrics.

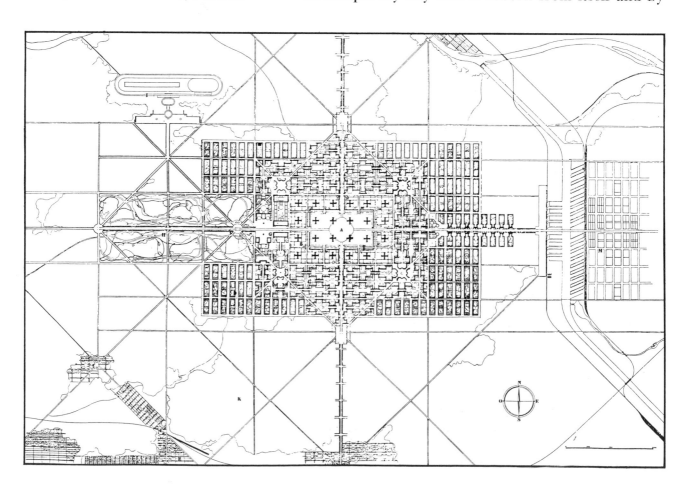

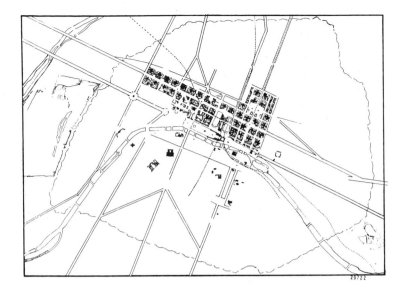

144. Plan Voisin, first study (FLC 29722).

itself rather than the modern city, unlimited and continuous in the pursuit of its own development.

"1922 Paris et une Ville Contemporaine" is the title
under which Le Corbusier published this work in
Oeuvre, exhibited at the Salon d'Automne of the same
year. It is "a work of the laboratory, which has as its
focus that of formulating the basic principles of modern urbanism . . . The objective is to establish the rules
of the game, to give an urbanistic structure to the large
contemporary city."[5]

That laboratory is Paris itself. Model and city are
closely linked in his experiments. The elements that
comprise it are found in the city, are commensurate
with it, its monuments, its locales. This operation of
commensuration and of opposition is not only a verification of the operability of the elements put into play in
relation to the city originally assumed as context. In
fact it contains one part of the theory that the model
alone cannot transmit. Paris is therefore at once the
site of application and the place of origin for Le
Corbusier's definition of urban theory. Paris furnishes the occasion[6] and the theoretical definitions of
the area of problems to confront: the problem of the
large modern city is first of all the one of its center. The
problem of architecture and of the plan. The model is
the representation itself of their hierarchy.

The sketch of a development plan for the center of
Paris is exhibited at the same Salon d'Automne, and it
is meaningful above all for its "writing." Annotated in
the drawing are the belt of the fortifications by Thiers,
the parks (Bois de Boulogne, Vincennes, the Senna),
and the new railroad tracks, the system of various
approaches from the north and the south, the "Grande
Traversée," the axis Louvre-Etoile, and the system of

[5] Le Corbusier, *Urbanistica*, p. 168.
[6] The occasion is provided by the debate on the localization of directional activity at St. Germain en Laye foreseen on the plan by Leon Jaussely, winner of the Competition for the Expansion Plan of Paris in 1919.

145. Plan Voisin, diorama.

[7] *Le Corbusier et Pierre Jeanneret—Oeuvre complète 1910–29*, W. Boesiger and O. Stonorov, eds., Zürich, Girsberger, 1929, p. 38.
[8] Le Corbusier, *Urbanistica*, p. 250.
[9] It is reasonable to believe that at the same moment in which Le Corbusier found the scale for the *immeuble-villas* confronting him at the construction site for the large department stores Bon Marche (*Oeuvre complète 1910–29*, p. 98), he might also have gathered the very similar nature of those elements in the already existing city.

Parisian monuments, completely absorbed into the plan on the right, isolated, like a constellation, from the one on the left. This system of representation is the matrix of many successive writings. Its importance consists in the articulation of themes that successive plans would develop; the theme of the urban center and of its persistence in the "true center" of the city, the street as urban problem and as "layout," the system of connection and origin of the urban settlement, for which "different cities have succeeded each other on the same ground," cornerstone of the new "historico-evolutionary" interpretation of the urban phenomenon that Le Corbusier applies and takes back to a concession that is very similar to the one of "operant history."

The plan seems to be placed at the center of the history, rather than on a specific site, of the city whose monuments are expressions of violent transformation, moments of accelerated rhythm.

The Plan is, up to this moment, the choice of a site on which it would be possible to undertake "a commercial operation at an infinitely larger scale than Haussmann's."[7] Le Corbusier sees the transformations, the large, open voids in the center of the city created in bringing Haussmann's plan to a conclusion: "An impressive expanse invites one, before being covered by constructions, to think . . . about so many things. This expanse is there, it has been created, it is an urbanistic event . . ."[8]

To him, the city of the 1800s presented a great opportunity that hadn't been fully exploited.

The definition of buildings of the plan is practically illegible, the two types, the *gratte-ciel* (skyscraper) and the *à redents* (with setbacks), seem to alternate in the same ground allotments and in the same contextual

146. City for 3 million inhabitants, diorama.

conditions, but most of all, the relation between the model and its implementation seem indeciphrable. As a theoretical construct, the rest of the model still has the form of the ideal city, and is actually the definitive drawing of the ideal city in the history of architecture. Its form is closed and complete, and has more oppositional symmetrical axes disposed to receive a system of internal differences, than perhaps are necessary in a theoretical model. Thus the two gates on the north and the south, in which the *redent* turns into two different modes, or the four plazas situated along the diagonal, none of which is identical to the other, closely recall the drawings of Patte for the Cité. It can be said, then, that there exists a tight interweaving between the urban model and the city itself. This includes the monuments, the building structure, the fundamental axes, Napoleon's grand layouts and Haussmann's diagonal webs.

The relation between model and plan is defined in 1925. At the Exposition Internationale des Arts Décoratifs in Paris, Le Corbusier constructed a full-scale apartment of the *immeuble-villas* that doesn't compare with the types on the plan and that would not compare with any other city plan.[9] An annexed part, the "*rotonde*," contained two large dioramas: Le Corbusier staged his *Ville Contemporaine* and the new plan, the *Plan Voisin*. The two dioramas were placed to directly confront one another, along the curving sides of the rotunda. A relation of images, the mirroring of figures, each one repeating the other, is established between model and project. The images blend together, the points of view equalize each other.

The figure is composed of irregular quadrilaterals, like the same system that divides the ground as a result of the rotations of the two generating axes, the Grande

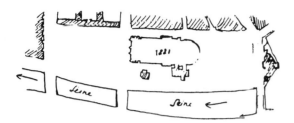

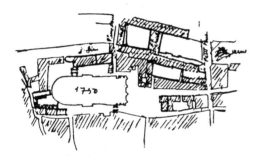

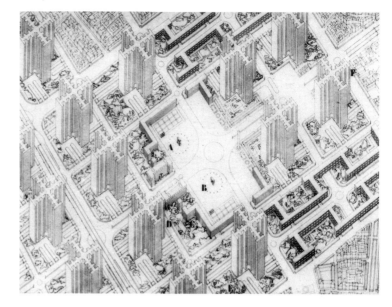

147. "From one group of houses, elements of the same nature, Rome erects its palaces and its temples. These are 'exposed.' Architecture is released from the urban magma (*Urbanisme*).
148. Notre Dame liberated, the entire isle was demolished and rebuilt (*Urbanisme*).
149. Plan Voisin, detail of the axonometric drawing of the Cité des Affaires (FLC 29723).

Traversée and the north-south axis that faithfully retraces the layout of the Boulevard Sébastopol. From the north the large axis enters the center crossing a system of slabs that recall a grand baroque system. The skyscrapers in Greek design have an autonomous orientation, slightly rotated in relation to the axes. The *redents* are a flexible system used to define a solid dialogue with the preexisting Louvre-Vendôme-Madeleine-Opéra-Elysée, along with which it constitutes a uniform weave, and out of which emerges the *Cité des Affaires* with a dimension projecting a tendency that the history of the city itself has proposed: "... The ascending lines of the interventions ... within the chain itself of tradition."[10]

The Palais Royal functioned as a link between the two systems.

On the left side of the drawing of the six skyscrapers, on the side of the large traversing avenue, the extension of the Cité des Affaires is suggested toward the west.

The plan does not resolve the ambiguity of being part of an urban foundation and at the same time being the principle of its progressive substitution; it is that same ambiguity that we find in the expansion operations of some projects (Cité de Réfuge and Centrosoyuz).

The problems of adaption to the complex conditions of the urban context is noticeable in the deformations of the *redent* that loses its character of *lotissement rationnel* (rational or logical lot assignment) transforming itself into an almost always peripheral construction system, even if absolutely different in density from the Haussmannian city block. In relation to the monuments, the *redent* continues to reproduce an environment made of spaces not too dissimilar from those of the existing city. In the working models of 1929, Le Corbusier would not put this part of the project into relief as it would totally disappear in successive plans. The model doesn't have a sufficient degree of generality; it is built too much on top of the city. The plan has a relation that is too close to the model.

The Ville Contemporaine would not serve as model for any other plan of the city, but is only alluded to in the *Etude sur Buenos Aires* of 1929. The five skyscrapers in Greek style rise, charged with light, over the dark horizon of the enormous estuary of the Rio de la Plata like those of Paris, in counterlight over the city that spreads out at their base.

In 1932 Le Corbusier took up his studies on Paris again with the idea of linking the strategy of carrying out the plan at the International Exposition, which was to be held in 1937 and that would have the house as its theme. This would furnish the opportunity to open the era of the "Grands Travaux" with the construction of the first leg of the Traversée (between the Porte Dorée and the Boulevard Sébastopol), the recovery of the eastern quarters and the construction of the Cité des Affaires, in successive stages. The idea of transforming the Exposition into an occasion for concrete and lasting interventions, the reorganization of the proposals and any perspective of a complex urban solution for

[10] Le Corbusier, *Destin de Paris*, Paris, Sorlot, 1941, p. 54.

150. Plan Voisin, planimetric drawing.

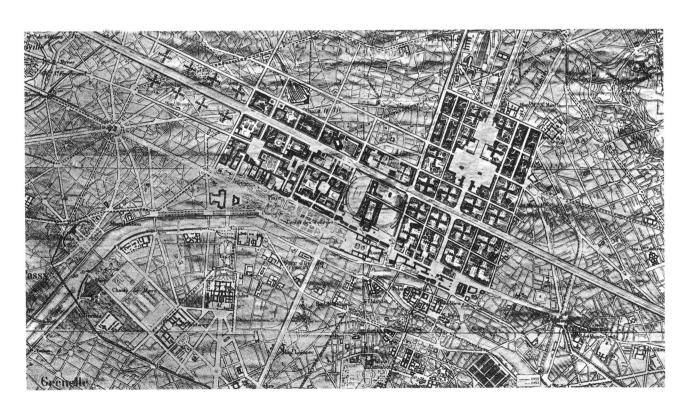

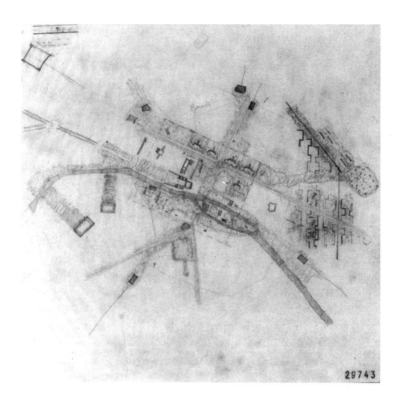

29743

Paris would not succeed. The Pavillon des Temps Nouveaux, a complex but temporary construction in iron and cloth with its 1600 square meters of exhibition space, would demonstrate the possibilities of modern urbanism. Le Corbusier exhibited the new plan called "Paris 37." The slogan is clearly built on the idea of its immediate feasibility. The new proposal made use of the technico-theoretic codifications of the CIAM of Athens (1933), above all the constructions of a new urban model, completely different from the preceding one, completed on the seventeen charts drawn up between May and June 1930 in response to a questionnaire on the transformations of the "Grande Mosca" that became the twenty charts of the Ville Radieuse. If in the Ville Contemporaine the order of the parts follows a rigid hierarchy and the definitions of the urban spaces mediate the relation between building and city, the new model affirms the principle of independence of parts also at an urban scale. The Ville Radieuse doesn't have form, doesn't have point of view, it is a purely theoretical construction. It is the structure itself of the relations that comprise it in respect to the double system of the Cartesian axes; relations among all the urban parts or functions along the vertical axis, inside each part along the horizontal axes.

This new system that favors positional relations represents, along with the basal organization of the installation in many of Le Corbusier's plans, one of the more obvious constants: for example, at Antwerp, where the topological and functional relations reapear unchanged with only the 45° rotation of the axis.

The east-west axis is the axis of relations within the residencial buildings that are arranged between the *lotissement à redent*, a system of similar relations between residences, utilities, and equipment. The latter make up a discreet ensemble of manufacturers in which recur some type-parts in which Le Corbusier seems to attempt the application of associative and configurational properties found in closed or open, symmetrical, assymetrical, speculative systems in simple or multiple combinations.

The Palace of the Soviets and the Centrosoyuz lend themselves to an analogical reading of this process and a comprehension of its significance: the constant compositional criteria are independent of each determination of dimensions or scale. The independence of

152. La Ville Radieuse, planimetric drawing (FLC 24909).

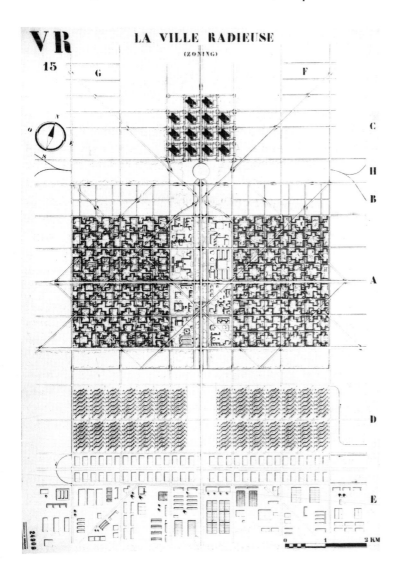

LE COEUR DE PARIS (AUJOURD'HUI POURRI) REVIT.
GRÂCE DÉLICIEUSE DE LA ZONE HISTORIQUE

LES QUARTIERS
IGNOBLES
OÙ IL FAUT
REMPLACER

153. Plan of Paris '37, photomontage of the center of Paris (FLC).

[11] See E. Kaufmann, *L'architettura dell'Illuminismo*, Turin, Einaudi, 1966.

parts and the idea of the city is an architectural principle. Its value is more than just a stylistic rupture with its Baroque foundation.[11] It is the presupposition of an option that in itself is an alternative that had never been introduced into the principles of human inhabitance nor in the relations between architecture and urban space.

The general frame of reference is now totally changed. The autonomy and degree of generality gathered in the theoretic model allow a greater articulation, an evaluation that is freer and more aware of the concrete opportunities of change. Plan 37, in ensemble and in its specific projects, is the representation of the great tension between model and city, between the idea of the city and the real city, between the parts and the whole, in the attempt to fill up areas that tend to be always more unfillable.

Redistribution and discontinuity of interventions characterize this plan that, having abandoned the strongly unitary criteria of the *Plan Voisin*, brings together different circumstances and at the same time renews the fundamental elements of urban form, the principal interpreter of whose development *is* Paris itself. It is a new idea of the discontinuity and measure of the unlimited development of the city.

The orthogonality of the two axes is not absolute. The Opéra, the Louvre, the Place de la République, and the Hôtel de Ville are the vertices of a single large

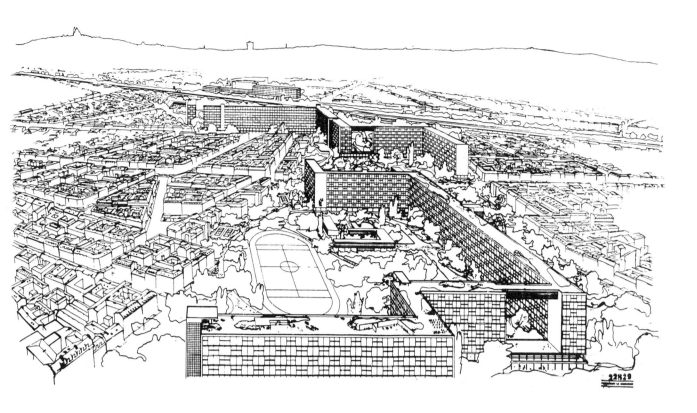

154. Îlot no. 6, bird's eye view (FLC 22829).

quadrilateral inside of which is the Cité des Affaires, now called the Cité de l'Administration since public and private business is contracted.

The position of the north-south axis with its absolute geometry, confirms the assumption of a new strategy in which the Cité des Affaires is considered a complete intervention with finite and congruent dimensions, having also the finite dimensions of the city, in the complex program of ground utilization.

To the north, four lots in "patte de poule" are aligned with the Traversée; to the south, the public urban utilities lean against the same large traversing avenue. A construction system with a different unity, utilizing the new "spine and lens" types binds the two large exterior lots, while an enormous central void pushes up to the Île and continues along the quays before hooking up with the Invalides and the Champs de Mars. Along the left bank of the Seine a vast area between the Pont Solferino and the Pont du Carousel, which comprise the Gare d'Orsay, is transformed into the new Government Center.

The *résidence urbaine* as element of the Cité des Affaires does not compare. The problem of the residence is reconsidered starting from the age-old demands for reconstruction of the eastern quarters. Le Corbusier takes into consideration the vast area between Buttes-Chaumont and the Père Lachaise cemetery and the Îlot no. 6 (one of the seventeen blocks

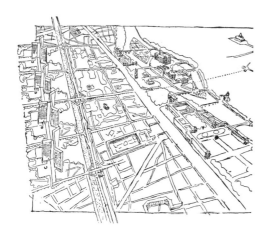

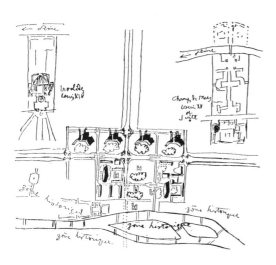

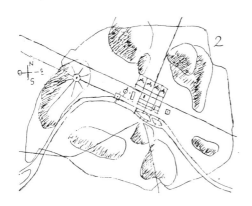

155. Plan of Paris '37, perspectival sketch (*La maison des hommes*).
156. Plan of Paris '37, summary sketch (*Destin de Paris*).
157. Plan of Paris '46, summary sketch.

declared unhealthy already in 1923 according to the sanitary records of P. Juillerat) that would be the motor for the entire operation of transformation.

Le Corbusier measures the applicability of the model at different scales. The area of the Îlot, the closest to the center of the city, with its elongated end toward the north, impedes the passage of the Grande Traversée that was starting to be built at this point. This surprising shift in strategy leaves the plan suspended between two concessions: the progressive substitution of the existing city, or better, of the metamorphosis that begins only with the origin of its form and the one of the plan as an aggregate of circumstances and partial modifications around an idea of the city. Also in this case the solution is not an immediate one, but intervenes only when Le Corbusier admits the contradictions between the role that the plan assigns to this area and its projection as a "concrete case of urbanization," that is, when the *redent* defines itself within the context of the real city, breaking the rule of its placement on the ground as defined by the model, conserving its properties and character as well. The model mediates the rapport of intervention/context not only in the definition of its building character, but also in the correlation of the parts (as one can deduct from the placement of the urban utilities along the traversal). It doesn't repeat the localizing and accessibility criteria. A symmetry is easily discernible in the western part of the plan where the Opéra can be found. The perspective with the caption that accompanies it—"The Opéra deprived of the space that Charles Garnier dreamed of giving it, seventy years later would find an indisputably favorable frame"[12]—completely interprets the analogy. This is one of the few vistas from inside the plan, a demostration of an idea of space but also an affirmation of the correct redistribution of the existing elements in the new urban system. All the same, the series of plans is not complete. A perspectival vista from the east in which the four skyscrapers appear by themselves, is published in *La maison des hommes*. The center of the representation is the large void that opens at their base. The monuments of Paris that Le Corbusier had multiplied and reproduced in a fabric "of their own nature," buried at the feet of the large *cube bâti* (built cube) and of the hill of Mercury (Montmartre), are brought to light, returned to a condition of pure archeology, immersed in a continuous grand design on the foreign ground of each form in the, above all, different geometric fabric of the *lotissements*.

In *Propos d'urbanisme*, written in 1946, he compares the last stage of development of Paris, the *Plan 7*, to a definitive text that will serve as an immutable frame for the new architectural projects successively drawn up for Paris. The four office buildings placed within the order of the large forms of the site rise up at the entrance of the valley between Montmartre and Buttes-Chaumont; "In front of these buildings, in successive stages, large green surfaces would be recovered from the actual concretion, allowing, nevertheless, the conservation of antique treasures."[13] Model and city are now clearly distinct. "In this plain, furrowed with useless buildings, which extends toward Saint-Denis, far from the testimony of the past concentrated on the banks of the river, four large architectural events will occupy a vast area, glorifying civilization that far from abdicating has given back to itself a line of conduct."[14] But that distance is already the same distance separating the plan from its realization. The plan has lost its function, it will no longer determine the existing conditions of architecture. From now on its "types," solitary like cathedrals, would be spread throughout the great European map, testimonials of a civilization that never fell. The Plan of Paris can be compared to other texts that Le Corbusier rewrote many times, in particular the Plan of Algiers, because the two projects have a similar symmetrical end. In Algiers the project-become-plan loses its control over the place; in Paris the four buildings that repeat the large parallel lines of the site would no longer need the plan. It is 1936 in which the plans of Paris and Algiers find a significant point of encounter. This rapport would later be underscored by an almost identical image common to both. In 1948 Le Corbusier realizes the mural painting at the Swiss Pavilion of the Cité Universitaire of Paris. A figure of a winged woman, symbol of the city that is reborn like a Phoenix, trusts its fate to the same hands that raise it in the figure of the book cover for *Poésie sur Alger* (1950). *Garder mon aile dans ta main.*

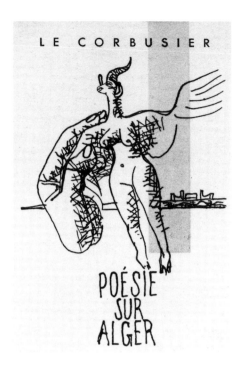

158. Book cover of Le Corbusier's book, *Poésie sur Alger*, 1950.
159. Plan of Paris '46, perspectival sketch (*La maison des hommes*).

[12] Le Corbusier, *Plans*, no. 4, April 1931.
[13] *Le Corbusier—Oeuvre complète 1938–46*, W. Boesiger, ed., Zürich, Girsberger, 1946, p. 142.
[14] *Le Corbusier—Oeuvre complète 1938–46*, p. 143.

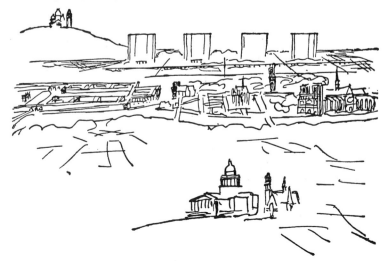

SOUTH AMERICA ALGIERS

Gianugo Polesello

The Plans for the Capital Cities of South America (Rio de Janeiro, Montevideo, São Paolo, Buenos Aires) appear in 1929 in the theoretical and practical experimentation of Architecture begun by Le Corbusier with the Plan for a Contemporary city of three million inhabitants and with the Plan of Paris.

The vehicles of communication for the new proposal (even if it is not its nature of being *one*, as much as a vehicle for showing architectural solutions, combinations, influences that are urban answers to the particular problems of each city evaluated in their singularity and, at the same time, *almost* as if in relation to a *theory*) are first of all the lectures "improvised in 1929 often before a changing audience," preserved later in notes taken during the return trip to France and successively transformed into a book in 1930.[1]

There exist, in addition, other books and other texts by Le Corbusier that link these experiments to a more complex case (complex because of the quantity of technical, ethical-political, economic-urban, etc. considerations that make up a much described circumstantial "emblem"), comprising the sequence of Plans for Algiers, starting with the Plan Obus of 1931.

One of the issues that doesn't concern critical history alone, is represented in this very sequence of experiments that is at times contradictory; however, it certainly cannot be organized in a chronological manner alone, and in this sense it represents a segment of theory even having the characteristics of a "reconstruction in time."

For example, the Plan Obus is transformed: it becomes Project B, assumes the "Fiorini tensile-structure," and is reduced in the process into the Marina with Project C.

But (and this is an expanded time span after the 1930s and during the first half of the decade arriving at the Plan of Paris in 1936) this type of experience is interwoven with others: the Plan of Moscow and the Ville

[1] Le Corbusier, *Précisions sur un état présent de l'architecture et de l'urbanisme*, Paris, Crès (coll. Esprit Nouveau), 1930; reissued, Paris, Vincent Fréal, 1960.

160. Prospect of Rio de Janeiro with steamship and highway-edifices seen from the sea (*La Ville Radieuse*).

Radieuse, the research on the mass-produced sky-scraper as "isolated architecture" and one based on the principle of *grandeur conforme* (uniform grandeur), etc.

Obviously there exist useful contributions toward the understanding of "plans" and "ideas" that he had been accumulating on urban issues such as the problem of the plan and its particular rapport that had been building up between architecture and urbanism before the hypotheses of substantial coincidence of *one* urban issue with *one* "plan issue."

In this sense Le Corbusier himself inclines toward his direct contribution or toward the supervisory operations and the construction of a text (*Oeuvre complète*) made up of images, written descriptions, aphorisms, slogans, drawings, and sketches.

In the text (and also in *La ville Radieuse* of 1933) the distance between Algiers and the South American cities is great: the South American experiences, as intellectual, visual, poetic experiences, end up being dominant.

To a dominant dimension for Nature, till then unknown, seems to correspond a reactive action, monotony, for example, and the insistence of the proposal to build a highway in a "plan outside of everything" descending from which the city would be developed.

These intellectual experiences and this new dimension of the "natural," appear most manifestly throughout the writings, through words; but to these classifications is almost juxtaposed the rational montage that makes up the "theorem Ville Radieuse" in seventeen charts.

If this appearance of separateness and almost contrast between the "cases" (Algiers, and the cities of South America) and the "theory" (La Ville Radieuse) is almost solicited in the texts themselves (*Oeuvre complète, La Ville Radieuse*), it is also described in the sustained critical attention given those plastic aspects of architecture that in a grand setting use architectonic characteristics (mass, contour, different levels, etc.)

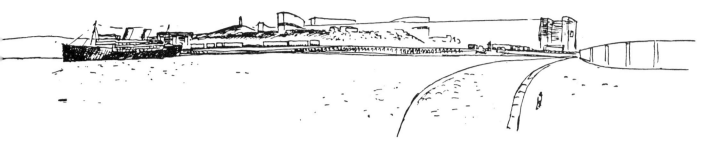

existing in Nature and Art, and that are proposed for a city on a specific site.

Obviously there are different ways of interpreting the text of *Précisions* itself that, with figure-symbol and with words, shows the repertory of ideas and concepts of Le Corbusier on industrial and contemporary civilizations, and the possible hypotheses able to give meaning to the inextricable tangle that makes up the tentacular cities (according to the expression in vogue).

In relation to these "different ways," I have found it useful *today* to point out (and apply) the analogies of similarities of situations that are presented in those plans that are still "contemporaneous" to us, if we wish to see them more in their technical generalities than in their poetic individuality.

Moreover, it doesn't help in trying to understand this problem (general and technical, because it concerns all contemporary cities that have been transformed in their internal structure through additive growth, repeated quantitative modifications leading to structural contortions) to have some description such as: "Le Corbusier adopts skyscrapers that use the *organic* lines of the *crescents* of Bath" employed by Siegfried Giedion to establish a "relation with the present," between an urbanism that had its very roots in the English practice of crescents or in the architecture of the 1700s and Baroque of the Plan Obus (text by S. Giedion: "Le Corbusier, plan of the skyscraper in Algiers, 1931. The late-Baroque spatial concessions are very close to contemporary solutions such as this one." It is the caption below an illustration on page 151 of the Italian edition, *Spazio, Tempo, Architettura,* that is the photomontage of an aereal view of Algiers from the east and that includes the quarters of the Marina and the hill of Fort-L'Empereur).

I want to state that the theoretical practice of the trip to South America, along with the plans and studies for Algiers, can take on great value for us today; not in

161. Prospect of Algiers with steamship, "Goodby to Algiers," July 1934 (*La Ville Radieuse*).

Siegfried Giedion's sense of activating a new architectural "linguistics," but in proposing architectural solutions partial to our cities, coherent with the necessary internal reasons controlled by technology and accomplished in the construction of new structures for the existing cities.

This is the problem that turns up in a superimposed reading of the "South American plans" in their ensemble and the Ville Radieuse or in a parallel analysis of the succession of plans for Algiers and for the (much later) plan of Buenos Aires, or, again, for the Plan of Barcelona.

There is no exegesis of Le Corbusier's complex of plans: everything stops with the Map of Athens or the Plan Obus, inserted between the Norm and the Exceptional, insisting (at least according to the communal sense that circulates in our Schools of Architecture) on the distinctions or, directly, on the separation between architecture and plan, and delivering, where the case lends itself, the plan through architecture.

We know that after the 1930 edition of *Précisions*, a new edition appeared in 1960 with a new preface by Le Corbusier; that the plan of Buenos Aires would assume the figure of a technically defined plan; that out of the South American intuition and reflections would come the Plan Obus and the sequence of successive proposals for Algiers.

But we also know that in 1930 itself, the "plan" for Moscow becomes *autonomous*, takes on the value of an *autonomous theory of the city*, of the big city, and is proposed as the "Ville Radieuse."

In the seventeen charts illustrating the Ville Radieuse, the existing city (inextricable, tentacular, radio-concentric, inaccessible) is not discernible: the "Ville Radieuse" is a general scheme, the general system of reference for the construction *of* the city.

It could also be said that it is in fact a substitute for the existing city, but is not antithetical to it.

In fact, in the architectural figures placed on the horizontal geometric plane, Le Corbusier separates the activities-functions that correspond to an organization-unity in the figure of the micro-city. Thus the Cité des Affaires, the Cité Residentielle, the industrial-productive one with areas for highway interchanges and large warehouses, are separated from each other by large green belts and barriers and interconnected by an *autonomous* network of roads for individual and mass transportation.

The reflections and propositions formulated in South America are not *all*; but one of the nodes within the study of the theory and practice of the city is the question of the compatibility between different researches and experiments, between the South American operation and its transplantation to Algiers, between the totalizing framework of "technical" urbanistic plans and the persuasiveness and efficacy of the timely and decisive architectural interventions.

In other words: to this simultaneity, or quasi-simultaneity, between Algiers (Plan Obus) and the Ville Radieuse, only one chronological notation corresponds. Or does a rapport between those of the "case/theory" type exist?

To answer this question, the record of some theoretical antecedents is called for, in the first place, the theoretical value of the concept "dominant." In the general scheme of La Ville Radieuse, the following proposition is written below: "*La résidence constitue l'élément primordial (de la ville)*." I maintain that this is the logical premise that rules the entire theoretical scaffolding and practice of Le Corbusier's work; even the South American studies.

That the modern urban residential concentrations are, in fact, haphazard extensions of a number of buildings; that those are without dimension or quality; negating every possibility of distinction and character at their interior, they are not emblematic of a place nor of any internal logic in their construction. They are dictated by uniformity, by inexhaustible, meaningless repetition, etc., which is verifiable in each one of our cities.

theless enumerated the true experiences of modern architecture and culture. This insistence on introspection in the analysis of the urban interior through non-architectural means (that is, without architectural analysis of the built city) has led to the negation of the constitutive material of the city itself, valued and consisting of its true civic dimension and role, and has led, on the one side, to the consideration of the residential problem in the city as merely a problem of regulating *extensive* growth and development, with little attention to the architectural and urbanistic problems that in the existing city are also greatly manifest; and on the other, to confining the role of architecture to a concern with the residential building and the new residential demands in terms of *housing* (one can say in the economic-technical sense) or in pure terms, singular architectural manufacture, considered in its individuality or in its group arrangements (the apartments or the Siedlung).

The problem of *building* the city today starting with the new redevelopment of this "material" is, it seems to

162. Sketch for lecture with the proposal for
Montevideo, 1929 (*Précisions*).

me, a problem common to many plans and studies that
appeared in that period and that, starting with the
South American studies themselves, takes shape after
the Plan Voisin.

Two procedural and foundational directions along
with a possible conjugation of architecture and
urbanism appear in those studies with a visual efficacy
(becoming extraordinary in the case of Algeria):
—the system "dominates," that is, the construction of
definite physical or functional configurations through
the study, the in-depth analyses that concern the city
in general (city="economic" fact in its historical dimensions) and the particular rapport of each urban
organization with the site, as a plot between technology
and nature. The "dominant" system defines difference
or analogies between situations, measures why it is in
possession of parameters, etc.
—the definition of an area of existence of the urban
phenomenon in which to intervene. That is, the question of the *grandeur conforme*, within a certain ho-
mologous institution, between technology (the technology of practical engineering and of the large constructions in the cases under examination) and Nature and
dimensions of the object phenomenon of the plan;
practically a consequent classification of the analysis,
built from reality, using concepts and categories that
allow the construction of a model that would be half-
way (a homology, in fact) between the city assumed in
all its materiality and nature and technology as an

Gianugo Polesello

[2] Le Corbusier, *Précisions*, p. 276.

ensemble; an archive of classified, catalogued, ordered experience that comprises the *rules* for the construction of the mass-produced and *the already built mass-produced* buildings, elements that are notable, known, reusable, true, and actually *outils* (useful).

Presenting the "products" of the South American trip in synthesis in *Oeuvre complète*, Le Corbusier gathered them under the title: "ÉTUDE D'URBANISATION EN AMÉRIQUE DU SUD, 1929: São Paolo du Bresil, Rio de Janeiro, Buenos Aires," declaring that the sketches presented evoke completely new concessions of urbanization using modern techniques whose principle consists in the establishment of large layouts for automobile traffic in the large inextricable cities. The construction of these roads would then allow useful answers to the question of new ground for building in as much as these same road constructions would also become artificial terrain.

In *Précisions* this objective is clear: "The builders of the machine age have not yet come to understand that the road is no longer a crust placed on top of the earth, but that it is a *horizontal construction*, a building: a *container* and not a skin."[2]

The projected highway-edifices are therefore the instrument for simultaneously resolving this declared double order of problems:

—the new demand for housing;

—the growing demand for transportation.

The various cases corresponding to the different cities do not have a precise analytical representation: the display of the localization of the existing or potential Cité des Affaires, of the harbor areas, the principal natural places, comes from them.

A sort of prevalence of some site-problems over other parts (but they are not yet parts, they are extensions) of the urban phenomenon are intuited, designing (as in a modern, mythic foundational act) the coordinates-categories over which more internal planning could take place without any successive actions.

The two bird's-eye view plan-sketches for Montevideo and for São Paolo use the same device: the horizontal elevated highway that climbs, like a Roman acqueduct, through external and internal valleys of the built city, the houses inside the three-dimensional road and beneath it.

In the case of Montevideo and São Paolo, the highway network becomes the only axis that appears on the summit of the hill near the Center, in the Cité des Affaires.

Here, where the road ends, the new architectural figures of the city find each other reunited: a cruciform

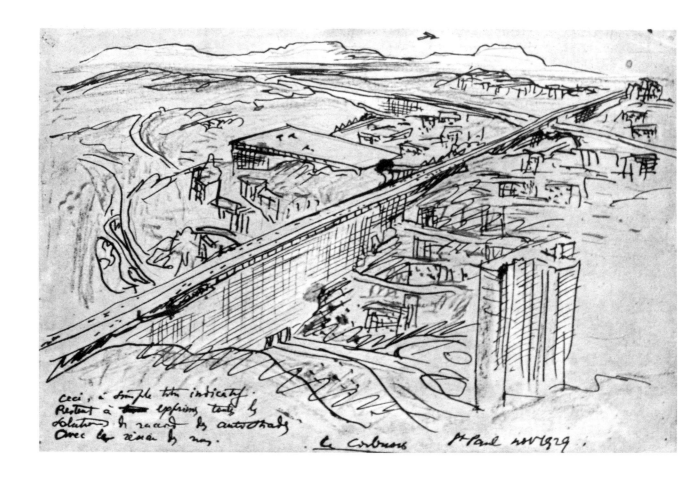

163. Sketch of the proposal for São Paolo, 1929.

[3] Ibid., p. 264.
[4] Ibid., p. 266.
[5] From the text of the same lecture, in 1929, in *Précisions*, p. 171.
[6] Le Corbusier, *Précisions*, p. 270.

skyscraper thrust into the earth, beyond the surface of the hill a forum, a parking lot for cars.

In São Paolo the "cross of streets" cuts across the entire city according to two orthogonal diameters of 45 kilometers.

The project recalls the "cross of Berlin" of M. Machler, taken up by L. Hilberseimer in *Grosstadtarchitektur* of 1927: ". . . if one were to proceed in this manner: stopping at one hill and another, from one summit to the other, a horizontal bar 45 kilometers long, and successively a second bar of the same genre, at approximately a right angle to the first, in such a way as to serve the four cardinal points. These bars are the highways of mass entry to the city, in effect, also of mass crossing . . . The highways I propose to you are gigantic viaducts . . .

What a magnificent appearance the place would assume! How much larger than the acqueduct of Segovia, how much more gigantic than the Pont du Gard!"[3]

In both cases (but it would be also thus in Rio and Algiers) the problem becomes opportunity, a point of departure for a functional twist of the urban machine and for its remaining in motion; the whole according to a procedure that the elements, the sites or functions, once ascertained, their transformative potential once evaluated, become the essential triggers for the process of restructuring, whether it is the shift from a given structure at the limits or its functional capacity to a new structure.

Only the case of Rio is formally different: here the highway-viaducts run sinuously from place to place becoming an "ensemble" of constructed places. "A branch of this highway can arrive at Pão de Açucar; this branch then develops, with an ample, magestic, elegant curve . . ."[4] etc.

In this design it is difficult to separate the distinct elements that comprise it, from one branch of the highway to another. Or, at least, it is more difficult to gather the meaning of an operation that in São Paolo or at Montevideo is more peremptory.

It is possible that the designs for Rio address a more general problem: they concern, in effect, the *scale* of the city, in the way that they concern the *scale* of the interventions, the *scale* of nature, etc. They repropose, additionally, a problem such as this one: "What is well planned will conquer. The city that is well planned will conquer. The country that has a well planned capital will conquer."[5]

And further still, in the same text: "When the solutions are truly comprehensive, and nature felicitously harmonizes with them: further still, when nature comes to be integrated, it is then that we have come close to *unity*."[6]

In respect to the other South American cities, Buenos Aires is assumed to be a different case, in that only much later will the "Plan" concern the city as a whole (like Barcelona, extraordinarily similar to Buenos Aires in some of its solutions), indeed recuperating the original "idea," pertaining to a new Cité des Affaires, a new airport, etc.; in fact, a new system of facilities (" . . . urbanism is a problem of facilities, implementation").

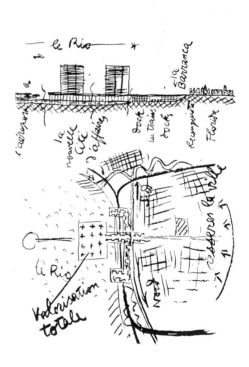

The Plan of Buenos Aires "explains" more than any other plan, perhaps, the events of the sequence of plans for Algiers: I mean that the centering of a place (as an emblem of an absolutely regular city, Buenos Aires, in its "*cuadras*" (city blocks) measuring 110 meters per side, with a congested traffic circulation, with a Cité des Affaires contained in its very interior), positioning it on the sea, in front of the City, creating a system of efficient grounds that allow the construction of new facilities, functional in its modern role as big city, as capital, the connection of this place with the internal territory, beyond the city, traversing its con-

164. Sketch for lecture with the proposal for Rio de Janeiro, 1929 (*Précisions*).
165. Sketch for lecture with the proposal for Buenos Aires, 1929 (*Précisions*).

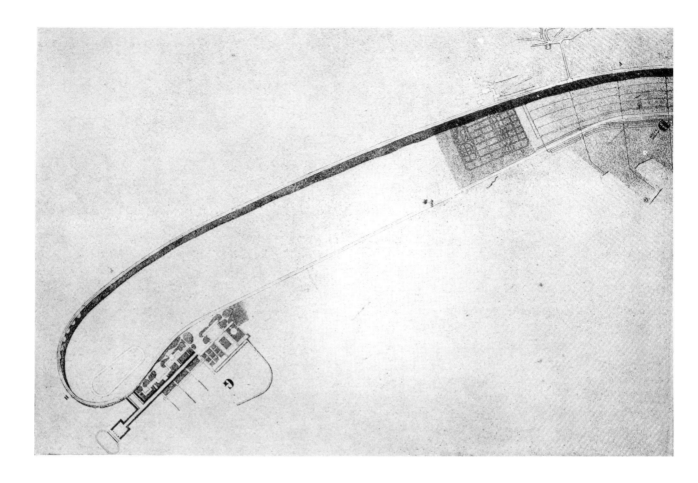

166. Algiers, Plan Obus, general planimetric drawing of the urbanistic intervention and principles.

structed parts with diagonals, etc.; all of this procedure shows up the "mechanics" of a "planning system" that joins urbanistic requirements to the programming of a territory through architectural actions, in a succession (also temporal) that maintains the unity of the ensemble's logic.

The "reduction" of the Plan Obus to the Plan C points up the analytical procedure as a backward process that operates through approaches and connections to the plan itself.

In this sense, in going from Plan C to the Plan Obus, it is possible to gather not only an assonance or analogy between the South American experiments and those that would be completed in Algiers, but it is possible to understand the technical value of instrument, procedure, of "pieces" tried out in South America (for example, the cruciform skyscrapers or the *logis* of the *immeubles-villas*) or inventions (the three-dimensional highways, the urbanized viaducts).

The large curvilinear layouts proposed for the front part of Baía di Rio, are closed up in Algiers and don't lead *anywhere*: they become a "crown," as Le Corbusier put it, placed in Algiers' head. But the Plan Obus does not consist in *this*.

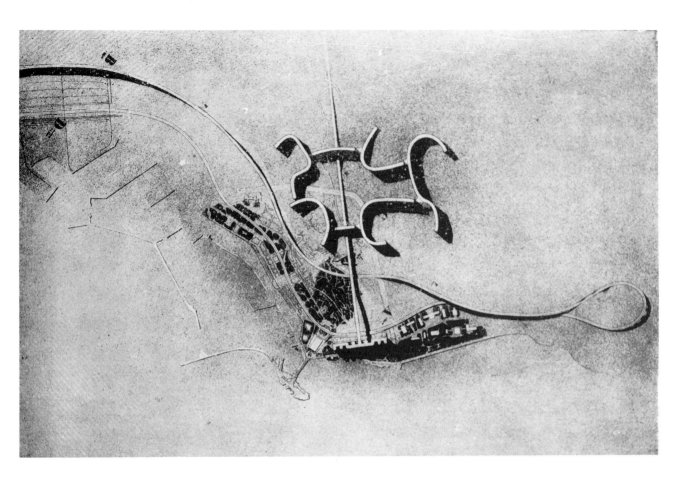

According to Le Corbusier, "the project is composed of three parts:

A—*Création d'une Cité des Affaires* . . .

B—*Création d'une Cité de résidence* . . .

C—*Liaison des deux banlieus extrèmes d'Alger: St Eugène à Hussein-Dey par une route autostradale établie à la côte 100* . . . (Link between distant suburbs of Algiers: St-Eugène to Hussein-Dey by a highway established at coast 100 . . .)"[7]

In fact, not all the relations between the three parts. have the same value: the relation A and B, in Plan B, would become a large axis linking Fort-l'Empereur to the Marina buildings furnished with the "Fiorini tensile structure," transformed into an architectural connection, with its own technical autonomy.

Thus the highway will loose its efficacy as container of residences along the hills overlooking the sea; the plan will "dry up" and "harden" at the Marina quarters, with experiments that would take up the scale of the isolated buildings, of the *localized* skyscraper.

It is the Marina quarter that will become the place for those facilities that should have made Algiers a capital ("*capitale d'Afrique, pointe sud du quadrilatère Paris, Rome, Barcelone, Alger*"). In

[7] *Le Corbusier et Pierre Jeanneret—Oeuvre complète 1929–34*, W. Boesiger, ed., Zürich, Girsberger, 1935, pp. 140–42.

167. Algiers, Plan B, perspective view (FLC).

their turn the quarters of the Marina would become, in Plan C, a complex place, organizing *all* of the new city on the sea, with its "extensions" and facilities.

In 1938, ten years after the trip to South America and the intuitive plans, the Plan of Buenos Aires is presented in the technical role of *Plan directeur* (Master plan). The original proposals, that had been completely accounted for on the estuary in the nocturnal view of aligned skyscrapers, are now confirmed and become one of the places of intervention *on* the city, also on the waterfront, expanded to the point of including the airport on the south and the Cité Universitaire on the north.

This is one of the few plans that Le Corbusier would draw up as "technical instrument," according to which judicial, and technical efficacy are attributed.

It is interesting and useful, certainly, to relate the dimensions (along with the problems) of the Buenos Aires of 1938 to the Buenos Aires of our time, to verify the retention of some (and which ones) of the choices at work then, etc.

There exists a system—unaltered in its persuasiveness, it seems to me—of foundational propositions, propositions that in their reciprocal re-

Gianugo Polesello

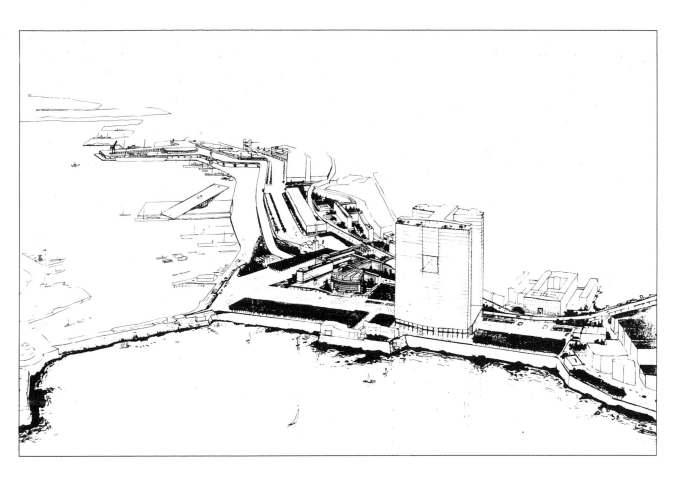

168. Algiers, Plan C, the proposed interventions for the Marina quarter (FLC).

lations *are* the plan. The perimeter of the plan is the limit of the geographical area that, from the Costanera Sur (including the projected airport), remains defined from the Riachuelo to the south and from the Avenue General Paz on the west before touching, in corre spondence with the Cité Universitaire, again with the Rio de la Plata.

In 1938, this natural and artificial layout comprised the entire city, its expansions, the surrounding areas organized into satellite cities, etc. Today this limit has been overtaken practically along the entire perimeter, but "the city" remains localized still in the original site, along the Rio de la Plata and the front that faces the estuary; it is still the "place" indicated by Le Corbusier in his plan, which included the airport, the harbor areas, the business district, all of the creative and productive part of the urban installation.

The question today is the practicality of any (or all) the solutions proposed for an urban area from now on deprived of dimension, an area that has gone past the demographic threshold of ten million, that maintains unaltered a foundation based on the grid of Spanish colonizations, that has undertaken its own, internal traffic structures, figures and dimensions of the "city in

169. Algiers, Plan H, perspective sketch with skyscraper of the Marina (FLC).
170. Buenos Aires, urban proposal; three "cuadras" (city blocks) measuring 400x400 meters organize the new city.

expansion" in which the roads from the interior of the continent cross the urban area to flow together in the center.

It is still, then, a place like Algiers or Barcelona.

That the updating of the Map of Athens could assume, at bottom, the characteristics of architecturally defined sites, of an ensemble of manufactured constructions with their own character; that the urban roads and the system of fast internal connections between the various parts of the city could result in a structural value of a purely functional (infrastructural) kind, without becoming actual *buildings*, was rather difficult to foresee.

The plan for Buenos Aires shows (can be used to show) fundamentally that:

—the metropolitan areas can *also* have an urban "government";

—the question of internal connections and interconnections becomes dominant in relation to problems of accessibility from outside in reference to physical systems (road axes, interior city, etc.) become finite elements; architecture is constrained to exert itself in a new field of "interior planning" of the city;

—the "zoning" can be "localized," or can solve strategic functions within "the government," within the urban actions of government in a metropolitan area;

—the "architectures" can, then, "be confused with," assume, the functions of zoning in those places in the city that assure, confirm the "necessity," the fixed points, the coordinates of the plan.

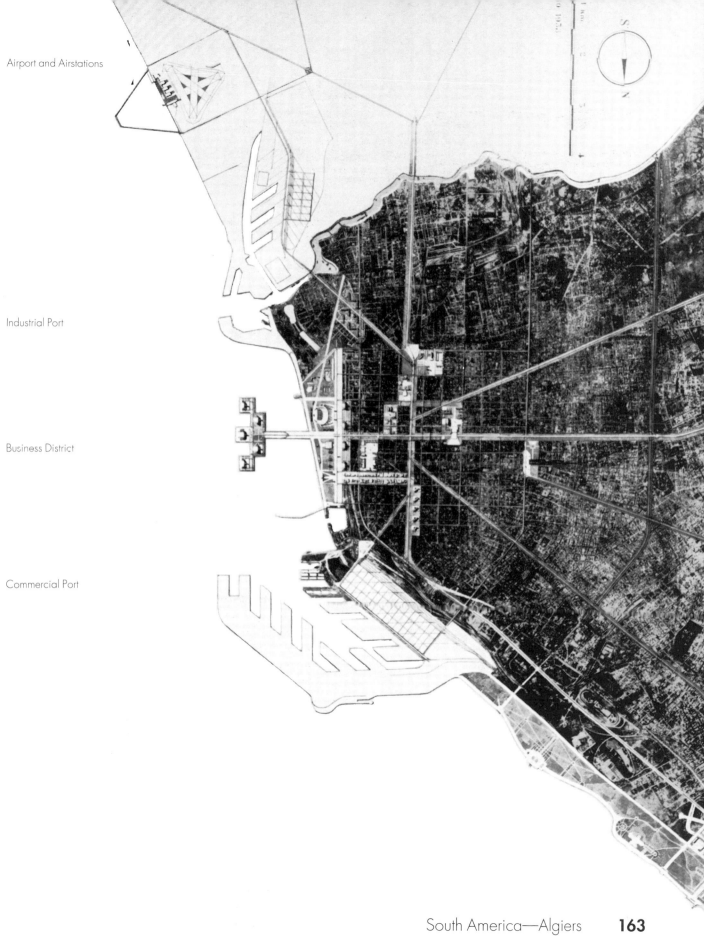

Airport and Airstations

Industrial Port

Business District

Commercial Port

LA VILLE RADIEUSE

Rem Koolhaas

In 1929 Le Corbusier realizes a Floating Asylum for the Parisian Salvation Army.

His barge offers accomodations for up to 160 *clochards*. They are arranged in pairs of double-decker beds along the length of the barge, which is made of *reinforced concrete*.

(Bums are the ideal clients of modern architecture: in perpetual need of shelter and hygiene, real lovers of sun and the great outdoors, indifferent to architectural doctrine and to formal layout.)

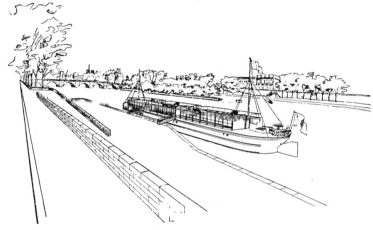

171. The floating asylum, Louise Catherine, Paris, 1929.

Le Corbusier's favorite method of objectification—of making his structures *critical*—is reinforced concrete.

Broken down in sequence, reinforced concrete construction proceeds as follows.

First, the conjectural structure of shuttering is erected—the negative of the initial thesis.

Then steel reinforcements—dimensioned strictly according to the rational principles of Newtonian Physics—are inserted: the reinforcing process of paranoiac calculation.[1]

Then a mouse-grey liquid is poured into the empty speculative counterforms to give them permanent life on earth, an undeniable reality, especially after the

[1] Reference is made here to the Paranoid-Critical Method, defined by Salvador Dalí as: "the spontaneous method of irrational knowledge based on the critical and systematic objectifications of delirious associations and interpretations . . ."; irrationally morbid conjectures, sustained by the crutch of Cartesian rationalism. I have treated this theme more comprehensively in terms of the responses of Le Corbusier and Dalí to New York in the chapter "Europeans: Biuer! Dalí and Le Corbusier Conquer New York", in *Delirious New York*, London, Academy Editions, 1977, pp. 199–233.

signs of the initial madness—the shuttering—have been removed, leaving only the fingerprints of the wood's grain.

Infinitely malleable at first, then suddenly hard as rock, reinforced concrete can objectify vacuity and fullness with equal ease: it is the architect's plastic.

It is Le Corbusier's all-consuming ambition to invent and build the new city commensurate with the demands and potential glories of the machine civilization.

It is tragic bad luck that such a city already exists when he develops this ambition, namely Manhattan.

Le Corbusier's task is clear: before he can deliver the city with which he is pregnant, he has to prove that it does not yet exist. To establish the birthright of his brainchild, he has to destroy New York's credibility, kill the glamorous sparkle of modernity. From 1920 he fights on two fronts simultaneously: waging a systematic campaign of ridicule and defamation against the American Skyscraper and its natural habitat, Manhattan, while carrying out a parallel operation of actually designing the anti-Skyscraper and the anti-Manhattan.

For Le Corbusier New York's Skyscrapers are "child's play,"[2] "an architectural accident . . . Ima-

[2] Le Corbusier, *La Ville Radieuse* (Paris: Vincent Fréal, 1964), caption, p. 129.

gine a man undergoing a mysterious disturbance of his organic life; the torso remains normal, but his legs become ten or twenty times too long."[3] Skyscrapers are misshapen "adolescents of the machine age," "handled nonsensically as the result of a deplorably romantic city ordinance"[4]—the 1916 Zoning Law.

They represent not the second (real) Machine Age, but the "tumult, hairgrowth, first explosive stage of the new middle ages . . ."[5] They are immature, *not yet* modern.

For the inhabitants of this grotesque congregation of architectural cripples, Le Corbusier feels only pity: "in the age of speed, the skyscraper has petrified the city. The skyscraper has re-established the pedestrian, him alone . . . He moves anxiously near the bottom of the skyscraper, louse at the foot of the tower. The louse hoists himself up in the tower; it is night in the tower oppressed by the other towers: sadness, depression . . . But on the top of those skyscrapers taller than the others the louse becomes radiant. He sees the ocean and boats, he is above the other lice . . ."

That he is exhilarated, not by nature but because he is eye to eye with the other Skyscrapers, is inconceivable to Le Corbusier, for there, at the top, these strange skyscrapers are usually crowned by some academic contraption.

"The louse is flattered. The louse loves it."

"The louse approves of these expenses to decorate the cork of his skyscraper. . . ."[6]

Le Corbusier's campaign of denigration is made possible only by the fact that his strategist has never beheld the object of his aggression—an ignorance which he carefully preserves for the duration of his attacks— and that for his audience, too, his imputations are unverifiable.

Le Corbusier's portrait of New York is an identikit: a purely speculative collage of its criminal urbanistic features.

In book after book, Manhattan's guilt is illustrated in a series of hasty paste-ups of grainy images—fabricated mugshots—that show no resemblance with his supposed adversary.

Le Corbusier's passionate involvement with New York is, in fact, a 15-year-long attempt to cut an umbilical cord. In spite of his angry obliterations he is still secretly nourished by its reservoir of precedents and models.

[3] Le Corbusier, *When the Cathedrals Were White—A Journey to the Country of Timid People* (New York: Reynal & Hitchcock, 1947), p. 89.
[4] Le Corbusier, *When the Cathedrals Were White*.
[5] Le Corbusier, *La Ville Radieuse*, p.133.
[6] Ibid., p.127.

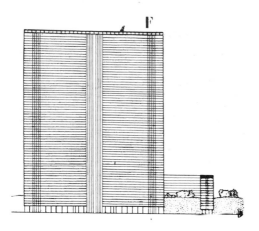

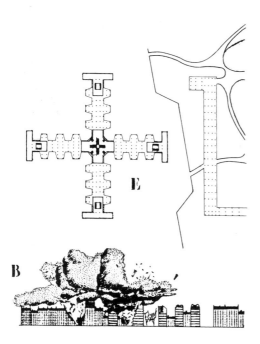

7 As quoted in Hellman, "From Within to With-out", *New Yorker*, April 27–May 3, 1947.

When he finally "introduces" his anti-Skyscraper he is like a prestidigitator accidentally giving away his trick: he makes the American Skyscraper disappear in the black velvet pouch of his speculative universe, adds jungle (nature at its purest possible form), then shakes up the uncompatible elements in his paranoid-critical top hat and—surprise!—pulls out the *Horizontal* Skyscraper, a Cartesian rabbit.

In this performance both the skyscraper and the jungle become unrecognizable.

The Skyscraper turns into a Cartesian (= French = Rational) abstraction, the jungle into a carpet of green vegetation that is supposed to hold the Skyscrapers together.

Usually after such paranoid-critical kidnappings of concepts from their natural contexts, the victims are forced to spend the rest of their lives in disguise. But the essence of New York's Skyscrapers is that they already wear costumes.

Before, European architects have tried to design superior costumes. But Le Corbusier understands that the only way to make the Skyscraper unrecognisable is to *undress* it.

The Cartesian Skyscraper is naked. In his blind rage, Le Corbusier has stripped Manhattan's towers, expecting to find the rational core of the true Machine Age.

Top and base have been amputated from the original Manhattan model; the part in between is stripped of its "old fashioned" stone cladding, dressed in glass and stretched to 220 meters.

It is exactly the rational Skyscraper that Manhattan's official Thinkers always *pretended* they wanted to realize, while in practice they steered as far away from it as possible. The make believe of Manhattan's architects—pragmatism, efficiency and rationality—has colonized the mind of a European. "To say skyscraper is to say offices, that is businessmen and automobiles . . ."[7]

Le Corbusier's Skyscraper means business only. Its lack of a base and a top, the merciless overexposures to the sun implied by the thin cruciform of its plan, all preclude occupation by any of the forms of social intercourse that have begun to conquer Manhattan, floor by floor. By stripping off the reassuring exterior architecture that allowed the ideological hysteria of the interior architect to flourish, Le Corbusier even undoes the Great Lobotomy.

He introduces honesty on such a scale that it exists only at the price of total banality. (Most desirable social activity being allergic to daylight.)

There is no place here for Manhattan's Technology of the Fantastic. For Le Corbusier, *use* of technology as instrument and extension of the imagination equals *abuse*. True believer in the myth of technology from the distance of Europe, for him technology itself is fantastic. It has to remain virginal, can only be displayed in its purest form, a strictly totemistic presence.

The glass walls of his horizontal Skyscraper enclose a programmatic void.

Le Corbusier names the Assembly of these Cartesian Skyscrapers implanted in their park—the remains of the jungle—the *Radiant City*.

If the Cartesian Skyscraper is the antipode of New York's primitive towers, then the Radiant City is finally Le Corbusier's anti-Manhattan.

"You are under the shade of trees."

"Vast lawns spread all around you. The air is clean and pure; there is hardly any noise . . ."

"What? You cannot see where the buildings are?"

"Look through the charmingly diapered arabesques of branches out into the sky toward those widely spaced crystal towers that soar higher than any pinnacle on earth."

"Those translucent prisms that seems to float in the air without anchorage to the ground, flashing in summer sunshine, softly gleaming under grey winter skies,

173. The Cartesian Skyscraper, section and plan: subway in the basement, surrounding park with elevated highways, sixty floors of offices, and, at top, "armored platform against aerial bombardments . . ."
174. The secret formula of Le Corbusier's Radiant City: the "City of Panic [Manhattan] . . . in the jungle" (*La Ville Radieuse*).

[8] Ibid.; first its floors were reconfigured by the Soviet authorities in Moscow, but, as the realized city demonstrates, the Stalinists preferred a pure manhattanism in the manner of the *Metropolis of Tomorrow* of Hugh Ferriss.
[9] Le Corbusier, *La Ville Radieuse*, p. 207.

magically glittering at nightfall, are huge blocks of offices . . ."[8]

In designing the Cartesian Skyscraper as universal accomodation for business, to the exclusion of those indefinable emotional services that have been built into the Ferrisian Mountain, Le Corbusier is the credulous victim of the pragmatic fairy-tales of Manhattan's builders.

But his intention is even more destructive: to *really* solve the problems of congestion. Marooned in grass, his Cartesian convicts are lined up 400 meters apart (i.e. eight Manhattan blocks—*but with nothing in between*). They are spaced out beyond any possible association. Le Corbusier has correctly perceived that Manhattan has "re-established the pedestrian, him alone." The essence of Manhattan is exactly that it is an ultra-modern supervillage *enlarged to the scale of a Metropolis*, a collection of Mega-"houses" where traditional and mutant lifestyles are simultaneously supported and provoked by the most fantastic infrastructure ever devised.

When he first strips, then isolates the Skyscrapers and finally connects them with a network of elevated highways so that automobiles (= businessmen = modern) instead of pedestrians (= medieval) can shuttle freely from tower to tower over a carpet of Chlorophyl-producing agents, he solves the problem but kills the Culture of Congestion.

He creates the urban non-event that New York's planners have always avoided (despite their lip-service to it): decongested congestion.

Through the twenties, as Manhattan is "removing stone by stone the Alhambra, the Kremlin and the Louvre" to "build them anew on the banks of the Hudson," Le Corbusier dismantles New York, smuggles it back to Europe and stores it for future reconstruction. So the Radiant City becomes a theoretical Metropolis in search of a location.

In 1925 the first attempt to graft it onto the face of the earth is made "in the name of the beauty and destiny of Paris."[9] The "Plan Voisin" is planned, it seems, according to the early Surrealist theorem *Le Cadavre Exquis*, whereby fragments are added to a body in deliberate ignorance of its further anatomy.

Lower housing blocks meander around eighteen Cartesian Skyscrapers that are arranged on a plain in central Paris where all traces of history have been scraped away to be replaced by "jungle": the so-called mobilization of the ground, from which even the Louvre barely escapes.

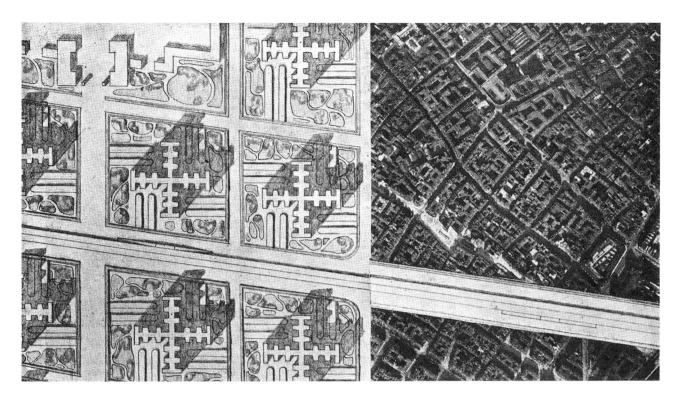

In spite of Le Corbusiers's dedication to Paris' future, this plan is clearly a pretext. The transplantation is intended to generate not a new Paris but a first anti-Manhattan.

"Our invention, from its beginning, was directed against the purely formalist and romantic conceptions of the American Skyscraper . . ."

"Against New York's skyscraper we erect the Cartesian skycraper, limpid, precise, elegantly shining in the sky of France . . ."

"Against New York, turbulent clamour of the giant adolescent of the machine age — I counteract with the horizontal skyscrapers. Paris, city of the straight line and the horizontal, will tame the vertical . . ."[10] Manhattan is humiliated in *Paris*.

The Radiant City is intended as the apotheosis of an experiment in architectural alchemy—one element turned into the other. But despite Le Corbusier's frantic efforts to outdistance Manhattan, the only way to describe his new city—verbally and even visually— is *in terms of its differences from Manhattan*.

The only way his city can be understood is by comparison and juxtaposition of the "negative" of Manhattan and the "positive" of the Ville Radieuse. The two are like Siamese twins that grow progressively together in spite of the surgeon's desperate efforts to separate them.

The Parisian authorities do not take the Radiant

[10] Ibid., p.134.

[11] See *New York Herald Tribune*, October 22, 1935.
[12] Le Corbusier, *When the Cathedrals Were White*, p. 197.
[13] Ibid., p. 92.
[14] Le Corbusier, "What is the American Problem?"; article written for *The American Architect*, published as an appendix in *When the Cathedrals Were White*, pp. 186–201.

Rem Koolhaas

invasion seriously. Their rejection forces Le Corbusier to become a Cartesian carpetbagger, peddling his horizontal glass Skyscraper like a furious prince dragging a colossal glass slipper on an Odyssey from Metropolis to Metropolis.

In 1935—twelve years pregnant with the radiant city—Le Corbusier sails for New York with the accumulated bitterness of a unwed mother, threatening, after the failure of all attempts to arrange an adoption, to lay phantom-foundling on the doorstep of his natural father and instigating a paternity suit.

At a press conference in Rockefeller Center a few hours after his arrival, Le Corbusier stuns New York's hard-boiled reporters with his Parisian diagnosis and remedy, which have survived the first confrontation with Manhattan intact.

After a cursory inspection of the New Babylon, he gave a simple recipe for its improvement.

"The trouble with New York is that the skyscrapers are too small. And there are too many of them."

Or, as New York's tabloids headline in disbelief, he finds "city all right as far as it goes . . ." but it is utterly lacking in order and harmony and the comforts of the spirit which must surround humanity.

"The skyscrapers are little needles all crowded together. They should be great obelisks, far apart, so that the city would have space and light and air and order . . ."

"These are the things that my town of Happy Light will have!"

"I believe within myself that the ideas I bring here and that I present under the phrase Radiant City will find in this country their natural ground . . ."[11]

"To reconstruct American cities and especially Manhattan, it is first necessary to know a place where the reconstruction can take place. *It is Manhattan, which is large enough to hold six million people . . .*"[12]

Manhattan itself is now one of the last remaining areas of the globe not yet exposed to Le Corbusier's hard sell.

But beyond this opportunistic urgency, there is a second, still more desperate motive: the real Manhattan confronts Le Corbusier—like the real America Columbus—with the fragility of his lifelong speculations. To secure the paranoid-critical reinforcements underlying his urbanism and prevent the collapse of his "system," he is forced (in spite of his almost irrepressible admiration) to persist in his earlier casting of the American Skyscrapers as innocent, even childish natives and of his own horizontal Cartesian Towers as the true settlers of the machine civilization.

Manhattan's Skyscrapers are Le Corbusier's Indians.

By substituting his anti-Manhattan for the real Manhattan, Le Corbuiser would not only assure himself of an inexhaustible supply of work, but destroy in the process all remaining evidence of his paranoid-critical transformations—wipe out, once and for all, the traces of his conceptual forgeries; he would finally become Manhattan's inventor.

The intransigence of this double motivation prepares the ground for a re-enactment—architectural this time—of the New World's primordial tragedy, the massacre of the Indians. Le Corbusier's urbanism unleashes exterminating principles which, with constantly augmenting force, will never cease to act until the whole aboriginal race—the Skyscrapers—are extirpated and their memory almost blotted from under heaven.

When Le Corbusier ominously condescends to his American audiences that "you are strong, we have reflected"[13] he warns them in effect that North American barbarism will make place for European refinement.

The Grid—"perfect in the age of the horse"—is to be scraped off the surface of the island and replaced by grass and a much wider network of elevated highways.

Central Park—"too large"—is to be shrunk, "its verdure distributed and multiplied throughout Manhattan . . ."

The Skyscrapers —"too small"— are to be razed and superseded by about a hundred identical Cartesian settlers implanted in the grass and framed by the highways.

So redesigned, Manhattan will be fit for six million inhabitants; Le Corbusier "will restore an immense area of ground . . . pay for the ruined properties . . . give the city verdure and excellent circulation; all the ground in parks for pedestrians and cars up in the air, on elevated roads, a *few roads* (one way) permitting a speed of ninety miles an hour and going . . . *simply from one skyscraper to another.*"[14] Le Corbusier's "solution" drains Manhattan of its lifeblood, congestion.

Sometimes a tourist returns from foreign lands unrecognizable. This has happened to the model of Manhattan on its paranoid-critical trans-Atlantic excursion.

The Skyscraper left as hedonistic instrument of the Culture of Congestion; it returns from Europe brain-

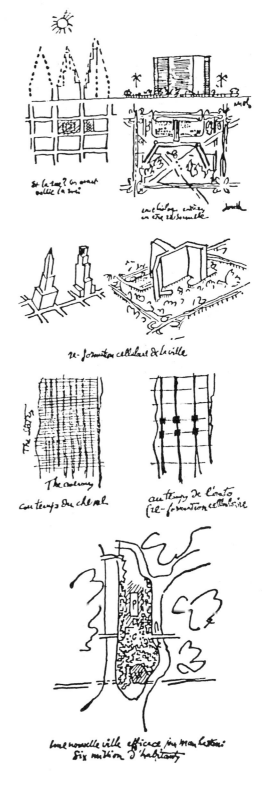

176. New York, first study for its transformation into the Ville Radieuse .

177. Paris and New York transformed into Siamese twins. "Two spirits confront each other: the French tradition of the Nôtre Dame, with its Horizontal Skyscrapers" and the American tradition, first explosive stage of a new middle age..."

178. Sketch of New York from a steamship.

washed, instrument of an implacable Puritanism.

Through a bizarre cross-fertilization of misunderstood rhetorics, American pragmatism and European idealism have exchanged ethos: the materialistic Philistines of New York had invented and built an oneiric field devoted to the pursuit of fantasy, synthetic emotion and pleasure, its ultimate configuration both unpredictable and uncontrollable.

To the European humanist/artist this creation is only a chaos, an invitation to problem-solving: Le Corbusier responds with a majestic flow of humanistic *non sequiturs* that fails to disguise the sentimentality at the core of his vision of Modernity.

The European's program for the true Machine Age is the efficiency of banality: "To be able to open your eyes on a patch of sky, to live near a tree, beside a lawn . . . to go simply from one skyscraper to another."[15]

Everyday life will regain its eternal immutability amidst the "essential joys" of sun, space, and vegetation. To be born, to die, with an extended period of breathing in between: in spite of the optimism of the Machine Age, the Old World vision remains *tragic*.

[15] Ibid.

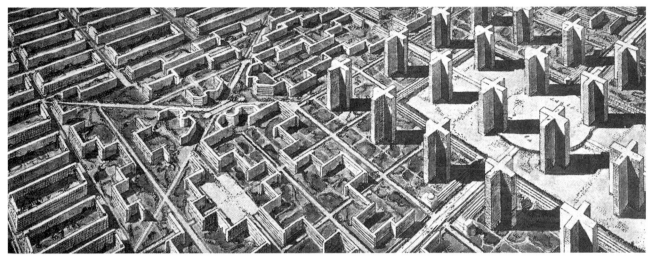

THE IMMEUBLE CLARTÉ

Christian Sumi

The Clarté is the first multi-family dwelling and at the same time the first construction in steel built by Le Corbusier and Pierre Jeanneret. Consequently, this involves the theme of the *Immeuble-Villas* (1922) as well as the *maison à sec*.[1] Starting with these two central themes (housing construction and industrialization of the construction), my interest as architect is mainly concerned with the questions inherent in the design methods and strategies in the relation between the individual phases of the design. Considering the influence of the illustrious client, the Genevan industrialist Edmond Wanner,[2] on the design, the questions of *concordance* and *coherence* of the design interest me above all others concerning the project.

The basic materials of my work, along with the archival material in Paris, are, on the one hand, the fascinating *photographs of the construction site* taken by the best architectural photographers of the time (Lucien Hervé of Paris, Paul Boissonas of Geneva, the Bauhaus instructor, Hans Finsler, and the perennial secretary of CIAM, Sigfried Giedion of Zurich), and on the other hand, the graphic reconstructions of the most important constructional details of the Clarté. The *relief* creates distance and allows free rein to speculations on Le Corbusier's work on the design and with it on part of modern thought, a thought process that in the daily work of the studio is always bent on the exploration of newer fields taking off from experience, from the plan, going against certain postmodern hypotheses.

Movement and speculative thought

"I have received your scheme whose idea is acceptable, but not perfect.

In fact, there are three main defects:

1) Orientation: . . .

2) Corridors: in spite of the two gardens that you

---

[1] On the thematics of the Immeuble-Villas, my contribution can be consulted in: Bruno Reichlin and Sergio Pagnamenta, *Le Corbusier—La ricerca paziente*, Lugano, 1980, pp. 63–68; and on the conception of the *maison à sec*, my analysis in: *Le Corbusier à Génève*, exhibition catalogue, Lausanne, 1987, pp. 93–111. The two texts appeared in an expanded version as a monograph on the Wanner and the Clarté designs in the series published by the Institut für Geschichte und Theorie der Architektur (GTA) of the ETH of Zurich, in the winter of 1988.

[2] On Wanner's personality also see my article in *Le Corbusier — une encyclopédia*, Milan, Electa, 1988, pp. 551–52.

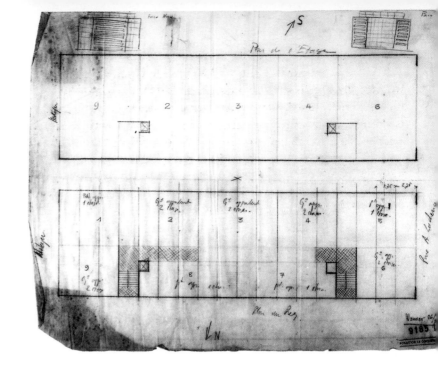

179. Edmond Wanner, design scheme for the Clarté (FLC 9185).
180. Immeuble Clarté, floor plans and ground floor.
181. Le Corbusier and Charlotte Perriand, *cellules de 14 m² par habitant* for one, two, and three persons.

foresee for lighting the corridors, it remains, however, that each of the corridors measures 12 meters without any lighting whatsoever. This is certainly bothersome and since it is why the disposition of the plot absolutely does not allow comparison to a general case, but leads rather to the resolution of a specific case, wouldn't it be better to treat it only as such, bringing out its greatest advantages?

3) *The apartments are too big*: in fact, in the apartments that you have foreseen, there are more than 200 square meters of habitable space per apartment, which is too much for the inhabitants we can expect in this part of town.

I am therefore sending you an outline of my idea that needs further development. The buildings will have 18 bays measuring 2.75 meters in width and will be distributed every two floors with 5 apartments on 2 floors and four apartments on one floor."[3]

This is the letter Edmond Wanner wrote in response to a first sketch for the Clarté by Le Corbusier. Le Corbusier's proposal refers to the Immeuble-Villas, conceived as *villas superposées* with a *rue intérieure*. Looking at the cross-section and the definitive plan of the Clarté, one can surprisingly verify that Wanner's requests (two stairwells instead of the *rue intérieure*, duplexes and apartments different in type and dimensions, and a continuous regular grid measuring 2.8 meters) come together in the design; more precisely, Le Corbusier has moved away from the initial idea of an Immeuble-Villa. This is amazing because Le Corbusier is rather well-known for his less than obsequious relations with his clients.

[3] FLC Archive, April 26, 1930.
[4] Le Corbusier, *La Ville Radieuse*, Boulogne, L'Architecture d'Aujourd'hui, 1935; reissued in Paris, Fréal, 1964, pp. 143ff.

178   Christian Sumi

A look at the year 1929 clarifies the situation. Now for the background of the CIAM Congress of Brussels (theme: "the habitat for *existenzminimum*"); Le Corbusier, with the young interior architect Charlotte Perriand, formulates a substantially new question on the home and proposes his *cellules de 14 m² par habitant*.[4] Unlike the Immeuble-Villas, this concept is distinguished by the large number of plans of different dimensions and by the extremely reduced number of surfaces, containing therefore exactly what Wanner requested. That is why Le Corbusier had only to turn to another model, adapting it to the specific requests, in order to respond to his client's wishes. Moreover, when Wanner requests the substitution of the *rue intérieure* with the two stairwells, Le Corbusier takes advantage of the opportunity to weave the concept of *cellules* more coherently into the lodgings, even orienting some of the bathrooms toward the stairwells.

Wanner's exacting and pragmatic critique constrains Le Corbusier to surpass, in a certain way, his own ideological obstacles and allows him to arrive at

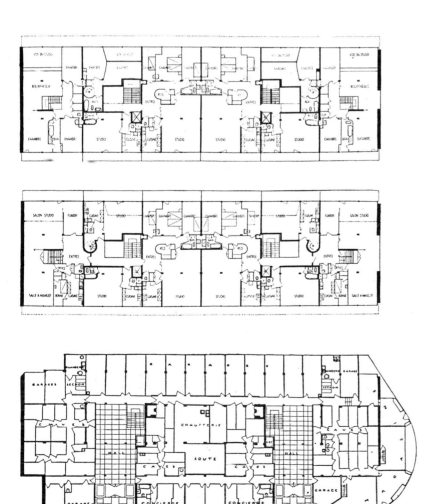

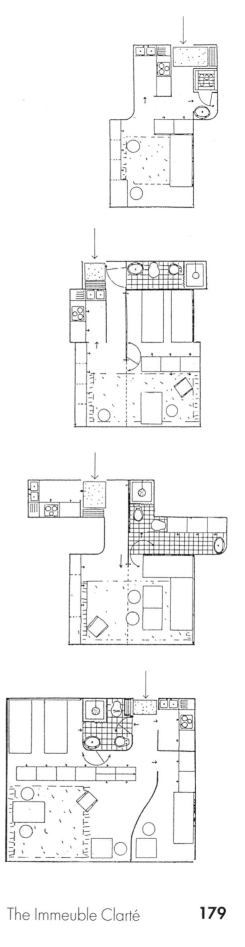

182. Immeuble Clarté, detail of the façade (H. Finsler, GTA).
183. The balcony of the Clarté, welded to a stanchion of the façade, serves also as *brise-soleil*.

[5] Le Corbusier, "L'Immeuble 'Clarté' à Génève = Das Haus aus Glas," in *L'Art en Suisse = Die Kunst der Schweiz*, no. 4/5, Geneva, 1933, introduction.
[6] *Le Corbusier—Oeuvre complète 1938–46*, W. Boesiger ed., Zurich, Girsberger, 1946, p. 104.

new possibilities, as, for example, the application of the principle of the *cellules de 14 m² par habitant* to the homes of the upper middle class. Wanner encourages him to reconsider the questions and relations that he would never have thought of first: "indecent" as a multi-family dwelling is, it should be served by two stairwells instead of a *rue intérieure*, and contrary to the principle of the Immeuble-Villas, should be made up of apartments that differ from each other and vary in size. The apartments are built into a steel structure with measurements of 2.8 meters: the minimal dimension of a room (with transversally placed bed and passageway), as much later Le Corbusier would justify Wanner's request.[5] Le Corbusier, then, succeeds in extrapolating the requests and wishes of Wanner in the direct client-architect relationship and takes them to a general level, a relative and broader content, allowing them to flow once more into the design on the conceptual level. In this way he acts exactly on the client's wishes; in other words, the client does not impose on his architect, and without knowing it, it works for him.

The centralization of the different levels of design

In 1940, eight years after the completion of the Clarté, Le Corbusier writes: ". . . in the Immeuble Clarté of Geneva, thus christened by the inhabitants, we have instinctively triggered a working approach for the *brise-soleil*. I design floors, these extend beyond the *pan de verre* across a balcony with a rather conspicuous projection measuring 1.5 meters, furnished with its own parapet. A first shadow is cast . . ."[6]

The logical origin of the *brise-soleil* in the sections of the Clarté's façade was developed, in reality, in a much more dramatic way than the one Le Corbusier had described in the retrospective exhibition. Very likely it was Wanner again who exhorted Le Corbusier to place a continuous balcony in front of the glass façade as substitute, in a manner of speaking, for the *jardins suspendus* every two floors, a request that must have contrasted profoundly with Le Corbusier's idea of the *pan de verre* as a flat continuous membrane. Nevertheless, Le Corbusier once again risks giving up his own ideas and responds to the demands of ulterior hidden implications, thus finding in 1945 one of the most important architectural elements for successive works: the sun-screen, a spatial grid suspended in front of the *pan de verre* protecting it from the direct rays of the sun. In the stairwell, Le Corbusier transforms the principle of the *brise-soleil*, one could say, into its opposite. He inserts concrete-framed glass blocks in the steps of the staircase and in the landings, thus eliminating, in this case, the unwanted shadow of the stairwell, truly creating a *canon à lumière* [light shaft] by means of the powerful emission of light from the roof.

In the same design, Le Corbusier interprets the same element — the overhanging slab — in two diametrically opposed ways: in the case of the balconies, as an element that effectively creates shadow and as an element that gives light. All of this takes us back to Le Corbusier's capacity for centering the design as it appears from a distance in relation to the levels that comprise it, even when this threatens to break up the client's wishes into separate sections. Thus Le Corbusier succeeds once again, contrary to Wanner's opinion in the letter quoted above, to establish, even in the case of the Clarté, a *cas général*, a solution that is distinguished by its general character and has validity well beyond a specific area of its application in Geneva.

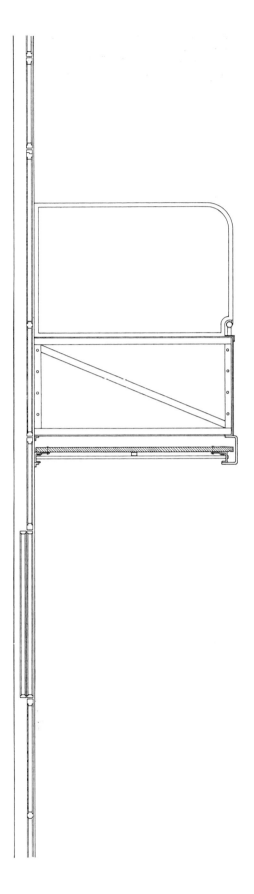

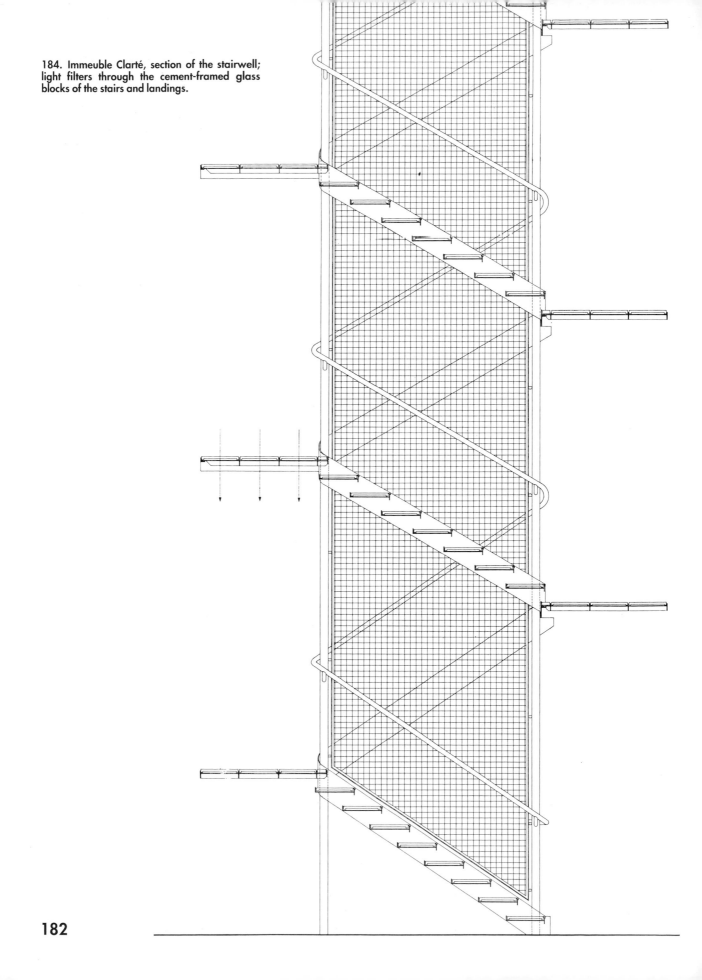

184. Immeuble Clarté, section of the stairwell; light filters through the cement-framed glass blocks of the stairs and landings.

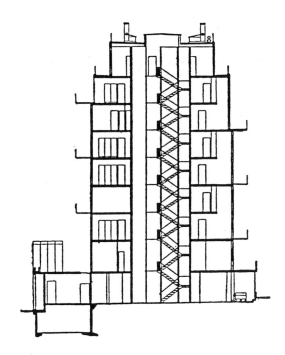

185. The stairwell as a *canon à lumière* (P. Bois-
sonnas).
186. Immeuble Clarté, cross-section.

"*Brise-soleil*, briseur de toutes sortes de difficultés"[7]

[7] Ibid., p. 107.

In Algiers Le Corbusier reworked the sunscreen in an office building (1939) thus going back to the multifunctional *brise-soleil*. The balconies of the Clarté also have more than one function. Beyond providing an external space for the apartments, they are a shield against the sun for the *pan de verre*, articulating the façade of seven floors in units of two floors each and seven establishing a relation with the two entrance doors that is out-of-scale. Moreover, they serve as a scaffold for cleaning, and during construction, as well as during the renovations of the façade in 1976, they were used as scaffolding for painting and assembly. From 1930 on, Le Corbusier sought to exploit the same constructive element in numerous ways; he thus criticizes naive mechanistic postulates of functionalism: the wish to see form and function always in a simple causal connection. In view of the infinite subdivision and dispersal of design and the functional specialization of form in the orthodox formalist manner, Le Corbusier's interest is directly beamed toward clarity and autonomy of form. For example, the balconies of the southern façade of the Clarté are not different from those on the north, even though obviously only the first serve also as shelter against the rays of the sun. And the general character of Le Corbusier's

187. Two interior perspectives: in the design for an office building in Algiers, in 1939, Le Corbusier uses an interior design of the plan for the Rentenanstalt of 1932; he substitutes the lake of Zurich with the sea of Algiers putting a *pan de verre* and a *brise-soleil* in front, "*briseur de toutes sortes de difficultés.*"

188. The steel columns: that "purist" welding of the Clarté and the bolted one of the Maison de Verre.

propositions (who is interested in knowing that only the balconies on the south function as a shelter from the sun?) confer not only a plastic-structural clarity on the Clarté (as its name suggests), but also its pleasant simplicity. The Clarté is certainly a *machine et laboratoire à habiter* (machine for living) in the positive avantgarde sense of the 1920s, but at the same time it has the grandiosity of the urban typology of nineteenth century bourgeois homes in Geneva, with their frequent alternation of entries by a floor-and-a-half and continuous balconies of reduced dimensions on the higher floors. But this means that in terms of his projects, for Le Corbusier the design themes and strategies remain convenient instruments only, and, more precisely, should not be architecturally thematized, as the application of steel technology at the Clarté and also the concept of the *maison à sec* demonstrate.

Christian Sumi

Architectural construction and language

It has become commonplace to consider the Clarté and the Maison de Verre of Pierre Chareau and of Bernard Bijvoet in Paris, also from 1932, as all the same, and to consider the Clarté as the younger sibling of the Maison de Verre. The presumed analogy of the two designs is founded only on the anecdote that Le Corbusier was "surprised," with hat pressed on head and a small notepad in hand, on the construction site of the Maison de Verre. This consideration surprised me, pushing me thus to the next comparison.

The steel columns of the Clarté are formed by two U-shaped sections joined by two arc-welded steel panels. The use of arc welding and the joining of the two Y-shaped sections create a hollow column with a neutral character not inherent in "construction in steel." In a contemporaneous commentary it was also said that "the elimination of the greater part of the joint covers, bolts, and brackets that have always made up the thickness of the otherwise pure lines of the columns or the beams, partially visible in the finished building, confer on the steel skeleton an appearance of lightness and a lift in height that, if one looks at the pictures, is more surprising by the fact that, given the elimination of the drill holes for the brackets, the beams could be relatively thin."[8]

The steel column of the Maison de Verre, instead, is formed by an iron sheet and by four angular bracketed steel sections with laterally applied slate facing panels. The two parts of the column are connected one to the other with supplementary brackets.

Le Corbusier and Wanner, with the choice of electrical welding (thanks to which the typical connective elements of steel construction have been eliminated) remove the column, in a manner of speaking, from the image of the traditional "construction in steel" and they subordinate it to the idea of Purist space. In Paris, in the last century, Chareau created an *industrie intérieure* with the bolted and bracketed column, anticipating Art Deco, with which he was marvelously successful.

Le Corbusier distances himself from techno-constructional themes. For him the thematization is not a priori, but gradual. The relation, the equilibrium between construction and architectural language, has been researched and defined case by case. In this sense the Clarté reproposes a certain current tendency to justify the growing design based on aspects and the regularity of the construction, thus removing it from the marshes of post-modern arbitrariness and

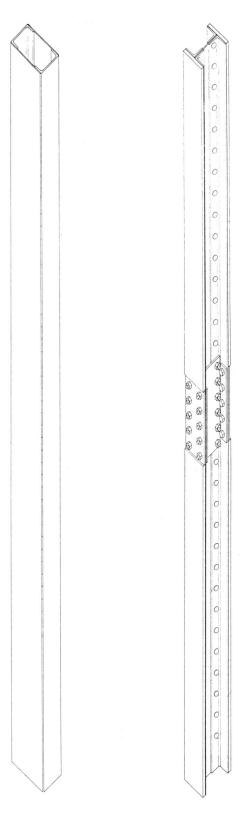

8 Le Corbusier, "L'Immeuble 'Clarté' à Génève = Das Haus aus Glas," technical information.

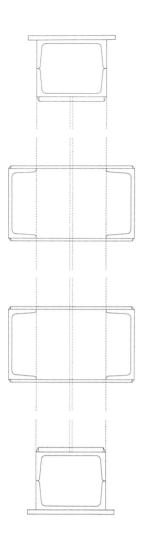

taking it into areas that are considered secure in the objective world of construction. The apparent fortuitousness between the constructional operative and architectural language turns out to be a mistake. The rapport exists at many levels and is more complex; more precisely, the construction is always presented as object of the author. In Le Corbusier's studio, the refined rapport with techno-constructional issues makes the determining contribution of the Genevan Pierre Jeanneret stand out in a obvious manner. In this way the Clarté is in part also a monument, in his native city, to this refined and intelligent builder who moved to Paris in the early 1920s to work with the cousin from La Chaux-de-Fonds.[9]

Le Corbusier around 1930

From the analyses of the Clarté it turns out that the design work by Le Corbusier in 1930 and after is distinguished by the contiguity and contemporaneity of various themes and strategies. Nevertheless, the architectural system conserves Le Corbusier's various classifications.[10] The system formulated in the five points for a new architecture is opened and the flexibility of its programmatic implementation is reexamined. Le Corbusier distances himself from the closed system of Purism and affirms its operability at a more general level. With this the five points are liber-

189. Immeuble Clarté, cross-section of the columns.
190. The construction site of the Clarté, photograph probably taken by S. Giedion (GTA).

Christian Sumi

191. Photograph of the construction site with a Zeppelin, probably taken by S. Giedion (GTA), "perhaps the elements of this building (the Clarté) could be defined as constructivist, but not its spirit. What can be grasped is the clear and measured language of the construction. Le Corbusier has finally taken the decisive step and taken possession of the machine." Peter Smithson, 1974.

ated, in a manner of speaking, from their Purist implications and become capable of being materialized in various architectural languages. This also means that Le Corbusier of the 1930s and after has more registers at his disposal, such as, for example, the thematics of the Immeuble-Villas and of the *cellules de 14 m² par habitant*, which he uses each time in a different mode and manner according to design needs, without however abandoning the general principle of his constructions of the 1920s. The presupposition of this liveliness and mobility is the functionalist-taylorist thought of Modernism with its push toward the breaking of everything into units in order then to put them back together according to new parameters and conditions. Le Corbusier's design is marked by the constant pleasure of seeing things always in a new way, each time using the speculative thought of Modernism as material for his own work. The interest isn't so much directed toward objects themselves, but to the potential relations they engender among each other structurally.[*]

[9] On Pierre Jeanneret's personality see Catherine Courtiau, "Pierre Jeanneret (1896–1967)," in *Le Corbusier à Génève*, pp. 112–17.
[10] The classification occurs on the level of the single structural elements (for example the different types of openings, *trou dans le mur, fenêtre en longueur* and *pan de verre*) as well as design experiences (the five points of a new architecture) and different kinds of compositions (the four compositions).
[*] The relief drawings of the Immeuble Clarté were executed by L. Lotti, P. Marmet, D. Rouge, C. Dumont D'Ayot, S. Horni, and P. Haegeli of the FAUG of Geneva.

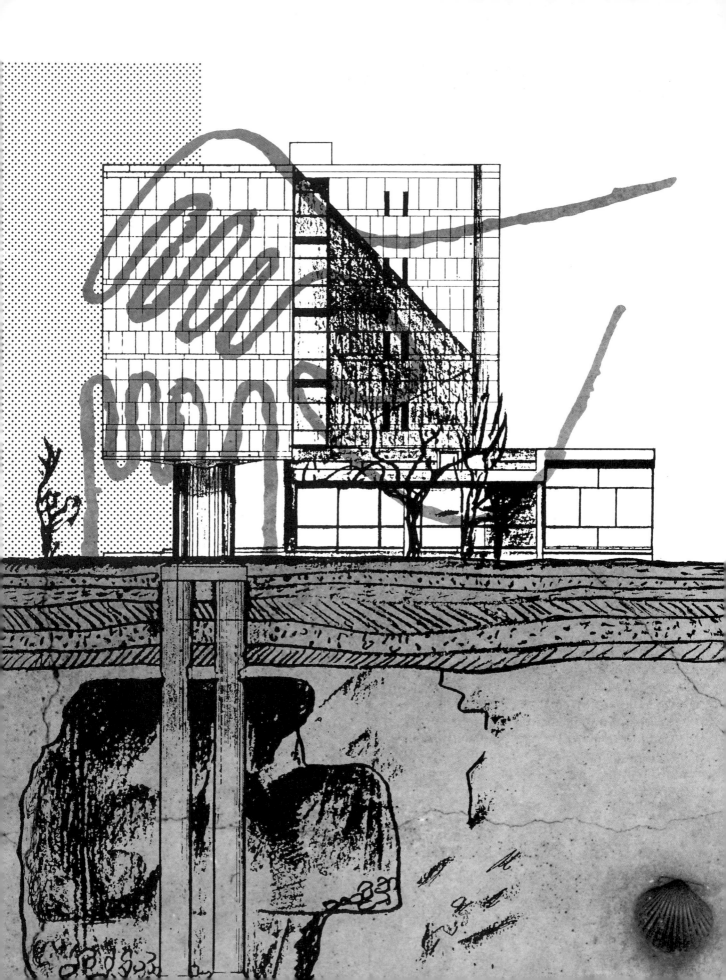

THE OPEN HANDS

ARCHITECTURE—ENGINEERING

Santiago Calatrava

The Engineer's Aesthetic, and Architecture, are two things that march together and follow one from the other: the one being now at its full height, the other in an unhappy state of retrogression.

The Engineer, inspired by the law of Economy and governed by mathematical calculation, puts us in accord with universal law. He achieves harmony.

The Architect, by his arrangement of forms, realizes an order which is a pure creation of his spirit; by forms and shapes he affects our senses to an acute degree and provokes plastic emotions; by the relationships which he creates he wakes profound echoes in us, he gives us the measure of an order which we feel to be in accordance with that of our world, he determines the various movements of our heart and of our understanding; it is then that we experience the sense of beauty.

Le Corbusier begins *Vers une Architecture* with these words; it is easy to see in them the will to take a position on the issue of the relation between architecture and engineering. By opposing the Cartesian givens of calculus to the capacity of "organizing forms" in order to reveal "deep resonances," he attributes to the architect the role of protagonist in the art of construction. Nevertheless, he nourishes a great admiration for the category of engineer that in that period included quite particular personnages such as Freyssinet or Nervi.

At the end of the 1920s Le Corbusier uses the structural elements (*pilotis*, large pillars, coves, etc.) in a more rigorous way, but with totally different ends than those of contemporaneous builders. Coves, roofings, cylinders, or cones are not evident in the strictly mathematical sense of those of Freyssinet or of Candela; they are rather imagined forms designed with great ability to satisfy exigencies of a plastic nature. The example of the pavilion on the roof of the Rentenanstalt in 1933 in Zürich is an emblematic

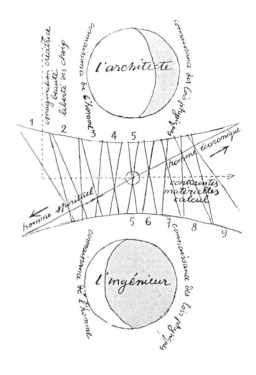

192. The material constrictions are placed on the horizontal axis, the conditioning of physics and calculus dominated by the engineer. On the vertical axis there is the liberty of choice (composition, elements, materials, etc.) with the duty of tending toward beauty in itself: this is the architect's job!

189

example whose longitudinal beams carry the horizontal force of the cone-shaped coves. Quite definitively, the structural elements in his work do nothing but contribute to the realization of form.

In the dual—Manichean—vision of Le Corbusier, the figure of the engineer and that of the architect emerge as indissolubly linked like those other complementary couples that populate the universe: day and night, good and evil, the full and the empty, the solar image of Apollo and the dark one of Medusa.

Even today, should the dual image have retained its fascination, the evolution of technologies (in particular the one of calculus, but also a structural analysis beyond any technology of materials) has modified not only the image of the architect but that of the engineer as well. The latter now possesses a new freedom, no longer tied to the rules of calculus or to a single structural model. The options from now on are released from rigid aprioristic parameters. To be able to build according to the laws of intuition, linked only to sensibility, is able to provoke emotions even today.

The problem of the industrialization of the building process has always been of great importance to Le

193. Swiss Pavilion, first design.
194. Construction site for the Swiss Pavilion (FLC).

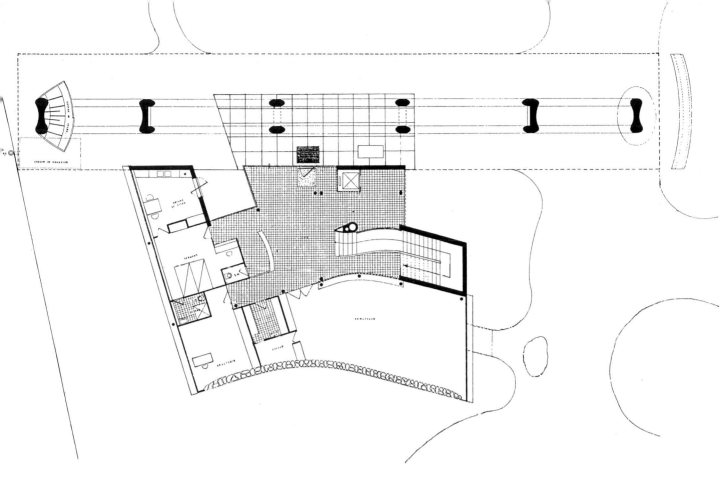

Corbusier. The Maison Dom-ino and the Pavillon de l'Esprit Nouveau are but two of the most famous examples. In these works the constructive-structural rigor given by the minimal use of constructive elements is tied to a criteria of economy that informs the entire first part of his work.

When the realization of the Swiss Pavilion at the Cité Universitaire in Paris is proposed to him, he decides to produce a manifestation of the *maison à sec* out of it and of the new construction technologies: a steel skeleton supported by a single row of pillars with stairs and entry on the side. This first solution presented various difficulties, not the least of which was the presence of some abandoned quarries in the basement. Obliged to discard the initial idea, Le Corbusier does not give up his proposition and decides to transform the entire building into a dual image.

To the light steel structure he opposes the material solidity of the base in *béton brut* [rough concrete]; to the stereometrics of the dry-mounted prism he opposes the curve of the stone walls of the atrium and stairwell; to the *pan de verre* on the south side he opposes the walls of stone on the north.

From the depths of the earth there emerge the sinuous forms of the pillars that raise the parallelepiped of the buildings. A large hand offers us a new technology.

The Open Hands   **191**

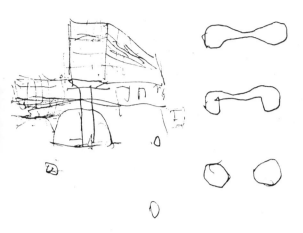

The Swiss Pavilion is to be considered the absolute fruit of a most advanced and rigorous interpretation of the science of building of that period. The optimization of the structure, starting with the methods of interpretation of the elasticity of materials, carried over to the distribution of the distances between the pillars or to the distribution of the mass of a roof, or of a plate slab, according to the lines of momentum. The pillars of the Swiss Pavilion are distributed according to a relation that does not have a discreet rapport: their distances are unequal, determined by the reception of the mass above distributed according to an ideal line of momentum in order to always have the maximum momentum on the supports. The use of two different construction systems for the two long sides of the construction determined the placement of the static axis of the superior prism from its geometric center: the "bone" pillars are aligned along this axis. Even their form in the plan is seen as an ideal line of pressure.

A manifestation of the thematics linked with the *maison à sec*, the Swiss Pavilion also expresses Le Corbusier's interest in the hidden part of buildings. The construction is not understood only as an external—visible—part of the "humanism" that would lead to the Modulor, it possesses a double life. Subterranean architecture, the large pillars entwine the grottos beneath.

Assuming a free form in the emergent part, the coupled giant immortalized in *L'Architecture Vivante* introduces a formal freedom into Le Corbusier's work through structural elements. In other words, it per-

196. Swiss Pavilion, sketch with the caverns underneath and the form of the pillars in the plan (FLC F25).
197. *Unité* in Marseille, sketches of the pillars (FLC 26738).

198. Philips Pavilion, the mounting of numbered panels (FLC).

tains to the first attempts at applied free plastic materials. To realize them Le Corbusier was constrained to fully exploit the possibility of reinforced concrete, using its plastic qualities. The diaphanous surface of the Esprit Nouveau would lead the way to the materiality of the *béton brut*. Extensive knowledge of the use of concrete would allow him to shape his architecture like a great sculptor. The *Unité* in Marseille, the chapel at Ronchamp, the buildings at Chandigarh and Firminy are closer to the plastic arts than Le Corbusier's experiments in sculpture.

In each case, this search would leave Le Corbusier's interest in aspects of technology unaltered. The enthusiasm with which he describes the "Benotto" foundation poles for the *pilotis* of the *Unité* in Marseilles is explicit testimonial to his fascination with them. From now on the rigorous use of mathematics and structural calculus in his work would be subordinate to its plastic application. All of the artifice of the Philips Pavilion can be seen in this way—a building that is not in the least orthodox from the point of view of constructional sci-

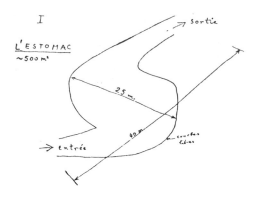

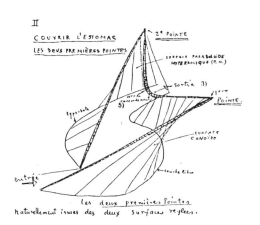

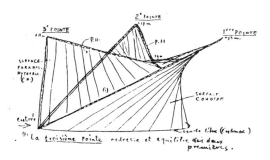

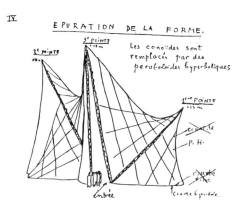

ence. It is useless to attempt to analyze those strange pillars and those very complicated coverings according to a structural model, since they have been shaped, one by one, over a bank of sand before being leaned against a mesh of steel cables.

To understand how the pavilion—made of hyperbolic paraboloids resulting from the development of linear elements spanning two lines based on a musical rhythm—was born, it is more useful to think about the musical compositions of Xenakis, of those elements of mathematico-plastic analysis of music or its interpretation through the development of so many linear elements progressing along two lines. But from the point of view of the science of construction it is all extremely irrational.

Le Corbusier and Xenakis have ideated a form and *then* thought about how to build it. In this way the laws of statics have completely been submitted to the will to form, to the plastic aspect of the building.

The entire Philips Pavilion is conceived to "provoke emotions." We can imagine how visiting this work must have been a truly plastic experience: to come upon its form, to enter it, guided by lines that are continually in transformation, to move accompanied by the music of light of the projections . . . "a gastric experience," the plan is a stomach with the entrance as esophagus. (Curiously, in Le Corbusier's work we find references to anatomy only on the plans, whereas they are rarely found in the three-dimensional work. Anatomy is order.

It is not by chance that there are anthropomorphic references in the organization of the Ville Radieuse.)

In spite of the power derived from the insertion of elements taken from the musical vocabulary of Xenakis, of his plastic music, the pavilion for the exposition in Brussels does not constitute the height of Le Corbusier's capacity to shape a building. Even by using the same kinds of contradictions, he achieves results of great beauty and poetry at Ronchamp: the roof that moves almost like a ship, the walls of stone that are empty on the inside . . .

In the work of Le Corbusier, architecture becomes an occasion—a pretext—to make plastic art on the grand scale; each of its elements (structure, form, color, relation to light) is applied to concur with a plastic effect.

The structural, then, is but *one* of the aspects that allows us to gather the complexity of Le Corbusier's work. Nevertheless there is no lack of admiration, of marveling, of surprise at the "and it is still standing."

All of his *recherche patiente* is pervaded by the attempt to assimilate, in different and even contradictory ways the rational rigor of the Maison Dom-ino and the irrationality of the Philips Pavilion, the world of the *forms of technology*, as far as the *engineers* have been able to realize it: airplanes and bridges, automobiles and silos, the elegant transatlantic ships that come from the pages of *Vers une Architecture*.

199. Philips Pavilion, design phases (*Poëme electronique*).
200. The Philips Pavilion at the International Exhibition in Brussels.
201. The hands of the engineer and the architect joined under the emblem of the ASCORAL.

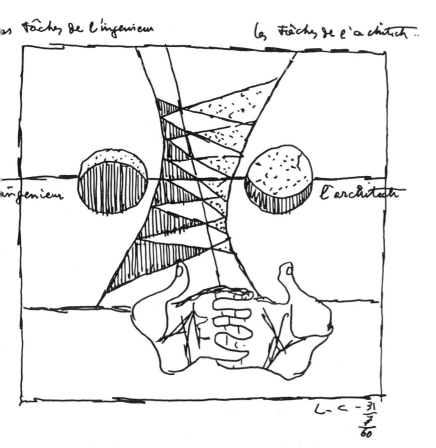

THE SEARCH FOR THE
ABSOLUTE

Jacques Lucan

Among the "five points to a new architecture" articulated by Le Corbusier, three specifically address the problem of superimposition: *pilotis*, the *plan libre*, and the *toit-jardin*.

The *pilotis* detach the building from the ground: "the house is up in the air."[1]

The *plan libre* has as a requisite condition the adoption of the *pilotis*: in the same manner as on the ground level, the garden can slide under the house across the grid of the *pilotis*; on the floor levels, the partitions are freely defined by the grid of the columns: "The columns, lined up like soldiers, do their work which is: to carry the floors."[2]

The *toit-jardin* is the last floor where the freedom of the plan is not fettered even by the grid of the columns. This floor represents the reconquering of a ground area equivalent to the one that covers the house, but it is now an "artificial" ground where only an ideal architecture is manifest. The *toit jardin* is detached from the immediate functional contingencies of the building, as it is oblivious to the contingencies of the construction: the columns end when they have supported the last floor.

We are interested here only in the *toit-jardin* but will first make a detour which might seem bizarre: we will examine a series of photographs of the Church, Savoye, and Stein villas, photographs that, for us, have always seemed enigmas, and that Le Corbusier may have left to the interpretation of his future exegetes.

The *toit-jardin* as offering

In the library of the pavilion of the Villa Church, at Ville d'Avray, several objects are arranged among the furniture that Le Corbusier and Pierre Jeanneret had just conceived with Charlotte Perriand and exhibited in Paris at the *Salon d'automne* of 1929: a camera is

[1] *Le Corbusier et Pierre Jeanneret—Oeuvre complète 1910–1929*, W. Boesiger and O. Stonorov, eds., Zurich, Girsberger, 1929, p.128.
[2] *L'Architecture d'Aujourd'hui*, no. 10, 1933, special issue "Le Corbusier et Pierre Jeanneret," p. 22.

placed at an angle of the room with its lens pointing at us; two open books are on the glass table; a gray hat with a wide black ribbon rests on the edge of the fireplace.[3]

This gray hat, is the very same hat that was left on the table of the *toit-jardin* at the Villa Savoye at Poissy, this time accompanied by a pair of sunglasses and two objects. The focus of this photograph strangely assumes an impossible position for the viewer: on the edge of the *toit-jardin*, on the other side of the "window" that opens onto the landscape at the extreme end of the ramp.

In another photograph of the kitchen of the same Villa Savoye, a coffee pot and a cut loaf of bread occupy a work table covered with white tiles.[4]

This last photograph is echoed by the one of the kitchen at the Villa Stein at Garches, where, still on a work table with white tiles, can be seen a pitcher, a teapot, and an electric fan that "observes" a fish placed there, open-mouthed.[5]

Other photographs, sometimes published, could undoubtedly complete this collection, all of them presenting "objects" left on tables: these have not been thrown there accidentally; they are arranged to form some strange, and perhaps disturbing compositions. They are either objects of current use, certainly chosen for their simplicity and uniqueness, or else things that evoke an absence: the bread that has just been cut; the hat and sunglasses that have been abandoned and await to be picked up again; the fish that waits to be cooked . . .

To qualify these compositions, we dare not mention the much too reductive word, "surrealist." These compositions that someone has staged, mark an interruption or an arrest of time, like an intrusion of time in an architectural setting: they belong to suspended time.

These compositions are absolutely deliberate on Le Corbusier's behalf. Between 1929 and 1931, it seems, the architect had thus populated the emptiness and solitude of some of his architectural works. The metaphor is evident: the objects and things are often placed on tables, as if on *altars*; they are *offerings*. And the triviality of some of these objects and of some of these things paradoxically only reinforces the enigmatic and dramatic dimension of the gesture.

We can now better understand the strange caption that Le Corbusier writes in the first volume of his *Oeuvre complète* for the photographs of the kitchen of the Villa Savoye,[6] his words of denial: "The kitchen is not exactly the sanctuary of the house, but it is certainly one of the most important places."

Why this need to specify at all costs that the kitchen is not a sanctuary? Why then does Le Corbusier choose the word to explicate a photograph?

If the kitchen is not *exactly* a sanctuary, at least the table is, without a doubt, an altar.

The table is a surface for offerings. It is thus the exact equivalent to the *toit-jardin* where the spectacle of a free and objective architecture is offered.

The *toit-jardin* as a place for meditation

What is Le Corbusier looking for in the *toit–jardin*? What does he want to offer?

Certainly, for practical and pragmatic reasons, for the polemic force of his architectural demonstrations, to set forth his will in proposing new modes of living, he never stops affirming that the *toit-jardin* is a place where activities often linked to physical culture can take place: gymnastics, running track, the solarium, etc. The projects in which the equipment necessary for these activities can be seen are numerous, in particular the track that can be found even on the roof of the *Unité d'habitation* in Marseille.

But is this the only goal that can be invoked? Certainly not.

[3] This photograph was published in *L'Architecture Vivante*, Editions Albert Morancé, Spring and Summer 1930, plate 18.
[4] This photograph was published in *L'Architecture Vivante*, Spring and Summer 1931, plate 34, and in *Oeuvre complète 1910–1929*, p. 29.
[5] This photograph was published in *L'Architecture Vivante*, Spring and Summer 1929, plate 12.
[6] *Le Corbusier et Pierre Jeanneret—Oeuvre complète, 1910–1929*, p. 29.

[7] Le Corbusier, *Précisions sur un état présent de l'architecture et de l'urbanisme*, 1930, p.154.
[8] Ibid., p. 159.
[9] *L'Architect*, October 1932.
[10] Le Corbusier, *Précisions*, p. 259.
[11] Le Corbusier, *La Ville Radieuse*, 1935, p. 230.
[12] Le Corbusier, *Les maternelles vous parlent, Les carnets de la recherche patiente*, no. 3, 1968, p. 13.

Far from the ground noise, the *toit-jardin* is a belvedere, an observatory, the bridge of the building as ship.

Thus, at the Villa Savoye, placed on "a vast convex lawn of a flattened dome,"[7] the view from the *toit-jardin* extends toward the four corners of the horizon, while domestic life rejoins "a Virgilian dream."[8]

Thus, after having come upon the higher, grass-covered terrace of the apartment of Charles Beistegui on the Champs Elysée in Paris: "The door closes: silence. One sees nothing else but the sky and the play of clouds and the burst of blue; it is a feeling of vast space, of the middle of the ocean,"[9] the middle of the ocean on top of the noisy universe of the city.

Le Corbusier found this feeling of *"grand large"* [vast space] again in Rio de Janeiro, during his trip to South America in 1929, when he climbed the "Favellas" to see "the sea, the roads, the ports, the islands, the ocean, the mountains, the estuaries": "the eye of man who sees vast horizons is superior, vast horizons confer dignity . . ."[10]

Or again, on the terraces of the houses of Algiers: "Arabs, are you the only ones to still have these daily contemplations during the beautiful hours of sunset? Sky, sea, and mountains. Beatitudes of space. Great distances for the eyes and for meditation."[11]

And, finally then, at Marseille on the roof that is "fabricated terrain"[12]: "The day of the opening of the

207. Le Corbusier looking up at the roof of the *Unité d'habitation* under construction.

208. The roof of Charles Beistegui on the Champs–Elysée in Paris (FLC).

Maternelle, the mothers, their children at their side, climbed up to the roof. They were dazzled by the splendor of the spectacle: sky, mountains, sea, islands . . . and architecture.

At the end of the afternoon, they came back to look for their little ones. Joy shone on the faces of the children. 'Tomorrow I will tell your father to come get you himself . . .'

The father came up: he was dazzled by the splendor of the spectacle: sky, mountains, sea, islands . . . and architecture."[13]

Freedom of play, or ineffable space

It is on the roof or the terrace of a building that time for meditation can be found, while we are removed from the tasks of daily life, a time for contemplation that begins with the embracing of the surrounding landscape and all its horizons. Le Corbusier searched ceaselessly for this privileged situation from the time, for example, when he conceived the Palace of the League of Nation in 1927 where on the *toit-jardins* it would have been possible to find oneself face-to-face with the magnificence of the Alps,[14] to the realization of the Capitol of Chandigarh from which the vast chain of the Himalayas can be seen.

On the roof of the *Unité d'habitation* in Marseille, we also can contemplate the mountains and the sea: we

[13] Ibid., p. 57.
[14] See: Le Corbusier, *Une maison—un palais*, 1928, p. 155, the caption for a photograph of a panorama of the Alps; and p. 154: "To order the whole composition so that it ends in the gathering of men up high, on an immense belvedere, facing the prestigious site, where even the most hardened of hearts are perhaps still open to such emotions, was a poetic intention."

The Absolute   **203**

are on a
plateau there, the
plateau of an *acropoli*. And, as
in Athens, "the Acropolis on its rocks and
supporting walls is seen from afar, all of a piece."[15]
Also, in Marseille the roof is a gathering place, a magic
place, a plateau placed above the regular and repetitive superposition of the apartments, raised to such a height that it is effectively a crown, the aerial crown of a building with terrestrial massiveness.

Therefore it is not by chance that Le Corbusier publishes a photomontage in which the maquette of the roof in Marseille is by itself, like a ship floating in the surrounding landscape.[16] The independence of this maquette in relation to the parallelepiped of the buildings is the mark that the roof of the *Unité d'abitation* in itself posseses rules of composition that borrow nothing from the floors beneath it, it posseses its own principles of coherence.

And like the rocks of Athens, the "buildings are amassed in the incidence of their multiple plans"[17]; also in Marseille the roof gathers an ensemble of singular architectural elements that etch a striking outline against the sky: these elements are arranged according to skillful balances and complex considerations.

To offer the spectacle of an *architecture libre* it is

[15] Le Corbusier, *Vers une Architecture*, 3rd edition, Paris, 1928, p. 39. See, in reference to this sentence, which does not appear in the first and second editions of *Vers une Architecture*: Jacques Lucan, "Acropole" in *Le Corbusier—Une encyclopédie*, Centre Georges Pompidou, Paris, 1987. This article treats the Acropolis of Athens as a major point of reference in the work of Le Corbusier.
[16] See in particular: Le Corbusier, *Les maternelles vous parlent*, p. 18; Le Corbusier, *Oeuvre complète 1938–1946*, p. 185.
[17] Le Corbusier, *Vers une Architecture*, p. 39.

necessary
that the latter not result
from the application of formulas or
principles that would immediately announce
their obviousness and their simplicity in the way, for
example, that the orthogonal grid of the loggias of the
apartments can if we consider them as representative
of a system of repetitions and superimpositions. An
architecture libre must not settle on programmatic,
functional, or constructional objectives as sufficient
justification.

The sublime dimension for an *architecture libre*
calls forth other exigencies.

Le Corbusier does not really seek to make a new
programmatic or typological demonstration on the
roof of the *Unité* in Marseille, even if the physical exercises require specific equipment that now belongs to
the repertory of "traditional" architecture. He mo-
mentarily turns his attention away from the problem

209. Roof of the *Unité* in Marseille, photomontage of the model and surrounding landscape.

which has preoccupied him for a long time, that is, the definition of a form for a collective dwelling; he solves this problem. He removes himself from the order of the orthogonal and regular grid of the lower floors; he forgets the famous principle of the "bottle" and "the cup-bearer" that allowed him to explain how the apartments in a general homogeneous structure are assembled. He comes back to the first language of forms, to his primordial affirmation: "Architecture is the masterly, correct and magnificent play of volumes assembled together under the light."

But in order for there to be play, that is, *liberté du jeu*, the forms must arise out of need, through "vital" necessity, imperious, beyond all objective reason, beyond all rational determinism.

Let us reread one of Le Corbusier's discourses that brings us close to the vision of the enigmatic "objects" placed on the tables of the Church, Savoye, and Stein villas: "Observe one day . . . in a popular little snack bar, two or three guests who have had their coffee chatting. The table is still strewn with glasses, bottles, plates, oil, salt, pepper, napkin ring, etc. Look at the inevitable order that puts all these objects in relation one to the other; they have all served, they have been handled by one or the other of the guests; the distances that separate them are the measure of life. It is a mathematically arranged composition; there isn't a false place, a hiatus, no trickery. If a movie director, unhallucinated by Hollywood, were there filming this still life, 'in the rough,' we would have a *witness to pure harmony*."[18]

What does Le Corbusier want to show here?

He wants to show that what is considered accidental is not accidental, that the fortuitous is not fortuitous.

That "accident" is stronger than will. That from "accident" the most extraordinary gifts can result, the most splendid offerings. That "accident" is the manifestation of a destiny or fate. That "the inevitable order that brings all these objects in relation one to the other" is the manifestation of a sacred dimension.

In this perspective, architecture is also a "witness to pure harmony" in order to be a gift to the community: the villas, while remaining private and, therefore, not part of a community, perhaps as in Marseille, also demanded the "trivial" metaphor of the offering evoked above.

The roof of the *Unité* in Marseille allowed Le Corbusier to find a space that he would often call "*indicible*" [ineffable], that is, which cannot be rationally described, a "mathematical place of consonance," a "place of visual acoustics."

In this place, a "message" that Le Corbusier specifies, on July 1965, in a last "*mise au point*" [refinement]: "The straight line that marries the axis of fundamental laws must be found: biology, nature, cosmos. Unbending straight line like the horizon of the sea."[19]

Some days later, on the 27th of August, he would definitively rejoin the horizon of the sea, leaving the shore in a final search for the absolute . . .

[18] Le Corbusier, *Précisions*, pp. 19–20.
[19] Le Corbusier, *Mise au point*, Paris, Forces Vives, 1966, p. 60.

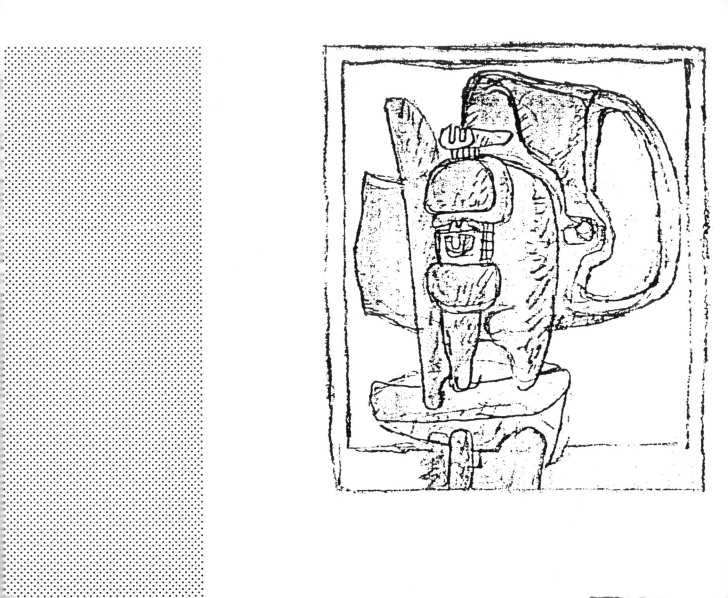

ON AN ANTIQUE
FRIEZE

Francesco Venezia

The truth about the extremely elongated contours of the Capitol of Chandigarh and the complex at Firminy came to me—by chance—in front of a frieze at the archeological museum in Palermo.

212. F. Venezia, sketch of the frieze on temple E of Selinunte.

What I saw then for the first time—and what I drew—was a rhythm.

Compressed between the horizons of the epistyle and the cornice, the monotonous stasis of the triglyphs alternated with the tumultuous disequilebrium of the decorated metopes. A kind of opposition, of conflict, took the form of narrative.

At the very moment in which the right angle cut with Doric precision into the triglyphs, it was as if seduced —again—by the oblique lines of the figures that made up the tangle of imagery in each metope.

Equilibrium. Disequilibrium.

Orthostasis. Animal tension of bodies.

It seems to me that this drama, represented in the

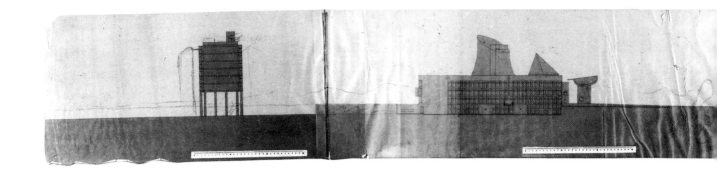

[1] "Incidenti a reazione poetica," *Domus*, March 1987; "Teatres i antres," *Quaderns*, Barcelona, Oct.–Nov.–Dec. 1987.
[2] And again the form of an absence; architecture appropriates structural technology: at Chandigarh and Firminy the use of concrete as material that finds expression in the imprint of a subtracted—and always absent—body, is pushed to the extreme.
In the time of contact between material and mould. Between arming and the other, of disarming, the transformation of time, is given form metaphorically.
To the point of adding the high–relief and depressed approach, brutal inversion of quality of the accident of light that shapes and excavates.
[3] At its greatest impact this idea has been expressed in Palestrina's plans, crowned with the pyramidal bulk by the ruins of temple of Fortuna Primigenia.
A great dialogue takes place between the sinuous ravines that furrow the plain—a tangle of snakes that is lost on the horizon—and the imminent layer of earth of the substrata of walls, ramps, terraces, regulated by the geometry of the square.
The presence of water, manifested below in the natural landscape (it is here that the subtraction stops its millennial action), is transferred to the ridge of the mountain in the system of depths and hollows supplying cisterns and caves accidentally revealed on the shattered form of the ruin.
The entire basement appears as a vast conveyance for the gathering of meteoric waters—a pluvial fountain in the shape of a city—metaphor of the surrounding landscape marked by erosion.
Time works equally on natural forms and on the forms of the building.
A study on the subject has been published in *Idee Prozess Ergebnis*, Internationale Bauaustellung Berlin, Senator für Bau- und Wohnungswesen, Berlin, 1984, with the title "Stadtgrundrisarchitektur–am Beispeil Palestrina"; Italian trans., "Architettura del suolo—l'esempio di Palestrina", in F. Venezia, *Scritti Brevi*, Naples, CLEAN, 1986, pp. 63–65.

frieze at temple E of Selinunte, is not dissimilar from the one planned (and put into action) at Chandigarh and Firminy.

We should substitute the epistyle for the density of the ground in which subterranean forces erupted—again; on the cornice, the substance itself of the sky; at the triglyphs and the metopes, the figures and the forms of the buildings.

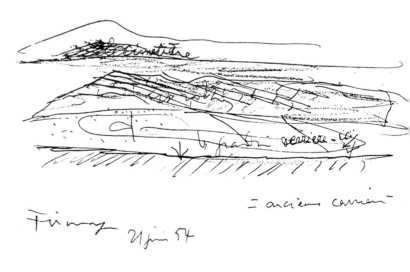

The extremely elongated contours push upon—and are supported by—the epistyle of the ground.

(The memory of the columnar giant, hiding in the basement, is not canceled, as it supports that outcropping fraction of the Swiss Pavilion in the Cité Universitaire of Paris.)[1]

Architecture at this point of the journey, no longer rises over an area (abstractly) shaped to receive it. Neither at Rio is there a form that is composed of those from the landscape. It is inserted rather into the geography and history of the site and intervenes

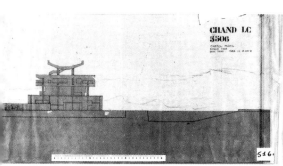

directly with the natural system in progressive transformations—at Chandigarh and at Firminy, through a process of reduction.

The construction adopts the form of an absence, and works on this in extending the labor of lifting or enclosing it as its own constitutive element: positioning the buildings on the water-eroded valley of Chandigarh, using as matrix of the design the system of abandoned quarries at Firminy.

The imprint of the phenomenon—erosion, excavation—comes into play in the creation of the new form.

(It can be observed at Ronchamp, up to the chapel, that the construction site had made an imprint on the ground to which he decides to give architectural form.[2])

The ground itself, living body, appears in the definition of the game of the parts and signs that, by and by, are incised into it.

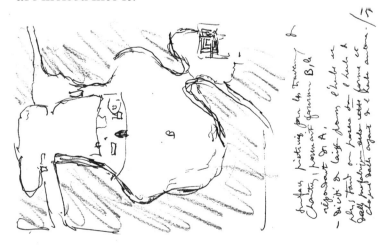

Thus, as in an autopsy, the action of time on the remains is the way to knowledge.

(Thoughts on the aesthetic autonomy of the ruins, and of each mutilated form; peculiarity and strength of the regeneration of aesthetic pleasure.)[3]

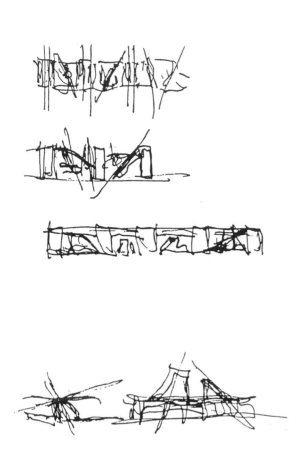

Opposed to this epistyle, the cornice of the sky is the seat of the inexhaustible battle between ground and clouds, reflected in its depths over the buildings below.

At Chandigarh and at Firminy the buildings are Towers of Shadow and Pluvial Fountains.

Towers of Shadow and Pluvial Fountains composed of parts in tumultuous conflict.

The years between 1940 and 1946 were fertile and decisive.

The felicitous state of "Les Heures Claires" of Poissy has been transformed into drama.

The square that contained and concluded the elegant mixtilinear play has been transformed into "metope" in the confines of whose weave an animal form struggles.

From now on geometry, measure, the affirmation of an abstract order—human—cannot exist if not through the pressure of an hydra.

The obsession of the Modulor would come out of the obsession with a bestiary.

In the extremely elongated contours of Chandigarh and Firminy each unsealed form is glimpsed between sky and earth in respect to the frame of the right angle: approach, inscription, penetration.

Fragmented forms, truncated volumes; a tension that is generated by compromised equilibriums.

The Tower of Shadow and the Pluvial Fountain of Chandigarh and Firminy are governed by geometry generating a rhythm.

Orthostasis. Animal tension of bodies.

Equilibrium. Disequilibrium.

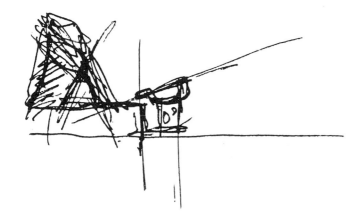

216. F. Venezia, Tower of Darkness and Pluvial Fountain in composite tumultuous conflict.
217. Chandigarh, the Secretariat and the Palace of the Assembly seen from the valley of erosion (FLC).

RONCHAMP

James Stirling

LE CORBUSIER'S CHAPEL AND THE CRISIS OF RATIONALISM

With the simultaneous appearance of Lever House in New York and the Unité in Marseilles, it had become obvious that the stylistic schism between Europe and the New World had entered on a decisive phase. The issue of art or technology had divided the ideological basis of the modern movement, and the diverging styles apparent since Constructivism probably have their origin in the attempt to fuse Art Nouveau and late 19th century engineering. In the U.S.A., functionalism now means the adaptation to building of industrial processes and products, but in Europe it remains the essentially humanist method of designing to a specific use. The post-war architecture of America may appear brittle to Europeans and, by obviating the hierarchical disposition of elements, anonymous; however, this academic method of criticism may no longer be adequate in considering technological products of the 20th century. Yet this method would still appear valid in criticizing recent European architecture where the elaboration of space and form has continued without abatement; and the chapel by Le Corbusier may possibly be the most plastic building ever erected in the name of modern architecture.

The south tower of the chapel, emerging as a white thumb above the landscape, can be seen for many miles as one approaches the Swiss border. The rolling hills and green woodlands of the Haute-Saône are reminiscent of many parts of England and Wales, and the village of Ronchamp spreads along either side of the Dijon-Basle road. After climbing a steep and winding dirt-track, leading from the village through dense woodland, one reaches the bald crown of the hill on which the chapel is situated. The sweep of the roof, inverting the curve of the ground, and a single dynamic gesture give the composition an expression of dramatic inevitability. The immediate impression is of a sudden encounter with an unnatural configuration of natural elements such as the granite rings at Stone-

218. The Chapel at Ronchamp as one arrives from the southeast.

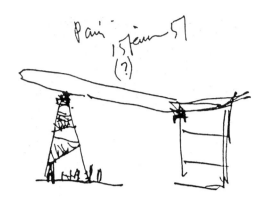

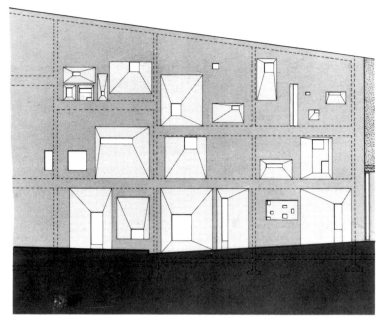

henge or the dolmens in Brittany.

Far from being monumental, the building has a considerable ethereal quality, principally as a result of the equivocal nature of the walls. The rendering, which is whitewashed over, has been hand thrown and has an impasto of about 2 inches. This veneer suggests a quality of weightlessness and gives the walls something of the appearance of papier-mâché.

Notwithstanding that both roof and walls curve and splay in several directions, the material difference of rendered walls and natural concrete roof maintains the conventional distinction between them. They are further distinguished on the south and east sides by a continuous 9-inch glazed strip, and though the roof is not visible on the north and west sides its contours are suggested by the outline of the parapet. There is a similarity between the chapel and the Einstein tower which is even less conventional, but only inasmuch as the walls and roof are fused into one expression.

The whitewashed rendering is applied to the interior as well as to the exterior and the openings scattered apparently at random over the south and north walls splay either inwards or outwards, similar to the reveals of gun-openings in coastal fortifications. On the inside of the west wall these openings splay inwards to such a degree that from the interior the surface takes on the appearance of a grille. It is through this grille that most of the daylight percolates to the interior, yet the overall effect is one of diffuse light so that, from a place in the congregation, no

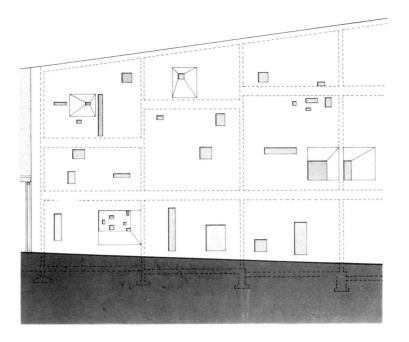

particular feature is spotlighted as in the manner of a Baroque church.

Where the roof dips to its lowest point, a double-barrelled gargoyle projects outwards to shoot rainwater into a shutter-patterned concrete tub. This element is surprisingly reminiscent of South Bank festivalia and something of the same spirit is conveyed by Le Corbusier in his stove-enamelled murals covering both sides of the processional entrance door. The same applies to the inscriptions on the coloured glass insets to the window openings. These linear applications suggest a final flourish and appear superfluous and even amateur in comparison with the overpowering virtuosity in moulding the contours of the solid masses.

The usual procedure in examining buildings—an inspection of the exterior followed by a tour of the interior—is reversed, and sightseers emerging on to the crown of the hill proceed to walk around the building clockwise, completing 1 1/2 circles before entering the chapel where they tend to become static, turning on their own axis to examine the interior.

Echoing the sag of the roof, the concrete floor dips down to the altar-rail which appears to be a length of folded lead. The various altars are built up of blocks of polished pre-cast concrete (probably with a marble aggregate) which are cast to a marvellous precision. The roof, together with the concrete alms-boxes and swivel-door, represents an incredible French ingenuity in using this material.

219. Chapel at Ronchamp, sketches of a section and of details of the roof and gutterspout, 1951 (FLC E18).
220. Interior elevation of the south wall (FLC 7252).
221. Exterior elevation of the south wall (FLC 7253).
222. The light that filters through the south wall.

Ronchamp **217**

223. Chapel at Ronchamp, interior view toward the main altar and the choir gallery.
224. Prospect and elevation of the south tower (FLC 7190).
225. Interior of the west tower.
226. Interior view from the altar of the south chapel toward the west chapel.

The wall adjacent to the choir galery stairs is painted a liturgical purple and the whitewash on the splayed reveals of the openings returns on to the purple wall to a width of 3 inches, thus resembling the painted window surrounds on houses around the Mediterranean coast. Small areas of green and yellow are painted over the rendering on either side of the main entrance and also on the reveals to the opening which contains the pivoting statue of the Madonna. The only large area of colour is confined to the northeast chapel and tower; this has been painted red for its entire height so that light pouring down from the top gives this surface the luminosity of 'Dayglow.' The three towers which catch the sun at different times of the day and pour light down on to the altars are in fact vertical extensions of each of the side chapels.

Even with a small congregation, the superb acoustics give a resonance suggesting a cathedral space and the people using the chapel do so naturally and without any sign of embarrassment. As a religious building, it functions extremely well and appears to be completely accepted. It is a fact that Le Corbusier's post-war architecture has considerable popular appeal. The local population, both at Marseilles and at Ronchamp, appear to be intensely proud of their buildings. Remembering the pre-war conflicts, it is difficult to ascertain whether the change is a social one, or whether it lies in the public or Le Corbusier. Garches is still regarded with suspicion by the public, either on account of its style or the manner of living of its inhabitants.

It may be considered that the Ronchamp chapel being a 'pure expression of poetry' and the symbol of an ancient ritual, should not therefore be criticised by the rationale of the modern movement. Remembering, however, that this is a product of Europe's greatest architect, it is important to consider whether this building should influence the course of modern architecture. The sensational impact of the chapel on the visitor is significantly not sustained for any great length of time and when the emotions subside there is little to appeal to the intellect, and nothing to analyse or stimulate curiosity. This entirely visual appeal and the lack of intellectual participation demanded from the public may partly account for its easy acceptance by the local population.

Basically it is not a concrete building, although it has all the appearance of a solidifying object; the walls, however, are constructed in weight-bearing masonry. The initial structural idea of outlining the form by a tubular metal frame wrapped over with

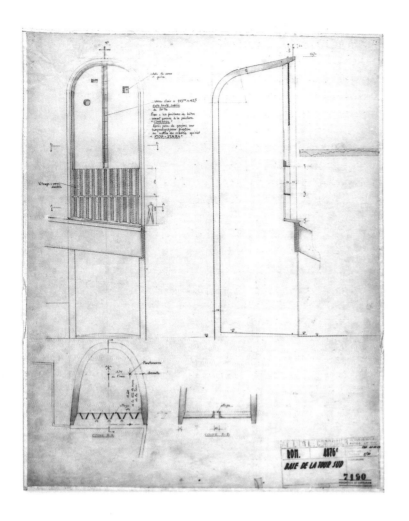

wire-meshing on to which concrete was to be sprayed for some reason was not carried out. With no change in the conception, this outline was filled in with masonry, rendered over and whitewashed to the appearance of the initial idea. The interior of the west wall became so interrupted with openings that it was found necessary to imbed in the masonry a concrete frame to form around the window openings. This freedom from the precept of the correct use and expression of materials, apparent in other post-war European architecture, has little parallel in the New World where the exploitation of materials and the development of new techniques continues to expand the architectural vocabulary.

With the loss of direction in modern painting, European architects have been looking to popular art and folk architecture, mainly of an indigenous character, from which to extend their vocabulary. An appreciation of regional building, particularly of the Mediterranean, has frequently appeared in Le Corbusier's books, principally as examples of integrated social

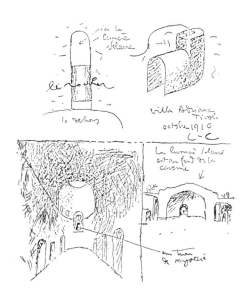

units expressing themselves through form, but only recently has regional building become a primary source of plastic incident. There seems to be no doubt that Le Corbusier's incredibile powers of observation are lessening the necessity for invention, and his travels round the world have stockpiled his vocabulary with plastic elements and *objects trouves* of considerable picturesqueness. If folk architecture is to re-vitalise the movement, it will first be necessary to determine what it is that is modern in modern architecture. The scattered openings on the chapel walls may recall de Stijl but a similar expression is also commonplace in the farm buildings of Provence. The influence of popular art is also apparent in the priest's house and the hostel buildings. The external woodwork is painted sky blue and areas of smooth rendering painted over in patterns are decoratively applied to the outside walls; their situation and appearance do not express any formal, structural or aesthetic principle. All the walls of these outbuildings are in concrete, and large stones have been placed in the mix close against the shuttering, so that when the boarding is removed the surface of these stones is exposed.

Since the Bauhaus, the fusion of art and technology has been the lifelong mission of Gropius, and yet it is this aspect which denotes his least achievement. The Dessau building itself presents a series of elevations each of which is biased towards either art or technology. The suggestion that architecture has become so complex that it needs be conceived by a team representing the composite mind may partly account for the ambiguity which is felt with buildings generated in this manner. On the other hand, Maillart, who evolved his aesthetic as the result of inventing theories of reinforcing to exploit the concrete ribbon, achieved in his bridges an integration of technique and expression which has rarely been surpassed. The exaggerated supremacy of "Art" in European Architecture probably denotes a hesitant attitude towards technology, which itself has possibly been retarded by our derisive attitude towards the myth of progress, the recent belief that true progress lies in charity, welfare, and personal happiness, having replaced the Victorian idea of progress as the invention and perfection of man's tools and equipment.

If the application of technology is of little consequence, nevertheless the appearance of industrial products still has some importance for Le Corbusier, as shown by the handrails to the stairs on the chapel. These handrails, which appear to be cut-offs from an extruded section of rolled steel joist, are in fact spe-

cially cast and the top flange is set at an acute angle to the web. The movable louvre is a logical development in resisting intense sunlight and it is surprising to find them above two of the entrances to the chapel; however, a closer inspection reveals that they are 4-inch static concrete fins set at arbitrary angles, suggesting movability.

The desire to deride the schematic basis of modern architecture and the ability to turn a design upside down and make it architecture are symptomatic of a state when the vocabulary is not being extended, and a parallel can be drawn with the Mannerist period of the Renaissance. Certainly, the forms which have developed from the rationale and the initial ideology of the modern movement are being mannerized and changed into a conscious imperfectionism.

Le Corbusier, proceeding from the general to the particular, has produced a masterpiece of a unique but most personal order.[*]

227. Chapel at Ronchamp, interior view from the north chapel toward the south wall.
228. Sketch made of a church during the *voyage en Espagne*, 1928 (FLC C11).
229. Sketch of the Serapeum of the Villa Adriana at Tivoli drawn during the *voyage d'Orient* (FLC).
230. The Chapel at Ronchamp with the ground-floor hostel.

[*] This essay was first published as "Ronchamp: Le Corbusier's chapel and the crisis of rationalism," in *The Architectural Review*, March 1956, pp. 155–61.

DOMINICAN MONASTERY OF
LA TOURETTE

Colin Rowe

The dimension of depth, whether of space or time, whether visual or aural, always appears in one surface, so that this surface really possesses two values: one when we take it for what it is materially, the other when we see it in its second virtual life. In the latter case the surface, without ceasing to be flat, expands in depth. This is what we call foreshortening. Vision in depth is made possible by foreshortening, in which we find an extreme case of a fusion of simple vision with a purely intellectual act.

José Ortega y Gasset, *Meditations on Quixote*[1]

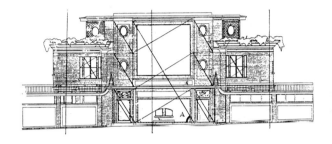

231. Villa Schwob at La Chaux-de-Fonds, 1916–17; elevation.

In 1916, at La Chaux-de-Fonds, Le Corbusier erected a house with a centrally disposed blank panel (fig. 231). Forty years later, and at a heroic scale, he has repeated something very like this device. At La Chaux-de-Fonds the blank panel is the central figure of a facade. At La Tourette a largely blank wall comprises the north side of the church (fig. 239). But in both cases, in the Villa Schwob and the monastery, as the building is first experienced, the focus of the visual field is provided by a motif without high intrinsic interest; one which, while it absorbs the eye, is unable to retain its attention.

In 1920–21, running through the articles in *L'Esprit nouveau* which were later to be collected as *Vers une Architecture*, there appeared the first public evidence of Le Corbusier's intense preoccupation with the Athenian Acropolis:

The apparent disorder of the plan could only deceive the profane. The equilibrium is in no way a paltry one. It is determined by the famous landscape which stretches from the Piraeus to Mount Pentelicus. The plan was conceived to be seen from a distance: the axes follow the valley and the false right angles are constructed with the skill of a first rate stage manager . . . The spectacle is massive, elastic, crushingly acute, dominating . . . The elements of the site rise up like

[1] José Ortega y Gasset, *Meditations on Quixote*, New York, 1961, pp. 68–69. This book first appeared in Madrid in 1914.

223

232. North wall of the Convent of La Tourette; view from the château.

[2] Le Corbusier, *Vers une architecture*, Paris, ed. 1958, pp. 39, 154, 166.

walls panoplied in the power of their cubic coefficient, stratification, material, etc., like the walls of a room . . . The Greeks on the Acropolis set up temples which are animated by a single thought, drawing around them the desolate landscape and drawing it up into the composition.[2]

It is not necessary to continue. But at La Tourette, while Piraeus and Pentelicus are alike lacking; while we are rather presented with a species of Escorial than a type of Parthenon; and while the old château, partly a farmhouse and partly a piece of Second Empire wish-fulfillment, is certainly not the most likely candidate for the role of Propylaea—though differences are so obvious that they need scarcely be stressed—there are still certain patterns of organization, e.g., a compounding of frontal and three-quarter views, an impacting of axial directions, a tension between longitudinal and transverse movements, above all the intersection of an architectonic by a topographical experience—which may, to the initiated, suggest that the spatial mechanics of the monastery's precinct are just possibly some very private commentary upon Acropolitan material.

But the casual visitor to La Tourette will have little conscious time for this precinct. He has climbed a hill, penetrated an archway, and arrived in a graveled courtyard to find himself in what certainly appears to be no more than the picturesque hiatus between two entirely discrete builindgs; to be a merely incidental space. To his left there is a mansarded pavilion. It carries a clock with blue Sevres figures. To his right is a kitchen garden of uncertain extent. But these, of which he is dimly aware, are the very subsidiary components of the scene. For right ahead, obsessively prominent and unsupported by any shred of conventional artifice, there is the *machine à émouvoir* which he has come to inspect (fig. 239).

Secretly the causal visitor is a little dismayed. He is no longer to be shocked by the absence of a preface to a work of architecture. He feels that by now he can take any lack of introduction quite in his stride. He is hardened to a very good deal. But he still scarcely expects to be so entirely cold-shouldered as here seems to be the case. A vertical surface gashed by horizontal slots and relieved by a bastion supporting gesticulating entrails; an enigmatic plane which bears, like the injuries of time, the multiple scars which its maker has chosen to inflict upon it; by any standards an inference of his own complete irrelevance—the visitor had anticipated something either a little less or a little more than this. And thus, while the three entrails, the so-called *canons à lumière*, might seem to quiver like the relics of a highly excruciating martyrdom, while the general blankness of the spectacle might seem to be representative of religious anonymity and while a variety of fantasies infiltrate his consciousness, the visitor, since he feels himself to be presented with a random disclosure of the building, is at this stage disinclined to attribute any very great importance to his experience (figs. 234/235).

The north side of the church this wall is instinctively known to be. It is doubtful if any other element could be so opaque. So much is evident. But, therefore, while the visitor interprets it frontally, he also attributes to this inscrutable visual barrier the typical behavior patterns of an end elevation. This wall may indeed be a great dam holding back a reservoir of spiritual energy. Such *may* be its symbolical reality. But the visitor also knows it to be part of a building, and he believes himself to be approaching, not this building's front, but its flank. The information which he is being offered, he therefore feels, must be less crucial than simply interesting. The architect is displaying a profile rather than a full face. And, accordingly, since he assumes that the expressive countenance of the building must be around the corner, rather as though the church were the subject of a portrait *en profil perdu*, the visitor now sets out to cross an imaginary picture plane in order to grasp the object in its true frontality.

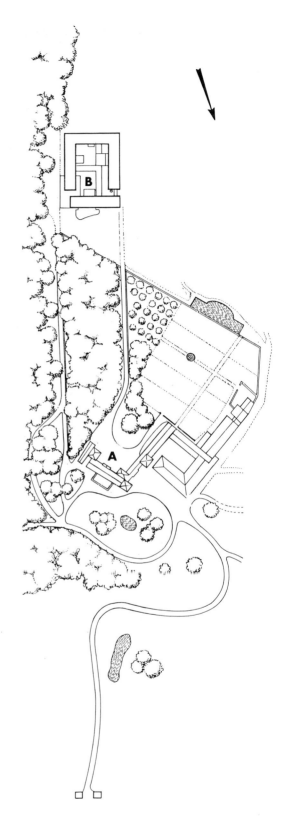

233. Site of the Convent of La Tourette at Evcux:
A) the old château;
B) the convent by Le Corbusier.

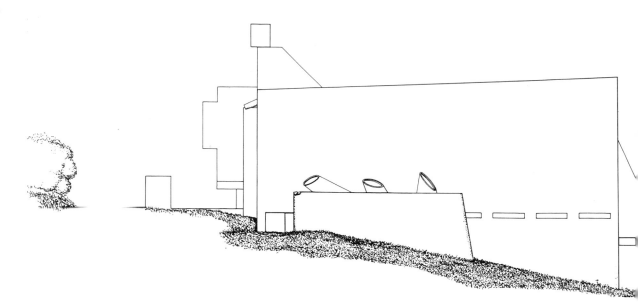

234. Convent of La Tourette; elevation of the north wall.

A certain animation of contour—the oblique cut of the parapet and the intersection with the diagonal of the belfry—will focus his eye and lead him on. But if, for these reasons, the building first insists on rapid approach, as he climbs the hill or moves along the alley within the trees, the visitor is likely to discover that, somehow, this gesture of invitation has vanished and that, the closer he approaches it, the more unsympathetic the building seems to come toward his possible arrival.

This is one aspect of a disconcerting situation; but another should be noticed: that, at a certain stage in the approach route, the building comes to seem utterly drained of importance. For, as one leaves behind the courtyard of the old château, which is the socket of the enclosure in which one had believed oneself to be, one is obliged to exchange a reliable womb for an unpeopled arena. The whole deserted sweep of the upper valley of the Turdine has progressively come into view; the field of experience is transformed, and the nature of the stimuli to which one is subjected becomes systematically more concentrated and ruthless.

Thus, the eye which was previously directed towards the left of the church façade, towards the point of entrance, is now violently dragged away towards the right. The movement of the site has changed. The visual magnet is no longer a wall. Now it has become a horizon. And the wall, which previously acted as backdrop to one field of vision, as a perspective transversal, now operates as a side screen to another, as a major orthogonal which directs attenton into the emptiness of the far distance but which, by foiling the foreground incident—the three entrails—also serves to instigate

Colin Rowe

an insupportable tension between the local and the remote. In other words, as the chruch is approached, the site which had initially seemed so innocent in its behavior becomes a space rifted and ploughed up into almost unbridgeable chasms.

This may be to provide too lurid an analysis: but, though it may exaggerate the intensity, it does not seriously distort the quality of an experience which is as unexpected as it is painful. It would be possible, and maybe even justified, to interpret this preliminary *promenade architecturale* as the deliberate implication of a tragic insufficiency in the visitor's status. The wall is exclusive. The visitor may enter, but not on his own terms. The wall is the summation of an institutional program. But the visitor is so placed that he is without the means of making coherent his own experience. He is made the subject of diametric excitations; his consciousness is divided; and, being both deprived of and also offered an architectural support, in order to resolve his predicament, he is anxious, indeed obliged—and without choice—to enter the building.

It is possible, but it is not probable, that all this is uncontrived. However, if one happens to be sceptical of the degree of contrivance, and if one is temperamentally predisposed to consider the game of hunt-the-symbol as an overindulgence in literature, then it will be desirable to continue an inspection of the building's exterior. It is not an easy decision to make. For the

235. The north wall framed with a view of the valley of Turdine.

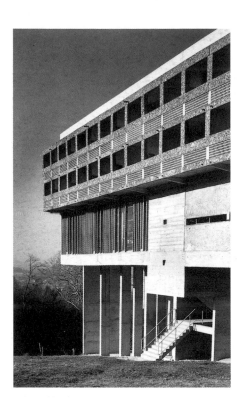

236. The balconies and the *ondulatoires* of the south facade.

vertical surface of the church wall slices both the higher and lower approach roads like a knife; and, when this psychological obstacle is penetrated, though something of the interior workings of the convent is at last presented, a further discovery is made. The visitor now finds that the anticipated frontal views never do, in fact, materialize. He becomes aware that the only surface of the building which actively encourages a frontal inspection is indeed exactly that north wall of the church which he had supposed was never to be interpreted in this way.

Thus, while other exposures, east and west, at the price of uncomfortable clambering around, may certainly be seen in frontal alignment, they are usually presented, and apparently intended to be seen, only in a rapid foreshortening. Thus, the south elevation, although generally visible in far less abrupt perspective, is still evidently to be seen from oblique points of view (fig. 236); and thus, though on three sides the monastery of La Tourette is entirely open to the landscape, the conditions of its visibility lead, not to the seeing of the real and tangible voids, but to a consciousness of solids (fig. 237), to an awareness of ranges of verticals implicated in quick succession, of the returns of balconies rather than the presence of the windows at their rear. While, in addition, since externally the building has an extremely high visual center of gravity, it must also be noticed that the same solidity, the same optical closure which issues from the lateral foreshortenings, is further affirmed by the vertical movements of the eye. Here again, as the eye moves up and down, there is a distinct tendency for it to register the density of undersurfaces and to infer the closest interrelation of horizontal memberings.

Once more, this elaborate divorce of physical reality and optical impression may possibly be uncontrived; but, to the degree in which it sustains images of concentration and inwardness, and in the manner by which it makes prominent the behavior of the approach facade, it is a phenomenon which may at least *begin* to suggest that we are in the presence of the most self-conscious resolution. On the Acropolis, the Greeks, we are told, "employed the most learned deformations, applying to their contours an impeccable adjustment to the laws of optics,"[3] and, though we are by no means on the Acropolis, if at this stage the patience can be summoned to reexamine the north wall of the church, there may now be detected admonitory signs which seem to rehearse the types of experience to which one is later subjected.

First, just as at La Chaux-de-Fonds, where the

[3] Ibid., p. 170

blank panel generates a fluctuation of meaning and value and is incessantly transposed from a positive to a negative role in the facade, so at La Tourette: the wall of the church, which is constantly invested with high figurative content and then deprived of it, acts both to call attention to itself and simultaneously to shift attention outward onto the visual field of which it is the principal component. But, while at La Chaux-de-Fonds the fundamental structure of the ambiguity is simple, while this structure is confined to a plane and causes largely an oscillation in the evaluation of surface, at La Tourette we are presented with a far more evasive condition. It is a condition which involves above all readings of depth; and, while from it there issues a series of disturbances scarcely amenable to any accurate generalization, there are still two approximate tendencies which might be noticed: that the building tends to revolve, to pivot around an imaginary central spike, and, at the same time, that the building also tends to a supremely static behavior.

As has been inferred, Le Corbusier presents the north side of his church to the visitor in very much the same way that in *Towards a New Architecture* he chose to illustrate the Parthenon (fig. 238). He provides, that is, a type of foreshortened frontal perspective which gives importance to the receding orthogonals, but which firmly insists on the priority of the transversals. He offers, in other words, a modified three-quarter

238. Foreshortened view of the Parthenon (A. Choisy, *Histoire de l'Architecture*).
239. Foreshortened view of the north wall of the convent.

[4] Ibid., p. 39.

view rather than a definitely oblique condition; and the visitor is thus made aware of the monastery's western exposure as a significant, but as a nevertheless subordinate, component of the principal figure.

But not to labor this point: at the same time that he does this, it is remarkable that Le Corbusier has also built into this frontal plane a depth which by no means exists in reality. The oblique cut of his parapet should now be noticed. It is a line so slightly out of the horizontal that the eye has an instinctive tendency to 'correct' and translate it for what average experience suggests that it should be. For, being eager to see it as the normal termination of a vertical plane, the eye is consequently willing to read it, not as the diagonal which physically it happens to be, but as the element in a perspective recession which psychologically it seems. Le Corbusier has established a 'false right angle';[4] and this *fausse équerre*, which in itself infers depth, may also be seen as sporadically collaborating with the slope of the ground further to sponsor an intermittent illusion that the building is revolving.

Something of the vital animation of surface, the small but sudden tremor of mobility, in the area between bastion and belfry certainly derives from the torsion to which the wall is thus subjected; but, if this phenomenal warping of surface may be distinctly assisted by the real flexions of the bastion wall itself, then at this point it should also be observed how the three *canons a lumière* now introduce a counteractive stress.

For the spectacle of the building as seen on arrival is finally predicated on a basis, not of one spiral, but of two. On the one hand there are the pseudoorthogonals which, by the complement they provide to the genuine recession of the monastery's west facade, serve to stimulate an illusion of rotation and spinning. But, on the other, are those three, twisting, writhing, and even agonized light sources—they illuminate the Chapel of the Holy Sacrament—which cause a quite independent and equally powerful moment of convolution. A pictorial opportunism lies behind the one tendency. A sculptural opportunism lies behind the other. There is a spiral in two dimensions. There is a contradictory spiral in three. A corkscrew is in competition with a restlessly deflective plane. Their equivocal interplay makes the building. And, since the coiled, columnar vortex, implied by the space rising above the chapel, is a volume which, like all vortices, has the cyclonic power to suck less energetic material in towards its axis of excitement, so the three *canons à lumière* conspire with the elements guaranteeing hallucination to act as a kind of tether securing a tensile equilibrium.

Now it is of the nature of optical illusions not to be apparent. They would have no value if they were. To operate, their behavior must be insidious; and to be justified, they must, probably, be something over and above 'mere' exercises in virtuosity. An estimate of the critical problem which they present—how surface becomes a revelation of depth, how depth becomes the instrument through which surface is represented, how a feeling of almost Romanesque density may be induced by a largely perforated construct—can scarcely be reached without some theory of the role which dissimulation must necessarily play in all perceptual structures; and such a theory can scarcely be presented here. Indeed so much time has here only been devoted to this matter—to this frontispiece which is also a profile, to these voids which act as solids, to this manifold intercourse between the static and the mobile—because, in certain ways, these manifestations seem to constitute an important datum which, if we fail to interpret it, may hopelessly distort any analysis of the building which lies behind these externals.

"The struggle goes on inside hidden on the surface" says Le Corbusier in another context;[5] and if, for the moment, enough may have been said to suggest the perceptual intricacies of La Tourette even before the building has been entered, it must now be possible to approach it with entirely opposite and wholly conceptual criteria in mind. Thus, though the normal way of seeing a building is as here described—from the outside in, since the normal way of conceiving one is supposed to be from the inside out, it may now be convenient to withdraw attention from the more sensational aspects of the monastery and to consider instead its ostensible rationale.

240. Convent of La Tourette, interior of the chapel of SS. Sacramento.

[5] Le Corbusier, *Creation is a Patient Search*, New York, 1960, p. 219.

241. Plan of the roof:

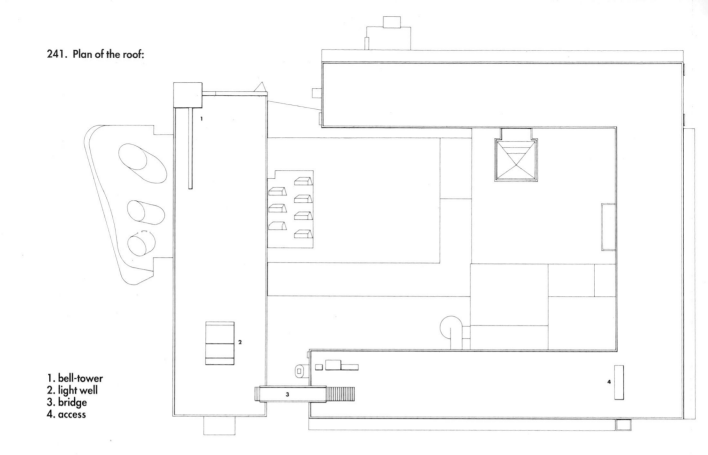

1. bell-tower
2. light well
3. bridge
4. access

242. Plan of the second level of the cellars:

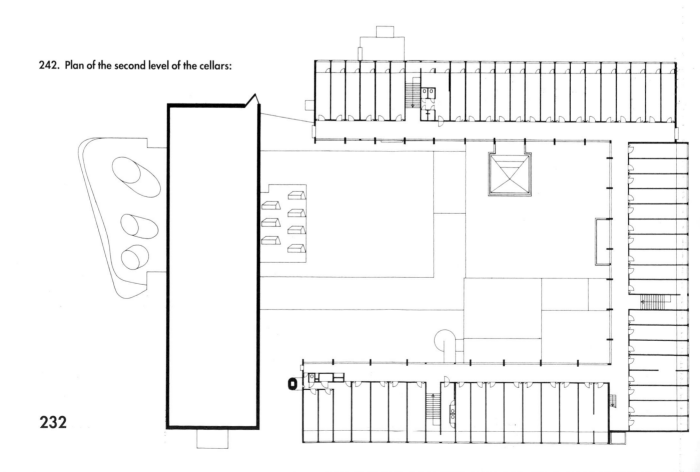

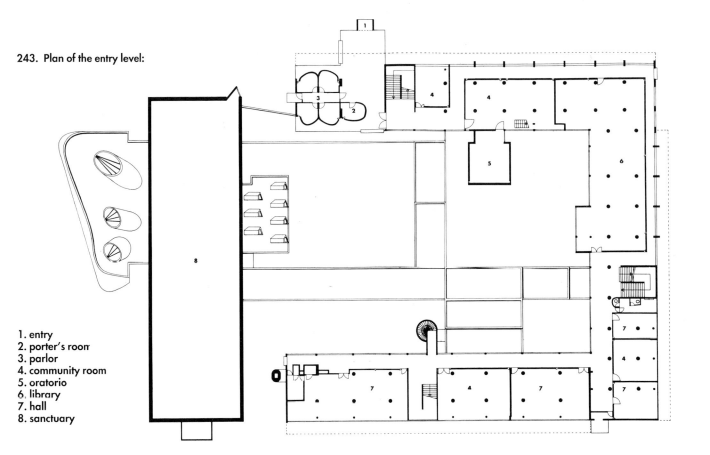

243. Plan of the entry level:

1. entry
2. porter's room
3. parlor
4. community room
5. oratorio
6. library
7. hall
8. sanctuary

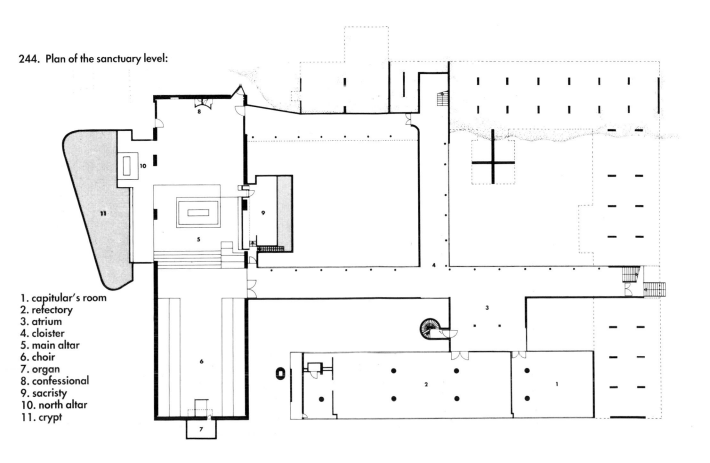

244. Plan of the sanctuary level:

1. capitular's room
2. refectory
3. atrium
4. cloister
5. main altar
6. choir
7. organ
8. confessional
9. sacristy
10. north altar
11. crypt

The program for the building was explicit. There was to be a church to which the public could, on occasion, be admitted. There were to be one hundred cells for professors and students, an oratory, a dining room, a library, classrooms, and spaces for conference and recreation. There was a certain problem of institutional decorum. But, though the architect was therefore subjected to certain very definite limitations, and though he was involved with a religious order whose regime was established rather more than seven centuries ago, it cannot truthfully be claimed that the operational requirements with which he was confronted were so very rigid and inflexible as to predicate any inevitable solution.

It is possible to imagine the Wrightian version of this program: a major hexagonoid volume, proliferating by an inward impulse a variety of minor hexagonoids, terraces, and covered ways. A Miesian solution can be conceived. Embryos of the Aaltoesque, the Kahnian and a whole forest of other variants swarm in the imagination. But the number of choices available to any one man, like those available to any one epoch, are never as great as those which, in fact, exist. Like the epoch, the man has his *style*—the sum total of the emotional dispositions, the mental biases, and the characteristic acts which, taken together, comprise his existence; and, in its essential distributions (though with one great exception), Le Corbusier's building is coordinated very much along the lines that previous evidence of his style might have led one to predict.

The solution which he has presented—a quadrilateral pierced by a courtyard; with the church on its north side; with the cells deployed to east, south, and west in two tiers immediately below the roof; with the library, classrooms, oratory, and principal entrance on the floor below this; with the refectory, chapter house, and major circulations at the still lower level adjacent to the floor of the church—is entirely evident from the published plans of the building; and, like all Le Corbusier's solutions, it is both a highly generalized as well as a highly particularized statement.

It could be said that La Tourette, like any other building by any other architect, is primarily determined by a formal statement which is felt to be a logical one. Obviously it reflects Le Corbusier's insistence on volumetric economy; and it would be reasonable, therefore, to suggest that the final premises of the arguments on which it is based are not really susceptible to empirical proof. Secondarily, the monastery would seem to be determined on the basis of category, i.e., by its relation to a series of propositions which

Colin Rowe

postulate the ideal form of the Dominican establishment, conceived in the abstract, and presumed to be valid irrespective of the circumstances of place or time. And, finally, these more or less aprioristic deductions are brought into antithetical connection with specific conditions of locality.

The site was allegedly of Le Corbusier's own choosing. It could be supposed that other architects might have chosen otherwise. But, if a superb prospect verified the selection, it does also seem probable that this particular terrain was chosen for its inherent difficulties. For at La Tourette the site is both everything and nothing. It is equipped with an abrupt slope and a lavishly accidental cross fall. It is by no means the local condition which would readily justify that quintessential Dominican establishment which seems to have been preconceived. Rather it is the reverse: and architecture and landscape, lucid and separate experiences, are like the rival protagonists of a debate who progressively contradict and clarify each other's meaning.

Above all, the nature of their interaction is dialectical; and thus the building, with its church to the north, liturgically correct in orientation, separated from but adjoining the living quarters which face the sun, is presented as though it were a thesis for discussion; and thus the site inevitably rises to function as counterproposition. There is a statement of presumed

245. Convent of La Tourette, the slope of the ground establishes a modulation between the canted piers and pillars.

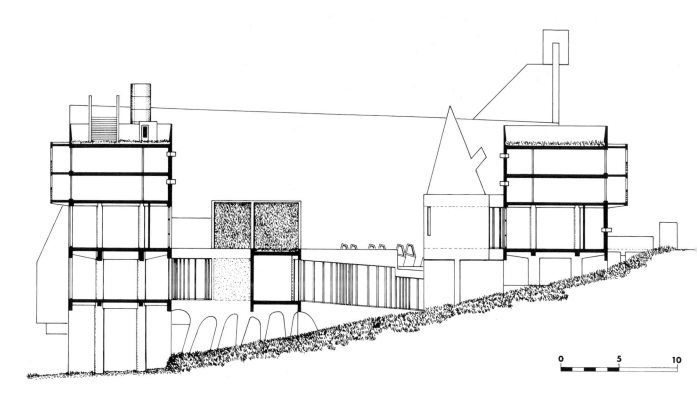

246. Convent of La Tourette, east-west section.

universals and a contrary statement of particulars. There is the realist proclamation and the nominalist response, the idealist gesture, the empiricist veto. But if this is a procedure with which Le Corbusier has long since made us familiar, and if such is his particular mode of logic, there is, of course, here in the program a curiously pragmatic justification for its exercise. For it was, after all, a Dominican monastery which was here required. An architectural dialectician, the greatest, was to service the requirements of the archsophisticates of dialectic; and there was, therefore, a quite specially appropriate dimension which inhered to the approach.

But, if the building thus answers to the ethos of the institution, this was surely the mere accident of parallel attitudes, of equivalent rigor. The architect scarcely set out deliberately to provide the plastic analogue of scholastic debate. It was only that his state of mind and that of his clients were coincident in their astringent quality, and that both parties were ironically aware of their common identity and difference. Above all, it was not a case of the architect mimicking scholastic reasoning so much as it was the presence, on both sides, of irreproachable intellectual integrity which has disinfected the logical conclusions of the argument of all those conciliatory flavorings which are apt to be the outcome of attempts to bring religious institutions and modern architecture into accord. At

Colin Rowe

La Tourette there are no turgid atmospherics. There is nothing ingratiating or cheap; and, as a result, the building becomes positive in its negation of compromise. It is not so much a church with living quarters attached as it is a domestic theater for virtuosi of asceticism with, adjoining it, a gymnasium for the exercise of spiritual athletes. The figure of the boxer and his punch bag on the terrace of the 1928 project for Geneva has become conflated with the image of Jacob wrestling with the Angel.

However, this is to discuss effects before causes. The play on spiritual exercise as physical gymnastic may be one of the more invigorating themes at La Tourette; but it is a result rather than a determinant, and the immediate causation of the building, apart from the dialectic of architecture and site, ought now at least briefly to be noticed. While, since Le Corbusier has always been frugal with ideas and has never mistaken mere experiment or intellectual profligacy for thoughtfulness, the more obvious causation is not far to seek.

There is the famous structural scheme for the Maison Domino (p. 35), with its conception of space as something horizontally stratified like the layers of a Neapolitan wafer; and there are the corollaries to this drawing: A denial of the spatial expression of the structural cell, a relegation of the column to the status of punctuation or *caesura*, and a penetration of the resultant product by a labyrinthine construction of miscellaneous partitions which propagate a centrifugal stress. This seems to be almost all. Basically, it is all by now very old; and, as a result, there appears to be very little to say about the living quarters of the monastery taken by themselves.

There are the usual elements of wit: an entrance which is possibly a little too Japanese, and the five parlors adjoining it; a spiral staircase which parodies something from a mediaeval building; and the astonishing Ledolcian fantasy of the oratory as seen from outside (fig. 236). But these are the *quodlibets* of the scholastic discourse; and more important are the distinctions of emotional tone which the different levels of the living quarters support. These are affected by an orchestration of light. There is a movement from the brilliance and lateral extension of the refectory and chapter house, through the more somber tonality of the library and the oratory, up to the relative darkness and lateral closure of the cells. There are the progressive degrees of concentration and intimacy; but if, in their turn, the cells—each equipped with its own blank white panel—are like a hundred private

247. Convent of La Tourette, balcony of a cell with its "blank panel."

recapitulations of the church, it is now necessary to close the circuit and to approach this most problematic element.

And, in this context, let us first notice Le Cobusier's passion for walls:

The elements of the site rise up like walls, panoplied in the power of their cubic co-efficient, stratification, material, etc.; like the walls of a room.

Our elements are vertical walls.

The ancients built walls, walls which stretch out to meet and amplify the wall.

There are no other architectural elements internally; light and its reflection in a great flood by the walls and the floor, which is really a horizontal wall.[6]

The inordinate significance which the vertical plane has always possessed for Le Corbusier has been somewhat obscured by his own polemic, so that we are apt to think that the logical development of the Maison Domino structure is no more than its packaging in a suitable cellophane envelope. And, in such an envelope, the conceptual reality of this scheme is, of course, entirely clear. There are pancakes supported on pins. It is all visible; and it is all somewhat like the diagrams which recur again and again as we turn over the pages

[6] Le Corbusier, *Vers une Architecture*, pp. 149-50.
[7] Le Corbusier, ibid., p. 145. This statement is a quotation given without source. (Does it derive from Gaudet?)

of *Précisions* or the earlier volumes of the *Oeuvre complète*.

But, although brilliant and cogent analysis of conceptual reality has always been one aspect of Le Corbusier's achievement, he has rarely, in his constructed works, paraded analysis as solution. He is one of the few architects who have suppressed the demands of neither sensation nor thought. Between thought and sensation he has always maintained a balance; and therefore—and almost with him alone— while the intellect civilizes the sensible, the sensible actualizes civility. This is the obvious message; and thus, with Le Corbusier, the conceptual argument never really provides a sufficient pretext but has always to be reinterpreted in terms of perceptual compulsions.

Hence, at La Tourette, all elements can be referred to two distinct structures of argument. The inclination of the parapet of the church *may* be related to optical desiderata; but it may also, *and just as well*, be related to the necessity of articulating a functionally distinct volume as something to be identified as separate from the other three sides of a courtyard. Hence also, even though the plan may be "the determination of everything . . . an austere abstraction, an algebrization and cold of aspect,"[7] the generational prime cause of Le Corbusier's buildings may be just as much a matter of their horizontal planes.

"The floor which is really a horizontal wall": an assertion of this order would have offended the structural sense of Frank Lloyd Wright. Nor would the inference that floors and walls are interchangeable planes, capable of identical determination, be any more acceptable to a Miesian rationalist. But, though it is not so much a definition as a casual aside, this sort of pronouncement could very possibly be pressed into service partly to explain the church, the most audacious innovation which La Tourette presents. For, if floors are horizontal walls, then, presumably, walls are vertical floors; and, while elevations become plans and the building a form of dice, then the complete aplomb with which Le Corbusier manages his church may, in some faint degree, be explained.

The quality of the church, in which chiaroscural effects reach their maximum, in which negation becomes positive, is not to be photographed. But, perhaps as a form, it is to be related, not as at first may appear to a late Gothic prototype—some King's College Chapel or Franciscan structure in the Valley of Mexico—but to Le Corbusier's own (and contemporaneous) Boîte à Miracles from the Tokyo Museum (fig. 249). This 'Box of Miracles,' intended as the stage of an

248. Interior of the sanctuary from the organ and the choir.

open-air theater, although it scarcely displays the same attenuated volume, does show the same slightly oblique cut in its roof, a similar entrance condition from the side, and an identical hangarlike appearance. To borrow a term from Vincent Scully, it is one of Le Corbusier's *megaron volumes*,[8] one of those tunnel spaces compressed between vertical planes which, deriving from the *Maison Citrohan* (fig. 250), have persisted in his work alongside those more advertised *sandwich volumes* where the pressure of the horizontal planes is the more acute.

A history of the crossfertilization of the megaron and sandwich concepts throughout Le Corbusier's career would be entirely relevant to the discussion of La Tourette; but it is scarcely an account which can fall within the scope of a short critique. Here one can only distinguish that Poissy is a sandwich and that the Maison Citrohan is the basic megaron, that the sandwich concept emphasizes floors and the megaron concept walls. But though, like all oversimple classifications, this one, if pressed, could easily become facetious, what is remarkable about it is that such a differentiation of species is less easily made than at first seems likely. For we are faced, yet again, with a house like Garches and we ask what it is. Is it a sandwich? Or is it a megaron? Do we feel the pressure of the floors or do we feel the pressure of the end walls?

The hybrid condition of Garches perhaps establishes some rather crude platform from which to view the intervening years. A megaron which is anxious to become a sandwich (or vice versa), it partly illustrates a line of development leading through to Poissy and to the Le Corbusier of the early thirties. But, at Garches, there are also those two frontispieces, the entrance and the garden elevations, which are scarcely connected with either the sandwich or the megaron idea. In terms of the lateral walls of the house they do not logically exploit the theme of an open-ended box. In terms of the floors, these facades conceal rather than expose the reality of the structural components. They are articulated—by a series of horizontal dissections and antigravitational cuts—so as to *comply* with a structural argument; but, in terms of an entirely literal induction from the physique of the building, they can only be considered a *non sequitur*.

Like so many other Corbusian elements they are obedient to the exigencies of the eye rather than those of the work, to the needs of the conceiving subject rather than the perceived object. They are the stimulants of heightened sensation. Their predicament is optical. Their logical reason for existence is stereographic. They delineate. They are the superficies by which the eye measures the specific gravity of the block behind, the two-dimensional surfaces on which the density of a three-dimensional substance is registered and inscribed, they are the planes which volatilize the reading of depth.

But this is to parenthesize. For, though the ability to charge depth with surface, to condense spatial concavities into plane, to drag to its most eloquent pitch the dichotomy between the rotund and the flat is the absolutely distinguishing mark of Le Corbusier's later style, the cerebrality which typifies Garches is not prominent at La Tourette. In spite of its dialectic, the Dominican convent is far from an intellectualistic building; but if, like Garches, it presents itself as a single block, then, unlike Garches, it is a block which, if examined in terms of plan, appears at first to contain in the church a major violation of all logical consistency (figs. 241–44).

To a block one attributes a structural continuity, a textural consistency of space, and a homogeneity of spatial grain or layering. While recognizing it to be hollow and to be empty, one still conceives of its emptiness as, in some way, the metaphor for a block of stone or a block of wood. It is exploitable only on the condition of collaborating with the nature which it has been assumed to possess.

Or so it might have been thought. But, at La Tourette, these precepts—which one may believe Le Corbusier himself to have taught and which one may feel to be a norm of procedure—are conspicuously breached, and breached with a sophistication so covert as to provide a new area of experience. By cramming a Tokyo-type megaron, the church, and a Poissy-type sandwich, the living quarters, into the closest proximity, by jamming two discrete elements into the same volume, from the violation of a unity of conception, it has become possible, simultaneously, to manipulate all spatial coefficients. In other words, by a combination of themes that one might have thought were obliged to remain forever separate, Le Corbusier has been able to instigate sensations of both tension and compression, openness and density, torsion and stability; and, by doing so, he has been able to guarantee a visual stimulus so acute that only very retrospectively does the observer begin to be aware of the abnormal experience to which he has been subjected.[*]

[8] Vincent Scully, *Modern Architecture*, New York, 1961, p. 42.
[*] This essay was first published with the title "Dominican Monastery of La Tourette, Eveux-sur-Arbresle, Lyons," in *The Architectural Review*, June 1961; it was collected in Colin Rowe, *The Mathematics of the Ideal Villa and Other Essays*, Cambridge, Mass., MIT Press, 1976, pp. 185-203; published in Italy by Zanichelli of Bologna.

LE CORBUSIER AND THE DIALECTICAL
IMAGINATION

Kenneth Frampton

Although the Millowners Association Building at Ahmedabad of 1954 and the Carpenter Arts Center, Harvard of 1964 are barely more than a decade apart, the development to which they belong has its antecedents in a labyrinth of creation that runs as far back as the late twenties; a convoluted history that it is difficult if not impossible to unravel. Suffice to say that the villa projected for Carthage in 1928, was in some way, a primary motivation behind a great deal of Le Corbusier's Indian work, which begun with his first sketches for Chandigarh in 1951. Between the Carthage Villa and the Ahmedabad building there lie a number of intermediate steps that demand our attention.

In the first instance the interlocking section of Carthage—with its 'cornice-like' parasol—was a device expressly contrived for the purposes of cross ventilation and sun control, and it is easy to see how it would have asserted itself, like some unfulfilled after image, once Le Corbusier was confronted with a climate where the relentless sun of high summer and the torrential rain of the monsoon would successively demand first shade and then shelter—this last being essential to the tradition of alfresco sleeping on the roof during the rainy season. As many observers have pointed out, the most striking formal precedent for this parasol construction was Akbar's Fathepur Sikri, erected towards the end of the sixteenth century. Thus the parasol of Carthage rises out of the creative memory in the very first designs for the High Court and the Governor's Palace at Chandigarh, and in the sketches for Chimaubhai and Huthessing houses projected for Ahmedabad in 1952.

In the second instance, some note requires to be taken of a book published by Le Corbusier in 1928 under the title *Une Maison—Un Palais*—ostensibly a defence of his disqualified League of Nations competition entry of 1927—but in fact the paradoxical asser-

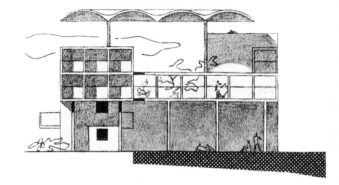

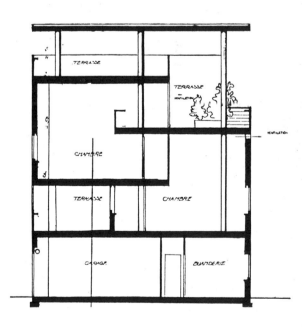

252. Ahmedabad, Casa Chimaubhai, elevation of the first project, 1952.
253. Villa Baïˇʋu, Carthage, section of the first project, 1928.

243

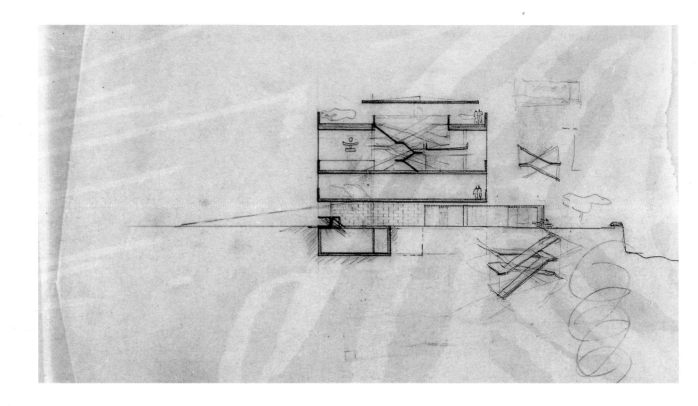

254. The Millowners Association Building, section of the *avant projet* (FLC 6943).
255. The Millowners Association Building, section of the project as realized.
256. The Millowners Association Building, second floor plan and first floor plan.

tion of a Neo-Palladian principle that was central to his work. This principle argued that by virtue of honorific treatment a house may become a palace and conversely, that a palace may be graced with all the convenient informality of a house. Both the Millowners Building and the Carpenter Arts Center are public structures which exemplify this curious reversal; for where the former was projected from the outset with all the deportment and frontality of a palace—including in the *avant projet* the facing of the façade in dressed stone—the latter, inserted between the classical proprieties of the Fogg and the Harvard Faculty Club, deployed, within a syntax that was at least honorific, its burgeoning figurative masses as though they were the projecting wings of some Gothic Revival house.

The Millowners Association Building, Ahmedabad

Within this cultural spectrum, the design development of the Millowners Association Building affords us adequate clues as to the nature of its discourse. The factors of shade and cross ventilation, that were given such priority in the Cart age section, emerge here, in the *avant projet*, primarily in the structuring of this 'palace' about a three story, breeze-hall entry, which, appropriately situated at the first floor, was allocated to the accomodation of the executive. The long access

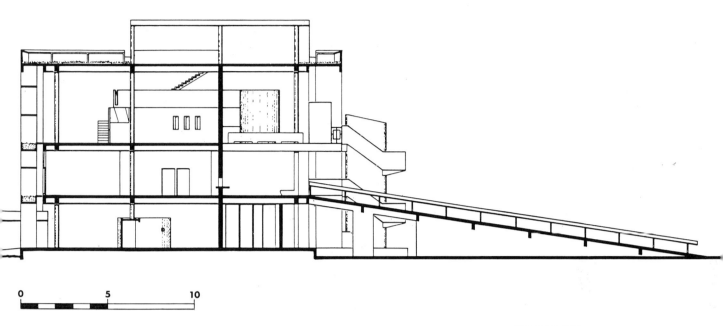

0   5   10

ramp to this honorific level—similar to devices in the
Villas Garches of 1927 and Savoye of 1929—served, in
conjunction with the relegation of the clerical staff to
the ground floor, as a means for establishing a 'palatial' hierarchy.

In the final version, this breeze-hall was reduced in
scale and transformed into a double height, sun-
screened space that constituted the programmatic climax of the entire composition. In the final rendering
of this space, the profiling and surface treatment em-
phasize the contrast between the static interior volume
of this in-situ concrete prism and the free-standing
shell form that is poised within it. The parabolic inner
track of this shell, cutting like a visual blade against
the inverted, saddleback clerestory roof, is emphasized by the diagonal plywood lining of its acoustical
interior, patterned in such a way as to contest its cubic
containment.

The very play of this form as an elliptical 'figure' set
against a rectilinear 'ground' suggests that we may
think of the Millowners Building as being the intro-
verted classical model, for which the Carpenter Arts
Center was eventually destined to become the extro-
verted anti-thesis. And this dialectical opposition—
which is such an essential part of Le Corbusier's
imagination—expresses itself at Ahmedabad at an intrinsic level in the double articulation of the entire
composition. Not only is the meeting hall set against its

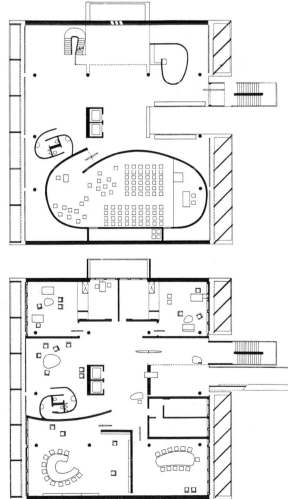

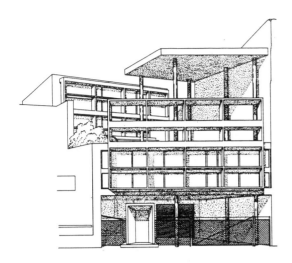

container, but also the elliptical outline of its plan is brought into conflict with the inverted parabolic section of the parasol. To the same end, the free-standing dog-leg stair, giving access to each floor, stridently proclaims itself on the entry façade as the sculptural focus for the access ramp rising to the first floor, just as the crustacean form of the hall presents a pregnant counterform to the orthogonal framing of the adjacent 'minstrels' gallery. And what is true for these basic elements applies with equal force at the next level of detail. Thus the concrete exterior, in the very same way as the 'diagonal' in-situ concrete *brise-soleil* of the front are set in opposition to the *appliqué* orthogonal sun-screening of the rear—the latter being drawn from the modulating frame of the 1949 Currutchet House. Similarly the closed elliptical form of the bar and cloak-room is set to oppose the open counterform of the dog-leg stair leading to the gallery and the roof. (This last reintroduces the theme of the *promenade architecturale* most fully elaborated in the 1926 *avant projet* for the Villa Garches.) Finally, with symbolic overtones that are specifically erotic, we are confronted with the interlocking shell-like enclosures of the male and the female toilets, attached like a composite limpet to the side of the hall.

257. House of Dr. Currutchet at La Plata, 1949.
258. The Millowners Association Building seen from below the entrance (FLC).

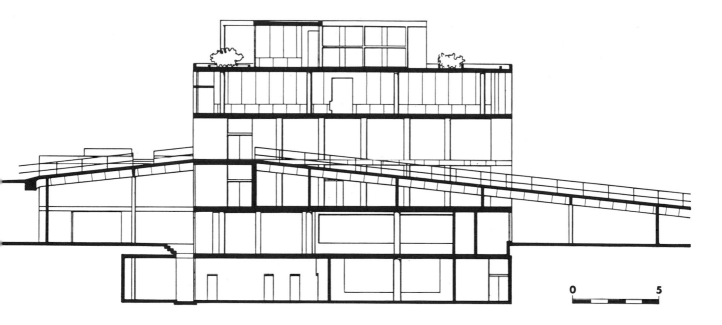

The Carpenter Center for the Visual Arts

These last binary forms, situated at the very core of
the Millowners Building, return us thematically to the
Carpenter arts center at Harvard where their interlocking ellipses, previously so discreet, have now been
expanded to such an extent as to erode and engulf the
orthogonal sun-screened cubic form that still constitutes the central mass of the 'model'. This diminutive
version of Le Corbusier's *prisme pur*—his third composition of 1929—still accomodates a vestigial breeze-
hall, although this feature is now little more than a
landscaped aperture for the passage of a pedestrian
ramp linking Quincy and Prescott Streets on the opposite sides of the site. This oblique axis, paralleling
the apex of the ramp, establishes the initial dialectic of
the scheme, partly through disengaging its binary elliptical masses from the buildings that flank its sides—
the Fogg Art Museum and the Faculty Club, and
partly through focusing diagonally on the two quad-
rangular spaces of Harvard Yard that open on to
Quincy Street.

And this dialectic, concealed in Ahmedabad but
self-evident, not to say obtrusive, at Harvard, asserts
its dichotomous nature at every turn. The orthogonal
order of palatial frontality is thrown to the winds. The
viewer/user has no sooner started to grasp the argument than it is at once refuted. Drawn like arterial

259. Carpenter Center for the Visual Arts,
Harvard University, section of the project as
realized.

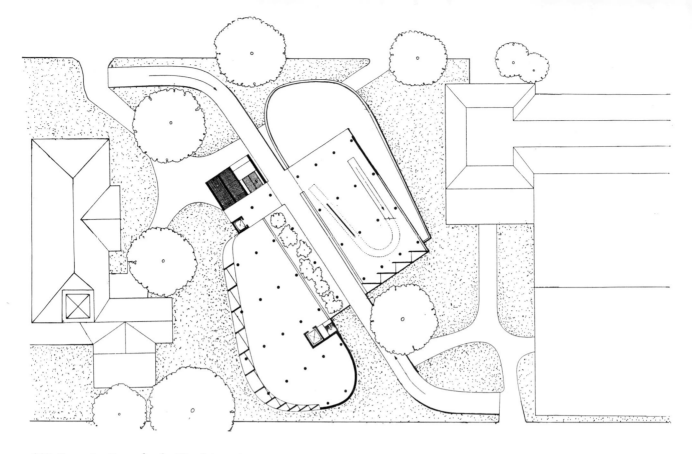

260. Carpenter Center for the Visual Arts, site plan.
261. The Carpenter Center seen from Quincy Street.

blood into the ventricle of the ramp, the pedestrian activates and dilates the lung-like forms of the major studios, which are situated to the north and south of the route on the first and second floors respectively. At the climax of the ramp, on the symbolic threshold of the building, the pedestrian is pinioned, so to speak, between the parabolic and the orthogonal; between the organic studio as the active-creative space and the rectilinear exhibition hall as the quintessence of passivity. (It is interesting to note that this same contrasting code was maintained from the time of the earliest sketches.) As with the breeze-hall at Ahmedabad, this point constitutes the nexus of the building, in respect of which all the other levels are subservient; the administrative and academic functions being relegated to the ground floor while the basement respectively contains the director's wing and the lecture hall. Finally the highly 'aspirational' third floor studio terminates the composition, both formally and symbolically, through reinstating the cube as the ultimate source of order. What is above is the *toit jardin* and roof-top atelier—the poet mystic under the stars; what is below, as a vehicle for everyday life, is the hypostylar hall of the dead. Above is the image of Paris as the fulfillment of the Enlightenment; below is the Nile as the alpha and omega of life.

Violating all the rules of classicism, but still committed to the essence of its spirit, the Carpenter Center is the crucial link between telluric force of Ronchamp of 1954 and the brilliant, creative burst of Le Corbusier's final years—the church for Firminy, the computer center for Olivetti, the hall for Strasbourg and the hospital for Venice of 1965. Nothing could surely be more Greek than this last design, laid out like a hospice in the underworld—a Minoan labyrinth suspended over a lagoon. "Life," Le Corbusier wrote towards the end of his career, "is without pity," and by it, he presumably meant this constant assertion of life in the midst of death. This is the endless tragic dialogue that we are aware of in the imagery of his architecture and painting; the complementary powers of architect and engineer, the diurnal rhythms of the sun and the sea, the lucidity of Apollo and the fertile ferocity of the Medusa. We are surely witness to a similar dialogical symbol at Harvard, where the Carpenter Center is not so much a building as it is a binary image. It is a three-dimensional epistolic condensation of his thought conceived of at an urban scale and while its composition is far from classical, we may fairly ask; in terms of substance, could anything be more archaic than this?*

* An earlier version of this essay appeared in T. Yoshizaka, "Le Corbusier, Millowners Building and Carpenter Center," *G.A.*, no. 37, Tokyo, A.D.A. Edita, 1975.

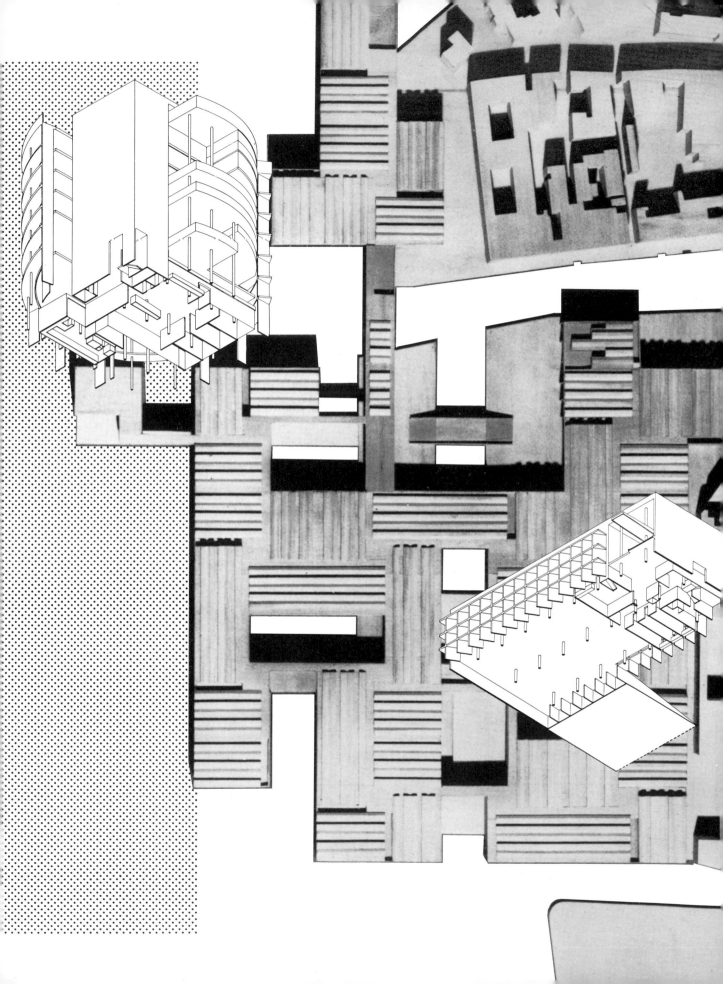

FORMAL AND FUNCTIONAL
INTERACTIONS

Alan Colquhoun

The French Embassy building in Brasilia and the Hospital in Venice seem to represent two extremes in the work of Le Corbusier. The Embassy refers directly to the concept of simple volumes intended to "release constant sensations" and to the related idea of the "surface," which form the basis of Le Corbusier's classicizing tendencies.[1] The Hospital, on the other hand, seems to derive from opposing tendencies which are typified in his investigations into patterns of growth, his interest in the irregular and spontaneous forms of folk architecture, and the direct tranformation of a functional organism into its appropriate form.

Yet if we look more closely, we can see that the polarity of these attitudes is present in both projects and that each owes more to its complementary principle than at first seems the case. The most immediately striking fact in the Embassy project is its division into two buildings of simple but contrasting volumes. An architect wishing to express the functional interaction between the residence and the chancellery would have developed his scheme in a single complex. But in such a solution it would have been difficult to avoid the administration's being overpowered by the residence. Le Corbusier has evidently wanted to make the ambassador's house carry the traditional meanings associated with embassies and to do this he has had to separate the two buildings completely.

The residence has the low cubic form of a villa, placed across the lower half of the site and looking toward the lake, dominating the site from the east and screening its upper half. The chancellery is situated near the western site boundary, where it has a more direct relation to the center of the city—a cylindrical seven-story tower, its height giving it views over the residence toward the lake, its cylindrical form enabling it to act as the complement of the smaller, rectangular mass of the residence. A driveway links the two

[1] Le Corbusier, *Vers une Architecture* (Paris: G. Crès et Cie, 1923) and Le Corbusier and Pierre Jeanneret, *Oeuvre Complète 1910–1929* (Zurich: Edition Girsberger, 1937).

251

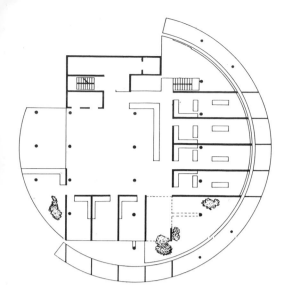

buildings and the opposite ends of the site, switching across the site between one building and the other and underlining their complementarity by giving the site rotational symmetry—a frequent device of Le Corbusier's.

The chancellery is the only example in Le Corbusier's oeuvre of a fully worked out cylindrical building (no plans of the cylinders at Strasbourg and Meux have, as far as I know, been published), but his early studies of simple solids, the photographs of grain silos in *Vers une Architecture*, and his drawings of Pisa indicate a lifelong interest in this problem. In this solution, a circular *brise-soleil* screen encloses an irregular orthogonal building, whose walls and floors extend only to the inner face of the circle at certain points. The impression of an object within an object which this gives is enhanced by the fact that the enclosing arc only extends for about three-fifths of a circle, allowing the corner of the enclosed building to emerge sharply from its sheath at the point of the elevator shaft and staircase. The effect of this is to slice off the circle in response to the driveway and to divide the building into an entrance and movement zone and a quiet working zone. Balconies prolong the *brise-soleil* on the driveway side, and their random spacing allows the lowest one to detach itself and to be read as a canopy over the entrance. A central hall on each floor, offset slightly from the center of the circle, opens into rows of offices facing north and east. These offices and their private balconies vary from floor to floor giving

constantly new relations with the inner surface of the *brise-soleil*. The cylinder is therefore hollowed out, and its interior surface is always felt as independent of the enclosed structure.

This concept of the simple solid differs radically from that held in the Renaissance. The Platonic form of the circle acts as a field within which a functional arrangement is established. It is necessary to express both the functional and the Platonic systems, since to express only the first would result in *apparent* disorder and to express only the second would deny the functional reality and assert a form that was empty of meaning.

It also differs from such circular schemes as the Dymaxion House, where the Platonic idea assumes the guise of mechanical determinism and becomes a sort of biomorphic absolute, saving man from the necessity of choice (of preferring one functional arrangement to another).

The same ambiguities exist in the ambassador's house, working within a different set of functional and formal determinants. The problem has been reduced to three elements: a main body consisting of the reception rooms and their offices, an "attic" containing the ambassador's private apartments, and a vast porch-vestibule linking the two and containing the main staircase. The entrance and reception rooms are on the second floor, and two broad ramps connect this level with the ground—one leading to the entrance porch from the west, and the other leading from the reception rooms on the east to a *parterre* surrounding a pool. From the southeast corner of this site the entrance ramp seems like a podium supporting the chancellery and, by suppressing the intervening ground, ties the two buildings together.

The motif of a porch at one end of a block is a recurrent one in the work of Le Corbusier. It first appears at the Villa Stein in Garches (though this itself is a derivative of the Pavillon de l'Esprit Nouveau) and reappears, slightly modified, in the High Court at Chandigarh. In the French Embassy it acts as a lens through which the chancellery is related to the ambassador's house and the lower end of the site (the two buildings are sited so that the chancellery can be seen through the porch from the east boundary and so that the offices on the east face of the chancellery look through it toward the lake). It is the eye of the building, the aedicule through which one enters its mysterious inner spaces and by means of which one also enters into relationship with the public space of site or city. Both at Garches and in the Embassy, its deep pen-

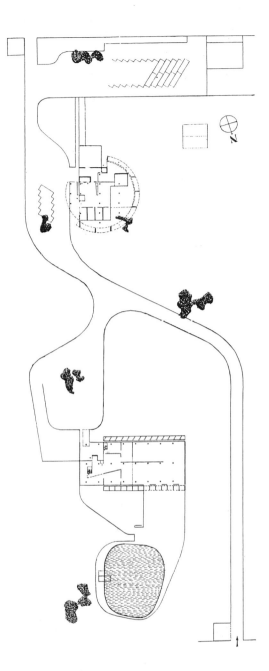

262. Chancellery of the French Embassy, Brasilia. Le Corbusier, 1964–65. Third floor plan.
263. Project for the French Embassy. Model viewed from the north.
264. Project for the French Embassy. Site plan.

Interactions **253**

265. French Embassy. Elevation with first floor of the Ambassador's residence.

etration at one end of the block activates the building diagonally and creates a countermovement to that implied by the strictly orthogonal shell.

The classical overtones of this porch are obviously intentional, and its position implies an ironical rejection of symmetry and gives it a curious, rhetorical independence. Equally subversive is the way in which it breaks through the solid wall of the attic and in doing so allows one to attribute to this floor an importance equal to that of the reception rooms—an importance which is reinforced by the "domestic" scale of their *brise-soleil.*

The apartment floor is a derivative of the director's apartment in the Pavillon Suisse. Here, however, the walls are not penetrated as they are in that building, partly because the linking action of the porch makes this semantically unnecessary and partly because at the Pavillon Suisse the *pilotis* necessitate the visual hollowing out and lightening of the top floor. Here the absolute privacy of the ambassador's residence is established, and roof patios form private open spaces which repeat, on an intimate scale, the public open spaces related to the reception rooms.

Both in this building and in the chancellery the *brise-soleil* belongs to the type first used in India, consisting of deep reveals supported independently of the main structure. The earlier *brise-soleil* structures were conceived of as projections from the glass wall. Their use as independent structures is one of the major developments in Le Corbusier's later style (although he continued to use them in their original form in certain late buildings). When used in this way they become perforated walls, which reestablish the transitional space between outside and inside lost when the solid wall was destroyed and replaced by a "dimensionless" and impenetrable skin. The continuous penetrability of this element at ground level made it possible to dispense with *pilotis* without implications of weight and massiveness and, in this way, also made it possible to put the principal rooms on the first floor. In the ambassador's house, the ground floor can be read as either open or solid, thus permitting it to be partially concealed by solid ramps, which give the impression of the ground floor rising to meet the second floor. Where rooms occur on the ground floor, the *brise-soleil* carries right down to the ground, but where the space is void the spacing is doubled to suggest vestigial *pilotis* without, however, destroying the surface value of the *brise-soleil*.

266. The Ambassador's residence. South elevation and plan of the second level.

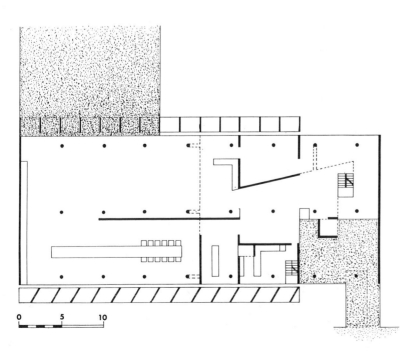

While the organizational problems in the Brasilia buildings are relatively simple, those in the Hospital at Venice are complex and specialized. It is possible (even within the height restrictions imposed by the site) to imagine a solution in which vertically organized blocks of different classes of accommodation would be related horizontally, but Le Corbusier has decided to separate the different classes vertically, so that each level serves a different purpose, and a cross-section at any one point is, in principle, typical of the whole organization. This has obvious advantages both from the point of view of administration and that of extensibility. But it also repeats the pattern of the city with its overall texture—a solid mass of building penetrated by canals and courts. In Venice, the city itself is the building, and the Hospital is an extension of this building spreading tentacle-like over the water.

The Hospital is sited near the northwest end of the Grand Canal and extends over the lagoon separating Venice from Mestre. The decision to contain the wards in a solid wall and to light them from the roof would seem to be justified by the proximity of the railway terminal and the industrial squalor of Mestre. The building covers a large area and is comparable in its mass and public importance to such groups as the Piazza San Marco, the Ospedale Civile, and the monastery of San Giorgio Maggiore. It therefore forms an important addition to that small but significant collec-

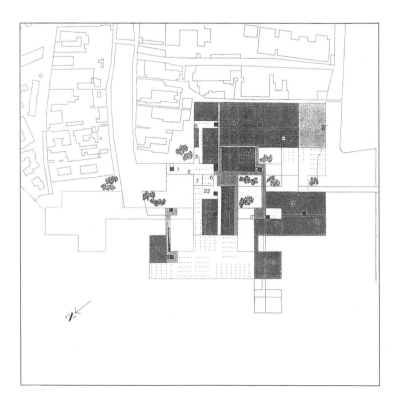

tion of buildings symbolizing the public life of Venice. The solution combines the monumentality suggested by this role with an intimacy and textural quality in harmony with the city's medieval scale. If built, it would go a long way toward revitalizing the "kitchen sink" end of a city which needs more than the tourist trade to keep it alive.

The ground level accommodation occupies an L, with an isolated block contained within the arms of the L. The reception, the administration, and the kitchen occupy the L, and the nurses' hostel the isolated block. A straight access system breaks through the L where gondola and car entries converge onto a common entrance lobby thrown across the gap. The gondola approach route is bridged by a route linking religious and recreational centers at its extremities. There is an entresol containing extensions of the ground level accomodation.

The analytical and treatment departments are on level 2a and are arranged freely around the cores. They include the operating theaters, which are organized around the cores in an analogous way to the wards above. Level 2b consists of a horizontal interchange system between all elevator points—patients using the central, and staff the peripheral, corridors. The ward block, which occupies the entire top floor, is both the largest department of the building and represents its typical element, and the organization allows

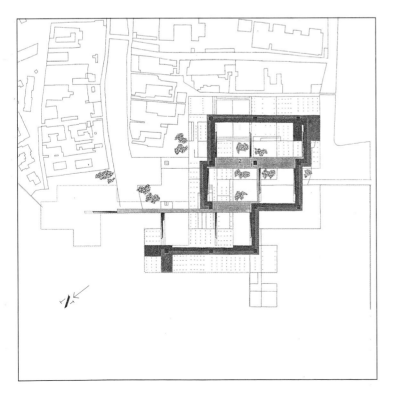

270. The Venice Hospital, first project, 1964.
Level 3 plan.
271. The Venice Hospital. Additive schema and
geometrical schema (drawing by the author).

this element to extend to the limits of the building with which it becomes identified by the observer, whatever position he may be in.

The basic unit of the plan and its generator is a square group of wards rotating around a central elevator core—which Le Corbusier calls a *campiello*. These units are added together in such a way that wards next to each other in adjacent units merge, thus "correcting" the rotation and making the independent systems interlock. An agglomerate of units creates a square grid with a *campiello* at each intersection.

The plan differs from those isomorphic schemes where the unit of addition is elementary (as implied, for instance, in the roof of Aldo van Eyck's school at Amsterdam). Here the basic unit is itself hierarchically arranged, with biological rather than mineral analogies, and capable of local modification without the destruction of its principle. It is obviously related to such matrix schemes as the Candilis, Josic and Woods project for the free University of Berlin. The concept of the top-floor plan is reminiscent of the Islamic medresehs of North Africa, where subcommunities of students' cells are grouped around small courtyards, forming satellite systems around a central court. As in the medreseh, the whole dominates the parts, and the additive nature of the schema is overlaid with a strong controlling geometry.

The geometric, as opposed to the additive, schema

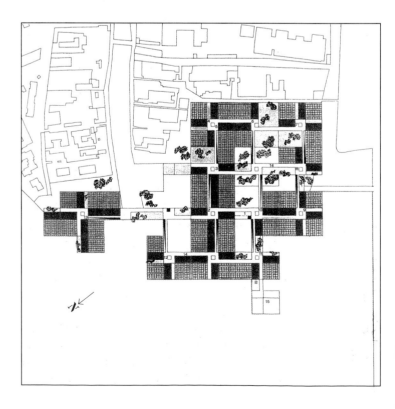

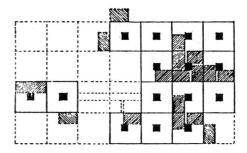

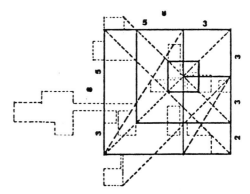

consists of a system of overlaid squares and golden-section rectangles. The smaller of the two squares establishes a center of gravity asymmetrical in relation to the scheme as a whole and related to it diagonally. This center is also on the intersection of the rectangles formed by dividing the total square according to geometrical proportion. The additive grid consists of eight units, which allows for division of the Fibonacci series into 8, 5, 3, 2. The center of the small square is the center of gravity of the treatment department and the main vertical circulation point for patients around which there is an opening in the top floor giving light to a ground-floor court which wraps around the central core. As at the monastery of La Tourette, the traditional court with circulation around it is modified by a cruciform circulation system on its axes—a typical Corbusian superimposition of functional and mythic orders.

The central core (which from another point of view is merely one of a number of equidistant elevator cores) assumes a fixed relationship with the southeast and southwest faces of the building only. Conceptually, the building can extend on the northwest and northeast faces, and these are developed in a freer way over the lagoon to the northwest and the Canale di Cannaregio to the northeast, where one assumes further extension could take place. (Between the first and second project a new site has, in fact, become available, and it is possible to see how extension has been achieved without detriment to the overall schema.)

The wards are grouped around the central light well, extending in a wing over the lagoon, and form a U-shape over the gondola entrance to provide ˘e echo of an *avant-cour*. From this "soft" side a bridge extends over the canal to an isolated ward complex on the opposite side.

Despite the uniqueness of this building in the work of Le Corbusier—a uniqueness that perhaps can be explained by the complexities of the problem and by the peculiarities of the site—a number of prototypes exist in his earlier work. At the Villa Savoye in Poissy the flat cube, projected into the air and open to the sky, was first established as a "type" solution. It seems clear that this sort of "type" solution cannot be equated with the *objet-type* discussed by Reyner Banham in his *Theory and Design in the First Machine Age*, since Le Corbusier frequently uses the same type in different contexts. We must assume that his concept of "type" relates to a mythic form rather that to a means of solving particular problems, and that, as with physiognomic forms or musical modes, a number of

Interactions

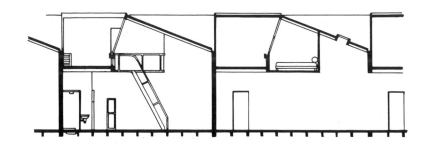

different contents can be attached to the same form. A similar idea is apparent in the project for the Museum of Endless Growth of 1930–39, also connected with the problem of extensibility as at Venice, though solving it in a different way. In the 1925 Cité Universitaire project a solid single-story block of studios was proposed, where the rooms were lit entirely from the roof.

There are also a number of projects where a building on *pilotis* extends over water, possibly stemming from Le Corbusier's early interest in reconstructions of prehistoric lake dwellings in central Europe. The monastery of La Tourette resembles such schemes through the way in which the building is projected over rough sloping ground which, like water, offers no foothold for the inhabitants of the constructed world suspended above it.

But in the Hospital scheme the potential symbolism of these forms has been harnessed to a new and unique problem. The space of the *pilotis* forms a shaded region in which the reflections of sunlight on water would create continuous movement. Over this space, which is articulated by numerous columns whose grouping would alter with the movement of the observer, floats a vast roof, punctured in places to let in the sunlight and give a view of the sky. This roof is, in fact, an inhabited top story, whose deep fascia conceals the wards behind. It is the realm of the sky in whose calm regions the process of physical renewal can take place remote from the world of water, trees, and men which it overshadows. But apart from its suggestions of sunlight and healing, it has more somber overtones. The cavelike section of the wards, the drawn representation of the sick almost as heroic corpses laid out on cool slabs, the paraphernalia of ablution, suggest more personal obsessions and give the impression of a place of masonic solemnity, a necropolis in the manner of Claude-Nicolas Ledoux or John Soane. Typical of Le Corbusier is the way in which the logic of a total conception has been relentlessly applied to the organization of the wards and has resulted in a solution which stands the accepted idea of "convenience" on its head. There is a civic *gravitas*, a ritualistic seriousness, about this scheme wholly at variance with a society whose values are based on the likely opinions of the "average man," and it is possible that such a *machine à guérir* may not commend itself to the committee in whose hands the fate of the building lies.

In spite of its different purposes and the different organizational patterns which these produce, the Venice Hospital resembles the Brasilia scheme in the way in which it evokes complex and overlapping responses. The analytical way in which the constituent functions are separated allows them to develop pragmatically around and within fixed patterns. The form is not conceived of as developing in a one-to-one relation with the functions but is based on ideal schemata with which the freely deployed functions, with their possibilities of unexpected sensuous incident, engage in a dialogue. The building is both an agglomeration of basic cells, capable of growth and development, *and* a solid which has been cut into and carved out to reveal a constant interaction of inside and outside space.

The impression of complexity, here as at Brasilia, is the result of a number of subsystems impinging on schemata which, in themselves, are extremely simple.*

* This essay first appeared in *Architectural Design*, no. 36, May 1966, pp. 221–34; it subsequently was collected in A. Colquhoun, *Essays in Architectural Criticism—Modern Architecture and Historical Change*, Cambridge Mass. and London, MIT Press, 1981, pp. 31–41.

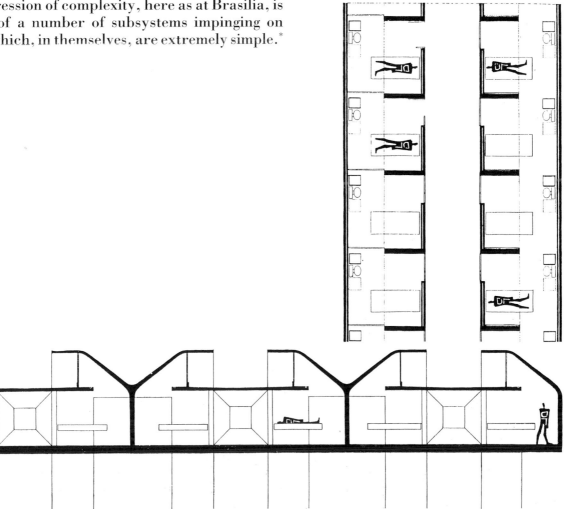

ARCHITECTURAL PROMENADES

Carlo Palazzolo
Riccardo Vio

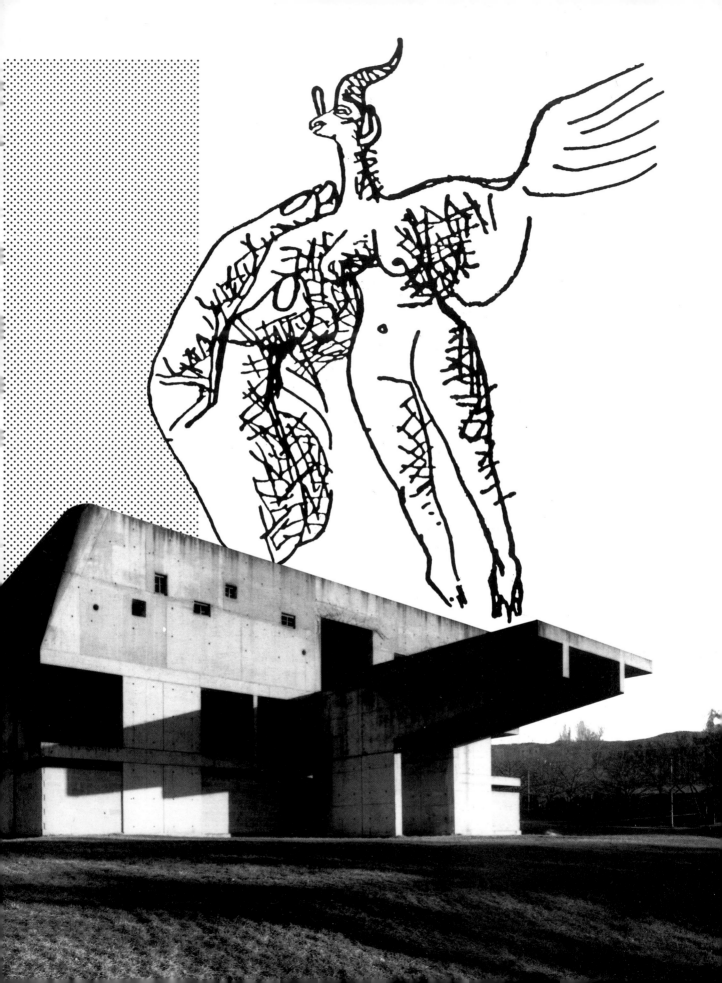

A building that is still a construction site and yet already a ruin dominates the quarries at Firminy: mutilated, unfinished, altered, it is the site's fulcrum. The elements do not besiege it, they consume it from within. The wall that was to protect it from subsequent damage isolates it completely—it creates in its interior a *world apart*.

Removed from nature by its creator, the church at Firminy seems to want to return to it, but henceforth bears the mark of a form given by man.

From the darkness of the crypt a *promenade architecturale* begins, a journey of initiation rises toward the grand hall. Here, dazzled by the blue of the sky, we sense the presence of the conedome, not yet realized—or perhaps already collapsed. Nothing exists "but the temple, the sky and the space of the tormented stones . . ."[1]

This late—and posthumous—work of Le Corbusier communicates sensations, emotions, suggestions that he had experienced in his youth at the climax of his *promenade dans les architectures*. On the Acropolis of Athens the Parthenon wavered returning definitively to nature and arising again at the hands of archeologist-restorers. Suspended between the real and the possible, it stimulated the exercise of a non-scientific anastylosis—the dream of a possible architecture. A phoenix that is reborn out of its own ashes, architecture arises from the ruins.

After his experiences in Paris, Berlin, and Vienna, confused by the multiplicity of architectural languages, the young Jeanneret realizes that in order to go forward it is in fact necessary to look back. To try to find clarity and to continue the journey as masters of the "words" of architecture, "le retour à zéro"—to go back and question the ancients—was indispensable. The stones that time has liberated from every barbarity are still there, ready to speak to "those who know how to listen."

[1] Le Corbusier, *Le Voyage d'Orient,* Paris, Forces Vives, 1966 (written in 1911); Italian translation, *Il viaggio d'Oriente,* Venice, Marsilio, 1984, p. 293.

274. Convent of La Tourette, the *toit-jardin* seen from the footbridge.

[2] Le Corbusier, *Urbanisme*, Paris, Crès (coll. Esprit Nouveau), 1925, p. 19.
[3] See Peter Handke, *Die Lehre der Sainte-Victoire*, Frankfurt am Main, Suhrkamp, 1980.

From Vienna, across the Balkans to the "Turkey" of Istanbul, from the "Persia" of Bursa to the "Byzantium" of Mount Athos, going back through space and time to the "Greece" of Athens—*promener dans les architectures* to the origin, the Acropolis of Phidias.

"Seen at first sight, nature has but an accidental aspect. The spirit that animates nature is a spirit of order; we learn to *know* it." In the same way, classical architecture is not just columns and pediments. It is necessary to grasp the spirit that created it without reducing it to mere academic formulae. Echoing the lesson of L'Eplattenier, Le Corbusier will conclude "we distinguish what we see from what we learn or know . . . We reject thus the aspect of things in order to adhere to what things are."[2]

In Athens nature and architecture do not present themselves as distinct—antithetical—but "d'un bloc." The Acropolis is not just a rocky outcropping, man has altered—completed—its form: he has made it the center of that landscape. Jeanneret grasps the bonds existing between nature and the temples. In the sketches of the *carnets d'Orient* Attica is like Cézanne's Sainte-Victoire, a landscape without even the relief of a bird.[3]

When he finally ascends the Acropolis, Jeanneret experiences first hand what Choisy had called "le pictoresque dans l'art grec"[4]: the accidents of nature or of history provoke the architectures, become opportunities to compose.

On the Acropolis the buildings present themselves as statues: in three-quarter view, autonomous, absolute. . . "cubes." By virtue of their placement they create "the masterly, correct and magnificent play of volumes assembled in light,"[5] but together they form a series of perspective views—*tableaux architecturales.*[6] Balanced asymmetries blandish the eye: without tiring it they offer it, one after the other, "those 'changes of scene' that keep the *promenade* from falling into weariness and boredom."[7]

The eye must not only be blandished, but also corrected. To permit the spirit to grasp the idea, the lines of the ancient temples were bent with great skill according to the laws of optics. Subtle distortions work in order that the "eye that sees" may not decieve the "mind that discerns."

Le Corbusier will attribute to Phidias, the sculptor, and not to Ictinus, the builder, this attention to the "visual." The marbles taken away from Pentelicus are

[4] See Auguste Choisy, *Histoire de l'Architecture,* vol. I, pp. 325 ff.
[5] Le Corbusier, *Vers une Architecture,* Paris, Crès (coll. Esprit Nouveau), 1923; reissued in Paris, 1958, p. 16.
[6] See Auguste Choisy, *Histoire de l'Architecture,* p. 329.
[7] Le Corbusier, *Urbanisme,* p. 58; italics the authors.

275. Villa Savoye, the "volumes assembled in the light" of the *toit-jardin* lead the eye toward surrounding nature (F.L.C.).

276. Le Corbusier continuously draws from the *carnets d'Orients*. Sketched separately in 1911, the antithetical shores of the Gulf of Corinth are recomposed in a single image in 1960 (*L'Atelier de la recherche patiente*).

8 Le Corbusier, *Vers une Architecture*, p. 163.
9 Le Corbusier, "Défense de l'Architecture: réponse à Karel Teige," in *L'Architecture d'Aujourd'hui*, special issue, 1933, p. 42; english translation, "In Defense of Architecture," in *Oppositions* 4 (October 1974), p. 95.

not utilized simply to create tangible forms: immersed in light, they also provoke virtual forms. "Moulding is the touchstone of the architect. Here he reveals himself an artist or simply an engineer."[8]

To satisfy the spirit, however, it is necessary to abstract from the senses; to understand the composition of the *Tableaux*; to dominate "the masterly, correct and magnificent play generated by the plan and the section."[9]

In the course of the *voyage d'Orient* Le Corbusier consolidates his method of observation and analysis. Searching for the "essence" of things, and not just their "appearance," even his own travel notes become more essential. Quick sketches completed with annotations replace the elaborate drawings of the *voyage d'Italie*.

The eye stops not only to register the temples of Athens or the mosques of Turkey, the immensity of the plain marked by the Danube or the antithetical shores of the Gulf of Corinth. The *carnets d'Orient* are filled with traditional houses, vases, utensils: forms born to respond to precise needs. Time and centuries of use reduced them to the essentials and manifested the logic that has generated them—their rigor.

The Serbian vases that appear in the page of *L'art décoratif d'aujourd'hui* are the beginning of the collection of *objets trouvès* that Le Corbusier will continue to collect for the rest of his life. The shell of a crab or the wing of an airplane, the spiral of a conch or of a turbine will serve as a constant stimulus to "observe, see, imagine, invent, create."[10]

From the *pilotis* emerging from the ground to the *toit-jardin*, where the "volumes assembled in light" echo the surrounding nature, the architectures of Le Corbusier offer *promenades architecturales*, paths of initiation through forms. Along these paths the *objets trouvés*, once again *outils*, present themselves as in a still life. Within the Dom-ino frame the architect has composed his *tableaux* according to the rules of the "Pavillonsystem."[11]

Fixed in sketches, photographs, quick notes, the experiences of the *voyage d'Orient* remained unpublished for a long time. Only some fragments will appear in Le Corbusier's articles and books. Before being reassembled, they will have to wait. A true spiritual testament, *Le Voyage d'Orient* will be published posthumously.[12] Thus, the modernist "Ange Exterminateur"[13] exits polemics to enter history.

The voyage, which in youth had been an instrument of learning, has become an instrument of teaching—an invitation to follow that path at the end of which await "houses-without-roofs."

[10] Le Corbusier, Carnet T70, August 15 1963.
[11] See E. Kaufmann, *Von Ledoux bis Le Corbusier: Ursprung und Entwicklung der autonomen Architektur*, Leipzig-Vienna, 1933.
[12] *Le Voyage d'Orient* was published as a book only after Le Corbusier's death (Paris, Forces Vives, 1966) although the chapters about the mosques and the Acropolis were included in the *Almanach d'Architecture Moderne* (Paris, 1925). Recently it has been published in a critical edition by Giuliano Gresleri, supplemented with hundreds of the sketches and photographs made by Ch. E. Jeanneret and his travel companion, A. Klipstein (Venice, Marsilio, 1984).
[13] Leon Krier thus entitles his caricature of Le Corbusier.

277. The Acropolis of Athens, 1911, Charles Edouard Jeanneret in front of the drums of the columns of the Parthenon and the Attic landscape.

The editors would like to thank the Fondation 'Le Corbusier/SPADEM for permission to reproduce figures 3, 5, 6, 7, 8, 9, 28, 31, 33, 36, 46, 49, 60, 73, 102, 108, 109, 110, 112, 114, 118, 120, 122, 135, 136, 141, 142, 143, 145, 146, 147, 148, 150, 155, 156, 157, 158, 159, 160, 161, 162, 164, 165, 166, 170, 171, 172, 173, 174, 175, 176, 177, 178, 180, 181, 186, 187, 192, 193, 195, 199, 201, 209, 231, 249, 250, 251, 252, 253, 263, 264, 267, 268, 269, 270, 272, 273, 276 as well as the illustrations that are marked FLC in the captions.

We further owe thanks to the following photographers and institutions: Archivio Gad Borel-Buissonnus, fig. 185; Bibliothèquo do la Ville, La Chaux-de-Fonds, fig. 277; Institut für Geschichte und Theorie der Architektur (GTA), Zürich, fig. 182, 190,191; Enrico Fedrigoli, fig. 218, 222, 223, 225, 226, 227, 230, 235, 236, 237, 240, 245, 247, 248, 274; Jacques Lucan, fig. 200, 210, 211.

The drawing in figure 265 is by Rosaria Gargiulo; figures 127, 128, 129 have been redrawn by Lorella Biasio and Sandro Tirri; 241, 242, 243, 244, 262, 266 by Luigi Marastoni; 68 by Enrico Rinaldi.

Drawings and photographs appearing without credit are the property of the editors.